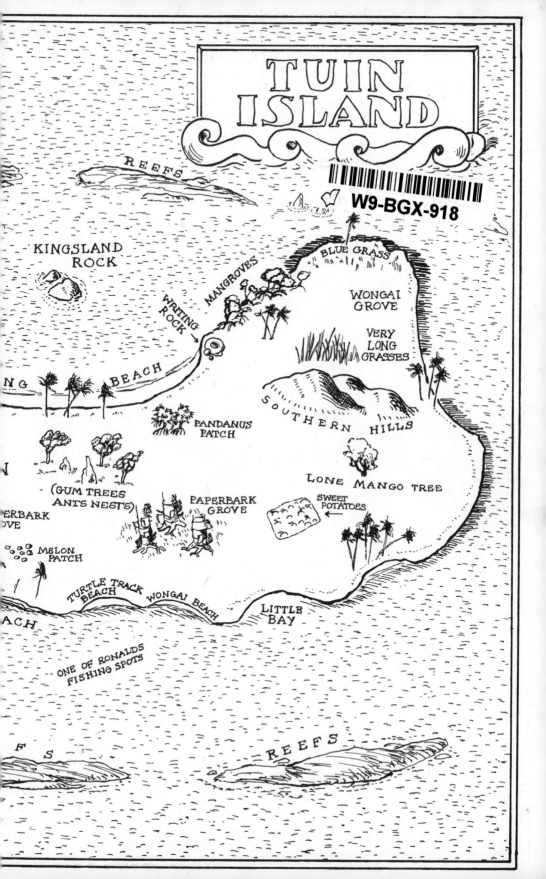

TUIN ISLAND

REEFS

KINGSLAND ROCK

BLUE GRASS

MANGROVES

WONGAI GROVE

WRITING ROCK

VERY LONG GRASSES

BEACH

PANDANUS PATCH

SOUTHERN HILLS

(GUM TREES ANTS NESTS)

LONE MANGO TREE

PAPERBARK GROVE

SWEET POTATOES

PERBARK OVE

MELON PATCH

TURTLE TRACK BEACH

WONGAI BEACH

LITTLE BAY

ACH

ONE OF RONALDS FISHING SPOTS

F S

REEFS

CASTAWAY

Castaway

LUCY IRVINE

RANDOM HOUSE NEW YORK

First American Edition
Copyright © 1983 by Lucy Irvine
All rights reserved under International and Pan-American Copyright Conventions.
Published in the United States by Random House, Inc., New York.
Originally published in Great Britain by Victor Gollancz, Ltd.
All photographs not otherwise credited are reproduced by courtesy of the *Sunday Telegraph*.
The illustrations in the text were drawn by Ley Kenyon.
The endpaper illustration was drawn by Ian Newsham.
The maps were drawn by Ted Hatch.
Library of Congress Cataloging in Publication Data
Irvine, Lucy, 1956-
Castaway.
1. Irvine, Lucy, 1956-
2. Tuin (Qld.) - Biography. I. Title.
DU280.T85178   1984   994.3'8 [B]   83-43196
ISBN 0-394-53542-1
Manufactured in the United States of America
24689753

ACKNOWLEDGEMENTS

Castaway describes events that took place on the island of Tuin off the northernmost coast of Australia, between May 1981 and June 1982.

There are certain individuals without whom the book would not exist. Principal among them is G. W. Kingsland, to whom, despite and, perhaps, because of all that happened, I dedicate *Castaway*.

Others I should like to thank, roughly in order of their involvement with the venture, are: The *Sunday Telegraph Magazine*, for their original sponsorship and permission to reproduce copyright photographs. Alan, Ross and Christine Gynther for their friendship and hospitality; Tim Baker; Kevin Robertson and family of Townsville; the Queensland Government Tourist Board for their help with our air fares from Brisbane to Horn Island; the Department of Aboriginal and Islander Advancement for their assistance in finding us an island; members and families of the O.T.C. station on Thursday Island; Captain Bert and the crew of the cargo boat *Torres Strait Islander*; Peter Close and Derek Hamilton; Gary Steer and Miriam Kin Yee; Mary Delahunty and Jock Rankin.

For invaluable help with the gestation of *Castaway* deepest thanks go to my father, who gave me the two things I needed most: a solitary capsule in which to write and endless encouragement; Ley Kenyon D. F. C. for unfailing moral support; my publishers, for their patient and sensitive handling of a volatile-natured first time author; Hilary Rubinstein, not only for his unerring professional instincts, but also for his kindness and understanding; my well-loved adopted Godfather, Sir Basil Bartlett Bt, for putting up with me with such gallantry throughout the final birthpangs of the book, and the Rosenblum family of Sydney, whose generous hospitality I can never adequately repay.

There are many others I should like to mention, particularly those among my personal friends both in Britain and Australia, but in my mind there is no doubt as to whom I owe the greatest debt of all: the native inhabitants of the Torres Strait, the Torres Strait Islanders. Without the Lui family, the Nomoas, the Nonas and the Chairman and First Lady of Badu, Crossfield and Teliai Ahmat, there would not only be no book, there would be no Lucy and no G . . .

CONTENTS

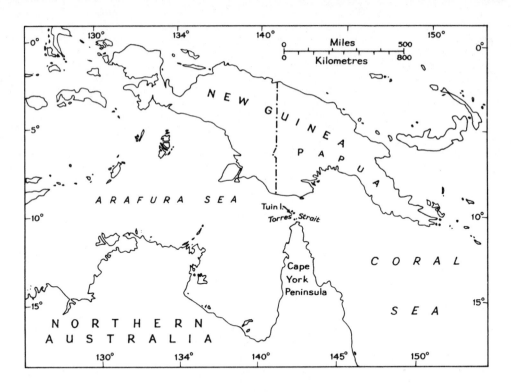

A Map of the Torres Strait showing Tuin in relation
to Australia and Papua New Guinea

Right: A Section of the Western Islands of the Torres
Strait

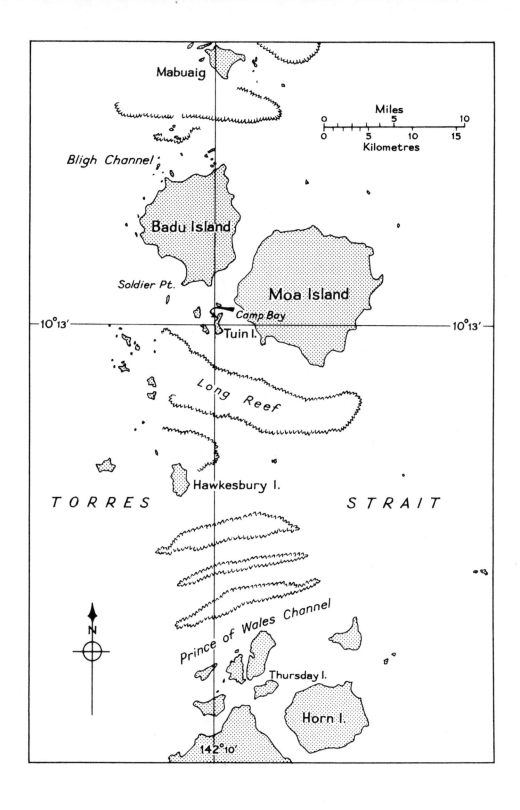

Mabuaig

Bligh Channel

Badu Island

Moa Island

Soldier Pt.

Camp Bay

Tuin I.

10°13'   10°13'

Long Reef

Hawkesbury I.

T O R R E S   S T R A I T

Prince of Wales Channel

N

Thursday I.

Horn I.

142°10'

Miles
0   5   10
0   5   10   15
Kilometres

PHASE I

Getting Away

SHOVEL NOSE AND BLUE STINGRAY

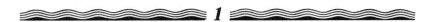

1

LANDINGS

An infinity of sea and sky bluer and more brilliant than in any dream. Our wake made a white streak across the blue so struck with glittering points of light it smarted the eye. We passed islands to our left and to our right; bottle-green bosomy mounds frilled about with white sand rising out of that electric world of blue.

Which one of them was to be our home for the next year? Its name, and the fact that it was situated somewhere in the Torres Strait where the Arafura and Coral seas meet between the northernmost point of Australia and Papua New Guinea, was all we knew about our island.

We were travelling in an aluminium dinghy, resting low in the water under the weight of five people and luggage for the two of us who were to be castaway. Our temporary companions were a young female photographer and the two silent Torres Strait Islanders who were manning the boat. G and I were squashed close together but each clamped stiffly in a separate world of anticipation. The sensation of waiting and the vastness of the sea and sky made the passage seem timeless. We skirted the edge of a reef across a long stretch of open water and then the dinghy made a decisive turn and the boy steering pointed ahead.

"Tuin," he said simply, the "u" sound an "oo."

The first impression was of a long narrow island with small hills to north and south muffled in dense dark green. Huge boulders, like gigantic molars, stood out in the middle of a wide-open bay. There was a long straight beach with light-coloured sand. And palm trees. But we were not going to land on this side of the island; the boys had been told to drop us where there was water. We chugged around the northern end, which flared out slightly from the island's length like the knuckle end of a bone. Closer in the hills looked higher, and where the tight vegetation of their slopes ended a jumble of dark rocks began. White spume from the shallow reef splashed the rough shoreline sporadically.

The water became calmer as we moved along the sheltered western side. We were on the edge of another very open bay but here the low tide had exposed a great expanse of smooth sandhills, making it impossible for the boat to take us far in. More palm trees were visible farther along the shore, but it was evident that the boat trip came to an end here in the shallows that washed the bewildering moonscape of sandhills, over which were dotted a few ragged heaps of salt- and sun-bleached rock. For all the distance of our beings G and I commented almost simultaneously, "Big, isn't it?"

No one had been able to give any solid information on the dimensions of the island. It had crossed both our minds that we could have been deposited on some minuscule atoll with one palm tree, a pocket hand-kerchief of sand, and somehow, miraculously, a fresh-water spring. Now, with the loss of the fanning breeze as the boat slowed, the intensity of the sun's violent heat and brilliance struck us fully, and the distance across the acres of sandhills to where the boys indicated there was water seemed immense. We all climbed out so that the dinghy could be floated in as near dry land as possible.

I noticed how gingerly the Island boys were stepping through the shallows, and wondered which one of the many poisonous sea creatures we had been warned about prompted this caution. Suddenly, one of them leapt several feet in the air and jabbered something in his own language. Following his pointed finger, I saw the cause of his alarm. Moving at speed away from a spreading cloud of disturbed sand was a blue stingray with red spots and a long black whip-like tail.

"Yikes!" I squawked.

"Ee-agh!" exclaimed Jackie, the photographer.

"Fuck that for a game of soldiers," from G, and we all, including the Island boys, made hastily for a dry sandhill each. Our noise and the scraping of the dinghy bottom on the sand scared up several more rays, which shot away as though by jet propulsion.

The boys helped us balance suitcases, typewriter, kitbag and boxes on the temporary safety of a rock, then we exchanged a shy, rather formal farewell, and they were gone. We stood for a moment beside our belongings. The dazzle of the sea made us lower our eyes after watching the boat go. Then we turned our attention inland and took in the long, utterly exposed trudge that lay between us and the nearest shade. G and I gathered up a load each and Jackie gamely lugged her tripod and camera cases. The heat seemed to bounce up at us off the sandhills, a breathless, blasting heat that dried the mouth and made distances waver before the eyes.

At the top of the beach a tall bony tree, its grey-green foliage pushed forward in a scruffy cowslick, grew out of the sandy bank of a long gully. The creek bed in the bottom was almost dry, but further up there were two tiny pools of water, each about the size of a washing-up bowl, and a third which was larger though very shallow and ringed about with ridges of sandy debris where it had evidently shrunk recently. A finger dipped in each confirmed that they were all sweet, a thin trickle from one into the other indicating that they filled themselves by slow seepage from inland.

G and Jackie lay recuperating under the scant shade of the tree. A tender vine of convolvulus, partially crushed by G's legs, trailed over the sandy bank. Sensibly, G was wearing a straw "Queenslander Anti-Skin-Cancer" hat. We had each been given one in Brisbane by well-meaning friends. Embarrassed by its carnival joviality at a difficult time when the prospect of ever actually getting to our island was looking more and more remote, I confess that I had purposely sat on mine and then surreptitiously lost it. Now, as I walked out into the sun again to fetch the next load off the rock, I tied a scarf over my head, banding it tightly to prevent sweat from my hair sliding into my eyes.

"She's nuts," commented G.

"Nuts," agreed Jackie faintly.

But mad-dogs-and-Englishmen though it seemed, the tide was coming in and if we did not bring it up soon our gear was going to get wet.

Eventually the heap on the rock was transferred to beneath the tree. While Jackie set up her equipment I rummaged for a billy (a can used for boiling water) with a cup of tea in view. I found a petrol drum, crumpled in at one end, which would make a good fireplace for the time being, and went to collect some dry kindling, glad to note that there was plenty about. When I returned to our pile of possessions for a cup to scoop up some water, all was in artistic disarray. Boxes were open and spilling their contents, the typewriter was trailing its guts in the sand, and the twelve emergency bottles of water we had brought, broken out of their cardboard shading, were broiling in the heat. Never mind, I thought, plenty of time to get organised later. Jackie was ready to take her photographs. She asked us to sit close together behind all the gear. G was looking very pink and sweaty. So, I imagine, was I.

At that moment the whirr of a helicopter made us all look up. It was coming in to land. G and I recognised it as having come from Thursday Island, the last outpost of relative civilisation off the tip of the Cape York peninsula. We had stayed there for a week after travelling up from Brisbane, and had met Bill, the chopper pilot, who had been intrigued enough by our venture to drop in now "just for the hell of it" before we were left in total isolation. Seeing the chance of a lift back to chilled orange juice on Thursday Island, Jackie took her photographs rapidly as Bill, who had stepped down leaving the chopper blades still whirling, explained that he could only stay a minute as this was an unscheduled stop. Already Jackie was packing up her camera ready to depart. It was just as well for her to go with him as other arrangements for her collection had been vague. (The boat that was meant to come for her never turned up.)

Suddenly I had an overwhelming urge to send a last message to my people. I found a crumpled unused airletter and scrawled a few loving words inside, then sealed it up, and handing it to Bill, hugged him and Jackie goodbye. I turned to G, who was standing innocently smoking a last cigarette cadged off Bill. His shoulders were slumped forwards and sweat filled the wrinkles at the back of his neck. There was a red weal under his left ear where the string of his hat had cut in. My eyes took him in and I thought, shocked, My God, what has this man to do with my life? On an impulse I snatched the letter back from Bill and dashed a squeal of impotent protest on the outside of the envelope: "It was so *unfair* of the Immigration Authorities to press this marriage! No two people could be less compatible."

Sixty seconds later the helicopter was gone and we were alone on Tuin.

It was perhaps about time that I asked myself what that man had to do with my life, what I had to do with his, and what we were doing stranded together on an island in one of the almost forgotten corners of the world. Less than a month before I had written a rather glib letter to a friend explaining how, as a complete contrast to working for the Inland [Internal] Revenue, I was going to spend the next year of my life on an island in the sun with a ginger-bearded Crusoe character I had met through an unusual advertisement in the travel section of a London magazine: "Writer seeks 'wife' for year on tropical island."

I recall noting with relief the quote marks around the word "wife" at the time. The only trouble was that we did actually have to get married, because for some reason the Australian Immigration authorities did not feel happy about allowing us to live as castaways on territory that came under their jurisdiction unless we had a certificate legalising our union. By that time I was so committed to the idea of the island that I would have done almost anything to get there. We had discovered that deserted although potentially habitable islands around the world are scarce. Most of them are either privately owned, secret naval bases or satellite tracking stations. Australia seemed to be our last hope. It was extremely unfortunate that G had suggested we marry a few weeks earlier and I had refused, as, having only spent a handful of weekends together, I felt it would be better to wait and see how things developed. I dithered for about a month over the decision, then gave in my notice, sold the piano and my books and gave away all the rest of my possessions bar two suitcases. We bought one-way tickets to Australia, went through the motions of a marriage and expected to be on our island within a fortnight. The discovery, on our arrival in Brisbane, that a suitable island had not yet been named, caused a great deal of strain and anxiety as the search began all over again, in a strange country and with no funds to fall back on. We had both taken a major step, not only geographically but also in the realms of mind and emotion.

The strings of habit do not all break at once, and recent past, however out of context it may be in the present, tends to order the lines of continuity between two individuals. In the first moment alone on an otherwise unpeopled territory, our choices of reaction were infinite. Our recent past, consisting of tense weeks of waiting for this very moment, hovered between us like a third presence, almost crippling spontaneity. Those weeks, during which a host of doubts had arisen in my mind concerning G's character, and he had been bemused and injured by the brusque and dismissive way I treated him as my fears deepened, had shaken the flimsy base of our relationship badly. The result was that now, under the surface, we were totally estranged. But the dream that had brought us together was now a solid thing. It was there under our feet in the warm grit of the coral sand, there in the pale-leafed tree above us and there in the very sweat on the palms of our hands. Less tangible was the sudden shock of the freedom that was now potentially ours: a private space, remote from the rest of the world, in which anything could happen.

The minute the helicopter was out of sight I took off all my clothes.

All white-bodied and beetroot-faced I stood facing G, nipples scrunched up in surprise at the sudden exposure. "Tea?" I asked, holding the word out in front of me like a screen.

G did not respond for a few seconds. He swung his hat by its string, slowly rubbing the back of his neck where it was sore from the sun. "Right," he said finally. "I'll start on the tent."

Little things make an immense difference in a situation where the whole structure of one's life, or at least the shape it takes on the surface, depends entirely upon one's own voluntary actions. "Start as you mean to go on" takes on a heavy significance. I was aware that, alone, perhaps neither of us would have taken cover so swiftly behind the banality of ordered activity overflowing from the old familiar world.

I knew exactly where to lay my hands on the tea, having packed and repacked the provisions box several times. In view of the 365 days that lay ahead, the stores seemed absurdly meagre, but they were only intended to keep us going until the vegetables we planned to grow were ready. We had:

1 packet leaf tea	2 kilos dried beans
200 tea bags	1 packet spaghetti
1 kilo porridge oats	1 large bottle cooking oil
2 packets dried fruit	1 kilo salt
1 packet wholewheat semolina	black pepper
6 packets brown rice (approx. 4 kilos)	

This minimal assortment had been bought with almost exhausted funds after the long and unexpected waiting period in Brisbane had eroded more than patience and nerves. I was relieved to have had the opportunity to add one or two items at the last minute. Somebody on Thursday Island had given G a box of twelve-bore cartridges. As we had no shotgun with us they were not very useful in themselves, but there was the possibility that they could be exchanged. We had travelled from Thursday Island on a cargo boat to an island called Badu, where we transferred to the dinghy that took us on the final leg of the journey. While G was filling our dozen emergency bottles of water on Badu, I had gone in search of the Island store manager, who willingly accepted the cartridges. In return I was given a jar of sandwich spread, chilli and soy sauces, a tin of butter, about half a kilo of white rice, some fish hooks and a toilet roll.

The little fire I had made in the petrol drum boiled up the water beautifully. I sprinkled in tea and knocked the leaves down to the bottom of the billy by tapping sharply on the side with a stick. G was sorting out tent pegs. The tea, though rather strong, was very welcome. We sipped for a moment in silence, then G said, "How about here for the tent?," indicating a flat patch of loose dry sand at the top of the beach.

"Looks fine to me."

We had agreed not to pitch the tent in the unknown green interior of the island until we had an idea of what might be lurking there. We did not relish the thought of unwelcome visitors slithering in at night. I recalled some sensible advice I had been given years before when accidentally stranded in the Negev Desert: as snakes tend to stay in the top layer of warm sand, if one scrapes down a couple of inches, making a sort of sunken mattress, they are less likely to come into the sleeping area. I mentioned this to G.

"No need to bother with that," he said confidently. "You haven't seen the tent yet."

With a flourish he shook a small puddle of ochre and mud brown cloth on to the sand and spread it out. On G's instructions I found the entrance and crawled inside to arrange the piping. He handed me each section from outside. The finished effect seemed surprisingly spacious with just me inside. It suddenly looked terribly small when G stuck his head around the flap and said, "O.K.?"

"Lovely," I said, "absolutely fine," and scrambled out hastily. It was a small two-man tent about the area of a modest double bed. I wished I had had a little more practice at living with someone at close quarters. However, during daylight hours there would be plenty of space.

The sun was already beginning to go down, so while G arranged the water bottles in the shade of a clump of bushes, and some in the lower part of the creek, I boiled up some rice for a bite to eat before bed. I was looking forward to fish tomorrow. With a little inner pirouette of excitement I realised just how much there was to look forward to tomorrow. The thought of being all day naked in the sun was delicious enough in itself, but there was the whole of our new world to explore.

We ate our rice under the shade of a broad-trunked tree set back from the top of the beach within the seaward curve of the L-shaped gully. Bushes behind the tree and a clear space in front of it made this a natural area for a camp, and although we were without doubt the only people on the island now, it was evident that we were not the first to have sat down here. We knew, from having spoken briefly to the Islander Chairman of Badu, that Tuin had occasionally been visited in the past by Islanders, but we had not realised that they would have left any traces. Close to where we were sitting was a lop-sided table made of split bamboos placed round side up on a supporting structure of rough wood. A bent slab of cracked board with a square bite out of one corner made another low table balanced on four rusty petrol drums. But the most blatant evidence of former use was a small shed shaped like a cube made entirely out of corrugated iron. It looked like the kind of third-class bathing hut teenage lovers break into on Saturday nights in Margate.

I had been wondering what we were going to do with the heap of baggage still lying on the other side of the creek. G had already looked around the door of the shed and found it virtually empty. "Just for tonight," he said as we shifted the stuff in. I acknowledged the sense but could not help feeling a little disappointed. I had not envisaged anything like corrugated iron on our island. However, it would keep our bags dry until our own shelter was built. I hoped we might make a start on that tomorrow. Information on the subject of rain had been as vague as everything else. Father Macsweeny, the Irish priest on Thursday Island who had kindly allowed us to stow our gear under his mission, had hardly finished telling us that we would see no more rain until November (it was then May) when there was suddenly a terrific downpour. Clearly, it was unpredictable.

Rice eaten, I went to wash the tin plates in the sea, which by now had come within thirty yards of camp. If the thin tide mark of shells was anything to judge by, it was unlikely to rise much higher tonight. The sun was a pale blob over the dark mass of an island a mile or so in front of Tuin. It was not to be a glorious tropical sunset, rather a gradual deepening of the blue of the sea with the occasional still hot white ray of sunlight piercing a rock with austere metallic glints. It had a strange, raw beauty which fascinated me.

G, taking the big brown-and-white sheet which had been a last-minute "useful item" donated to us by a friendly woman on Thursday Island, announced that he was off to "make the tent." I followed, carrying the pale-blue striped maternity smock (another "useful item") and muslin evening dress we were to use as top sheets. G did have a cotton sheet somewhere but it was becoming too dark to bother about finding it. Folded clothes would do as temporary pillows. While G spread the bottom sheet I could not resist wandering down to the sea again. Stooping, I lifted a double handful of water to rinse my face. Stars of phosphorescence winked and ran through my fingers in glimmering chains.

"I wouldn't go down there at this hour, Lu," came G's warning voice. "An old croc might come along and bite yer bum."

"Goodness, yes."

I was too entranced to be startled by the truth of this possibility, but nevertheless moved slowly away from the edge of the water. I went to the tree where I had thrown my clothes earlier, and dried my face on a pair of shorts, then hung them up with shirt, bra and pants on the lower branches. Tomorrow I would tuck them away in a corner of my suitcase. It would be a long time before they were needed again. I peered in towards the dark interior of Tuin, wondering what it was like in there and how far to the other side.

"What are you doing, Lu?" G's voice coming from the tent.

"Having a pee."

I did so, squatting beside a sprawling knot of vines, grey and mysterious in the darkness. Not a whisper of the sun left now, and the barest ripple of night-time cool on my skin. I made my way slowly to the tent.

G was already installed under the maternity smock. I lay down and arranged the muslin dress over me. I had brought this along with a number of purposes in mind: filtering water, tearing up for bandages, as a light covering to keep flies off food.

"Fishing tomorrow?" I said enthusiastically. "I can't wait to explore this place. Won't it be marvellous when we've made a raft, we can go all round—God, there's so much to do. Do you think we'll start on the shelter tomorrow?"

"All in good time. Take it as it comes. Aren't you tired?"

"Not a bit. If it were not dark now I'd like to explore all along this beach—and go for a swim."

He was tired. It had been a long day. Also, there was our painful, unspoken lack of physical rapport. He could not share my high spirits, and within a few minutes had folded himself away into sleep.

My thoughts galloped and jumped all over the place, a mass of open-ended questions. I lay awake for a long time on my back, enjoying the firm support of the sand under the thin groundsheet. Then I wanted to sleep but could not because I had to pee again. Black tea and excitement. Moving quietly so as not to disturb G, I sat up and opened the flap on my side of the tent. It had not grown any colder and the air on my face as I poked my head out felt soft and unutterably fine. I crept out and walked several yards away before squatting. There were small groups of stars very far away in the black. The sea was tickling the sand with barely audible wavelets. Near me was what appeared to be a very young pine tree of some sort. A tiny suggestion of wind gently stirred the delicate fronds of its branches. I don't know how long I stayed out there.

All at once the enchantment was rudely torn: "Jesus Christ, Lu, there are fucking things biting us! Lu? Where the hell are you?"

He sounded so irate, I laughed. "I'm out here. Must be mosquitoes. Don't shut the tent, I'm coming in."

G was by now very much awake. He was sitting up, flaying wildly about himself with a pair of underpants.

"Little shitfaced bastards, they must have been coming in for hours. We'll have to keep the netting zipped right up all the time."

After a few moments we settled down again, but not for long.

"Bloody things are still in here, Lu. I've just been bitten again!"

"Are you sure?" I had not felt anything since we had closed the netting.

"Of course I'm bloody sure. I tell you, I'm getting bitten!"

He dived a hand under the cover and raked his shins furiously, muttering murderous imprecations.

"That's better," he sighed, a moment or so later, wiping bloody nails on his shirt. "Scraped the tops off all the bites."

I was concerned that this was not perhaps the wisest thing to do in view of all the warnings we had received about small wound infections in the tropics. However, I knew how G felt: it was impossible to resist scratching. Where I itched, I rubbed vigorously but did not draw blood. It was not until a few days later that we were to understand that our nocturnal assailants were not in fact mosquitoes. They were sandflies, minute creatures that make their homes in sandy places near the sea. They do not so much fly as move about at lightning speed in a series of jumps, as if they all had miniature pogo sticks. They are so small that we could never determine whether they are more like a fly or a flea; they have the agility and persistence of both. Also, they carry the effect of a double sting. As if the irritation of one bite were not enough, a few minutes after each one there is a maddening recurrence of the same sensation. We were to name this phenomenon "après bite." It was this that had caused G to believe he was being bitten again after the tent had been sealed.

It was not long before G's even sleep breathing and the so-soft lapping of the sea were the only sounds in the night once more. At last, washed over by those two deep rhythms, I slept too.

Diary
Joy begins with the first hint of dawn. The body seems to know: one moment limp in sleep, the next, although no movement has been made, every muscle tinglingly alive. Up and out there to be with it when it comes—that first pale unfolding from behind dark hills. To the sea to crouch where it curls over the sand, over my toes and into my hands. I love to follow the tide as it falls and, at the same time, the sun rises. Make tea while I wait, and watch the little brilliance of the fire while sea, sand and trees are still grey.

Kneeling by the creek to measure water into the billy, I can see the breath of light expand. It is shot through from behind with a white intensity that dispels the first pallor and burns along the tops of the trees like a white flame. Gradually, a single hovering streak of hot silver extricates itself and nudges the first blue into the sky above it. It trails a yellow flare which spreads from side to side and way beyond the hills of Tuin.

There is time, until the billy boils, to swim or, if the water is low, to bathe instead simply in the morning air.

A narrow sand bar stretches far out into the sea in front of Tuin. A spit of sand. As the water goes down, its smooth, rounded back comes slowly into view, and all along its glistening length the sea meets and parts, meets and parts in a snaking white ribbon of foam until it finally parts and falls away into two separate seas. Then is a good time to cross the sandhills and go for a stroll into the blue.

The sun, an ever strengthening flare as it slowly begins to climb the upward curve of its long arc, washes the trees, the sand, the rocks, the sea, in their dazzlingly clear daytime colours. Morning Tuin is all green and yellow and grey and blue, lit with white and touched with silver.

Out there on the sandspit, between two seas, sometimes I walk right to the end and bend my body over backwards until my hands rest on the sand, just to say hello to the day upside down. Because I feel so happy.

2

OVERTURE
WITH MISSING NOTES

"I can't get it up."

"Oh, don't give up! Here, let me help."

"Ah, that's more like it. Come on, Lu, get a proper grip on the bloody thing."

"I'm doing my best. Oh God, it's bending again."

"Damn thing's got Brewer's Droop."

G's belly is shaking uncontrollably. He grasps the pole with both hands for one final lunge, gives an almighty heave, staggers, groans. It wavers, bends almost double, then topples gracelessly into the undergrowth.

"Shitting bloody pissquick thing."

He rubs sweat farther into his eyes and wobbles into the shade to take five.

"Let's sit down a moment, Lu. There's no way I can do it when I'm laughing."

We pant for a space.

"Let's have another go."

I wade through piles of mashed palm leaves to salvage the various sections of our peepa pole. The night tides have been high lately, washing the feet of these palms. No wonder they don't grow as tall as the ones further up on Palm Beach. G is lugging himself to his feet for the next effort. Heat seems to add pounds to our limbs.

I have discovered that the pole needs to be completely retied, and one of the ties, a chewed bit of orange packing string, is shredded beyond all use. What can take its place? There are no handy vines in this part of the island and I am wearing nothing but my knife and sheath belt. But hanging off G's back are the remnants of a denim shirt. Several strips have already been taken off this to bind the soles of a pair of broken thongs on to his feet. Now we rip off two more lengths and G proceeds to remake the vital peepa pole. His face, previously creased with laughter, is now set and tired. We need the liquid inside the nuts too urgently to make more than one failure amusing.

The peepas, large young green coconuts, hang in heavy clusters tight in to the top of the tree. They are attached firmly by strong orangy-green stems that do not want to let them go. It makes me cross that I cannot just shin up there and hack through the damn things with a machete. Earlier on, before our strength began to dwindle, we did both have a go. Unfortunately there were no conveniently sloping palms for our soft city bodies to practise on. I would get so far up a dead straight trunk, hugging it passionately with feet, knees, elbows and clasped hands like some kind of overgrown tree frog, and then, against all powers of will, start to slide. Quite sizable patches of skin stayed on the tree, the rest of me time and again returned ignominiously to earth, sans coconuts. G had more the right idea about how to climb, using mainly the power of feet and hands to pull himself up, but he was no more successful than I in actually reaching the top of the tree. So one day he dreamed up the peepa pole. It seemed simple enough. All we needed was a long pole with a fork at the end of it and a piece of rope double the length of the pole. We had brought with us one sturdy length of twisted hemp which served many purposes. At the time of the creation of the peepa pole it was acting as a washing-cum-fishdrying line. No matter, I soon transferred towel, rags and shark slices to the branches of a tree. The shark was too dry at that stage for the ants to bother much with it. A pole long enough to reach the top of one of our palm trees was slightly more of a problem.

First we took a stroll down Coconut Alley to find the shortest tree with the greatest number of peepas on it. It was still over twice the height of any of the saplings we could cut down and use. The obvious answer was to lash two together. This we did but found it still too short because the weight of the top sapling, despite the fact that it had been selected for its lightness and strength, made the whole thing bend. So G cut down a third and bound that on as well. It did not have a convenient fork in the top, so a small forked "extension" section was added. With the middle of the rope looped into this, the tackle was ready to use.

The idea was to lift the pole up so that the fork at the top lay just above a bunch of coconuts. This was G's job. He managed by first pulling it up straight in front of him with one foot pressed against the bottom, and then heaving it off the ground so that the base rested on his lower belly. My part in the operation was, theoretically, quite simple. All I had to do was run out to either side of the tree, taking one end of the dangling rope in each direction. Then, at the precise moment when G succeeded in manoeuvring the infuriatingly languid top section of the pole into position, I had to dash in and flip the rope out of the fork and around the stem holding the peepas. Of course, every time I tried and failed to flip it correctly I was jerking the end of G's delicately balanced contraption mercilessly. A cataract of colourful abuse hurled itself out of his mouth every time this happened. Then, fatally, he would begin to laugh. The pole would slide casually out of position and its long gently bobbing end drift aimlessly among the tops of the trees until G lost control of it altogether and it crashed to the ground. By this time I would also be weak with mirth, sweating and giggling and trying to produce suitable rejoinders to the fantastic list of names I had been called. The fact that I tried, and took the whole thing on the level it was intended, showed progress in our relationship. A mutual aim often sweeps aside the rubbish, particularly when it is something you both want pretty badly. In this case, coconuts.

As soon as G was in command of his muscles once more we would try again—and again and again until suddenly, either by accident or design, he would have it in the right place and I would hook the rope over the nuts and pull the two ends tight. Now I had to jump up and down with the rope producing a sawing action on the stems, and if G's guiding hand was no longer needed on the pole, he would come and join me and we would perform a bell-ringing act together. It was a joyous moment. We had what we wanted within our grasp and all that was needed was just one final bouncing effort and it would be ours.

"Look out, here they come!"

"Yippee!"

Whee . . . the big green footballs flew out from the cluster, one, two, five at a time. Satisfying thumps as they hit the ground all around.

And now, at last, what we have come for, the juice. G is tired out. He sits down and closes his eyes wearily while I run about collecting up the peepas. Some have short lengths of stem attached and I use these to knot pairs together for carrying. I am longing for a drink. The last liquid we had was well before the sun stood straight above and now it is already touching the edge of the stratus cloud that hovers above Tukupai Island to the west of Tuin. G must be thirsty too, but I know that if I don't play my cards right he might make me wait until we get back to camp. I select a perfect peepa heavy with juice and bring it to G with the machete. He opens one eye.

"I suppose you want me to open this for you, shithouse." I know he is going to do it on this occasion because he has opened the other eye and taken up the machete. He jabs the ground softly with the rusty blade. I am smiling and winsome, sycophantic as hell because I want that drink.

"O.K., O.K., you'll get your peepa juice, but I'm tired, Lu, and it takes strength, you know."

My God, I wish I had the strength to do it. The times I have taken myself secretly into a copse with the machete and a green coconut and slashed and wrestled and sworn until in the end the damn thing bursts and I am left sucking the juice off the grass. I know that G will always do it in the end, in his own time. I only wish I did not have to ask him. I always watch very carefully when he does it, hoping to learn how to place the blows without damaging the tender nut inside the thick, fibrous exterior. At last it is done. G passes it to me and I pierce the exposed end of the inner nut with my knife. The juice in these young peepas is so clean and clear it is like a bland sweet wine. Sometimes it even has a slight *pétillance*.

"It's got a fizz on it like beer, this stuff has. Do you think it's all right, Lu?"

"It's beautiful. I could drink another, but I suppose we should save it."

"You'd drink anything, you would, you little pig. It'll probably give us the screaming shits."

It didn't. Well, at least not that one.

Coconut Alley ran at the back of Crocodile Bay on a false beach blocked off from the sea by a thick forest of mangroves. What remained of the sandy part of the beach formed a narrow pathway between palms and mangroves. Beyond the palms lay a thickly wooded area cluttered to impenetrability in places with convoluted roots and woody, immovable vines. Further back still lay the part of the interior we called the Plain. We began going to the Alley together for green coconuts when our drinking-water situation was becoming a serious cause for concern. But I went there alone each day to gather fallen brown coconuts, and because the jungle of mangrove swamp on one side and the dark, shady woods on the other fascinated me. G had the misfortune to have been stung by four wasps simultaneously the very first time we went there. Enough to put anyone off.

Diary
Again G was not feeling up to starting on the shelter today. This is hardly surprising, he does not look well. I noticed how yellow the whites of his eyes were when I handed him his tea this a.m. But I must confess that I was disappointed. Something sank in me a little when I saw him take up his daytime sleep position not long after breakfast. He must be feeling very low.

I wandered slowly through the Plain, heading towards the paperbark trees. I try to collect a good bundle each day so that some can be put by to see us through the monsoon season. As I walked I kept my eyes peeled for half-hidden passion fruit vines in the long grass. I love the ones that sling themselves in fragile skeins between two trees. The tiny, pale orange fruit look so delicate against the armadillo-rough bark of a pandanus. Like thin eggshells against dark wood. I would love a boiled egg right now. Two, with toast. Perhaps I can find a scrubfowl's egg. Some flowering vines to the right looked promising, but the fruit was yet too green to be good. I stepped over them, careful not to cause any damage, and made my way to a clearing where the sun could more easily penetrate the parasol of foliage. Here one or two fruit were ready to eat and I sucked out the sweet seeds as I moved among the vines. How I adore these tiny orange explosions of sweetness! First I select the most deeply coloured, perfect specimens off the vine, pushing apart the soft cup of fronds surrounding each individual fruit, and then, poising it carefully before my lips between thumb and forefinger, deftly pop the skin so that only the honey-scented seeds flow into my mouth. Where there are only two fruit, I eat one and keep the other for G, where there are eight, eat four, keep four.

And where there were five, I ate three and kept two. The passion fruit were just beginning to ripen when we arrived on the island in May. They were the first wild fruit I tried, and when it was obvious that there were to be no ill effects, G enjoyed them too. He had a more cautious attitude to wild things than I, and although in most cases my somewhat rash experimentation went unpunished, there came a time later when I had to pay a high price for my greed.

Collecting passion fruit became my first major business-with-pleasure activity on Tuin. It took me away on my own with the justification behind it that it was a food collecting mission. I learned quickly where the most abundant caches of fruit were, and to get to these entailed a trek through the interior, Tuin's inner world. The wonder of stepping softly through a totally unmanned environment both excited and becalmed me. I became a receptacle for impressions. The sights and sounds and textures of Tuin numbed the analytical side of my mind. I was not conscious of thinking in words or of naming the things around me. Nevertheless, if I observed something potentially edible or useful, some mechanism inside would snap awake and a mental note would be made of how to find the spot again. An awareness of possible danger was not very pronounced. I left body-sense to take automatic precautions such as employing a stick instead of a finger to poke at interesting-looking insect nests or holes in the ground. But the first time G and I penetrated the mystery of the interior, it was altogether another story.

I had always rather assumed that with his previous experience of islands, and being the senior member of the team, G would take command of such things as exploratory expeditions. It was not in fact necessary for anyone to take the lead: whatever had gone before, we were both newcomers to Tuin. However, my initial ''other ranks'' attitude, a general show of willingness, demonstrated that whatever had happened to undermine it in Brisbane, I was prepared and eager to renew respect for G here on the island.

We had almost no idea of what to expect on entering the interior, so enthusiasm was tempered with a certain amount of caution. Extraordinary though it seems to me now, we wore clothes all over our bodies. This made sense as we did not know what snakes or poisonous spiders we might find, and an outer layer of garments, however thin, could offer vital protection. We decided to go in behind the palm tree nearest camp. It would make a good marker should we have trouble finding our way back. The tree stood to the south of camp and to reach it we had to cross a short stretch of loose white sand and pass beneath the branches of a larger version of the fir-like trees which decorated the top of Home Beach. It was not long after the sun had risen, a sensible time to explore before the heat became too oppressive.

Wearing sandals, we flapped our way rather awkwardly across the still cool sand and halted between the fir and palm for a moment while G adjusted one of the ties round his ankles. We had both thought it wise to arrange bicycle-clip-style ties around the loose legs of our trousers, against the possibility of unidentified creatures crawling up our legs.

G issued a businesslike warning: "You don't want to stand under any trees too long, Lu. Could be an old snake up there."

"Yes, nobody seemed to know anything about the snake situation here, did they?"

"Load of jerk-offs don't know their arses from their elbows, from now on we're on our own. Come on, you going in front?"

I was vaguely surprised and rather flattered.

"O.K. Hang on, I think I'll take a stick."

"Forward, Carruthers!"

So, with G holding the machete at the ready and me armed with knife and stick, we took the first cautious steps into the green.

I headed in the direction which seemed the least overgrown and G came close behind exhorting me to take care where I put my feet. He slashed away some creepers and branches that impeded our progress and whacked a few deep notches in treetrunks to mark our way. Every sound we made seemed magnified in the stillness that closed around us as we penetrated deeper into unknown country. So far so good. The ground was almost flat in this middle section of the island, and the trees, though close together, were mostly small gums, their grey-green leaves growing high up and allowing plenty of light to filter through. We skirted around tight clumps of pandanus with dark scaly bark and shock heads of leaves like twisted swords. Huge, woody cones hanging from some of their branches glowed a faint red at the end.

It is not easy to describe the atmosphere of that first trek. Both G and I were being ultra-casual in our manner and commenting on things in matter-of-fact tones. But underneath all this was an almost bursting feeling of trepidation and suspense. All our senses were on the alert. Our idea was to see how far it was to the other side of the island—if we could get there.

"My God, what do you suppose built that?"

I had stopped before a large, sandy-coloured edifice of fantastic shape. It must have been three feet across, two feet deep and at least six feet high. It was apparently unoccupied at the moment.

We concluded that it must be some kind of ant's or termite's nest and as we went on we saw them everywhere: little pointed yellow ones, squat square grey things, vast granite-like structures with crumbling "turrets," but never any sign of the builders. G tried hitting one with his machete and caused a minor landslide. Another was as solid as a rock and hurt his wrist when he clouted it. They were extraordinary.

I resolved to spy on them at some point and find out how they came into being.

The grass here was no higher than our waists and of mixed shades and thicknesses: some thin, hollow stalks like straw, others with broad, flat blades which cut like paper. Ferns not unlike bracken with strangely webbed leaves grew between boulders in the "rockeries" that dotted this Plain area. I noticed these same ferns growing up trees, in the crotches where branch joins trunk. Knobbly black excrescences bulged above our heads from gum branches like huge globs of tar, another kind of nest, presumably.

The going was not too difficult and we were beginning to relax a little and walk with less hesitation when all at once something happened which within a second had us clutching at each other and gibbering idiotically. Shocking, after the silence, we suddenly heard galloping, loud galloping. Something evidently large and fast was racing through the undergrowth, not far from where we were.

"Jesus Christ, Lu, what the fuck's that?"

"God knows. I thought there weren't any wild pigs and things on this island."

"We don't know what there bloody is."

Whatever it was, it passed without showing itself to us. Nerves wound up tight as springs, we pressed on. G swore murderously when the sharp spike of a baby screwpine on the ground stuck him in the heel, and I jumped about three feet in the air when a leaf fell down the neck of my shirt.

The pattern of the scenery altered as we approached the eastern shore. Rows of low bush trees, their branches forced in one direction by the wind, grew together in tousled hedges. A band of thick reeds divided the Plain from where the beach began. It was not without difficulty that we beat a narrow path through here. The voice of the sea, muffled by the trees, broke upon us without warning.

The eastern shore of Tuin was a revelation to me, so different from Home Beach, where we had made our camp. Here was the original untouched desert island beach: a long golden swathe of sand curving into a bay of coral at one end, black rocks swept by a lively surf at the other. The statutory palm trees swayed beatifically in the wind. The sun was hot, flashing points of brilliance on the sea, but the south-easterly wind, so much stronger here than on the western side, breathed a freshness into the warm air that was delicious. It made me want to dance and do cartwheels. We walked along the beach towards the bay at the southern end. There was a distinct skip in my stride, but I curbed my desire to leap about childishly as it was clear that, despite his comment, "Yes, it's nice over here," in response to my outpourings of pleasure, G was not affected in the same way. Time enough for us to adjust to the island in our own ways.

We had it in mind to find a second source of water somewhere in the south. The Chairman of Badu Island had intimated that there could well be more than one permanent fresh-water spring on Tuin. As we had been rather taken aback by the extremely limited supply of water in the creek beside camp, we made it a priority to search for a second source. Halfway along this beach, which was soon referred to as Long Beach, we came upon a deep-sided gully winding into a dense part of the interior knotty with tangled roots and interwoven branches. A wide pool, two to three feet deep, stood at its mouth, separated from the sea by a high bank of sand. The water in the pool was greenish and had evidently not moved for a long time.

"Shall we try it?" I asked.

"Yeah, dip a finger in, Lu."

I did, and discovered it to be mostly salt but not 100 per cent. We decided to come back next day with a spade and see what happened if we dug a trench to clean out the pool. There was a chance that good fresh water seeping through from inland could be trapped in some way before it mixed with salt. At this point G felt that it would be a good idea to start making our way back. The sun was high now and despite the fanning effect of the wind, we could feel how intense the heat of the day was going to be. It would be unwise to be caught out far away from a known source of water.

We re-entered the interior at the place where we had come out, beside a tree I was later to christen Lone Pine. We soon lost the exact route of our former footsteps, but found our way by the larger landmarks of anthills and specially noted trees. One of G's thongs broke which made negotiating thorns and inconsistencies in the ground awkward for him. He was irritated when I went too far ahead, carried away in my eagerness to inspect every new tree and plant minutely. We both still trod with great care. Just because we had seen no snakes on the way did not mean that there were none. When we came to the area of the galloping mystery, we halted. "That Thing," I said nervously, peering among the trees. "Yes, well, we don't know what it is, so don't go wandering miles ahead on your own. It was most likely just a big lizard, but it could have been a croc, and what chance do you think you'd have with that knife?''

We scanned the undergrowth for tracks, hoping to find a hint as to what it could be. There seemed to be no signs, so finally we continued on our way no wiser, G insisting that we stay closer together. He was limping now, after a particularly painful jab in the foot, his hat was on crooked and he looked hot and tired. The rift that had been between us since Brisbane was still there, deep and ugly, but already I was seeing evidence that G was indeed going to be different on the island, as he had always predicted. Here he was showing concern for my safety. I was touched. He grumbled on: ''It would be just like you to go and get yourself killed right at the beginning of the year. Then what am I supposed to do? You're always such an impetuous little bitch.'' I slowed down and we carried on for a while in silence.

''Cup of tea when we get back?''

''You bet.''

''Then fishing?''

''O Lu, there you go again! Let's do one thing at a time. What's the bloody hurry? You've got a whole year.''

''We need some fish for supper.''

''We can always have a bit of rice from the stores.''

''Those stores are going to have to be eked out. If we use rice every day we won't have enough to last more than a month.''

''All right, Sergeant Major, we'll get you a piece of fish for your supper. I had every intention of going fishing later, it's just the way you go on. Always in such a bloody hurry.''

There was plenty of time in which to learn to slow down, and to learn to curb—or hide—impatience. Everything lay ahead for us. Perhaps it was a good thing we did not know exactly what did lie ahead. For the time being, ambition and thoughts of the future went no further than making sure we had a fish for supper and wood for a fire on which to cook it.

And so to fishing.

Diary
Hurrah! Caught my first shark today, a baby Black Tip just the right size for a beginner. I went off on a lone fishing trip soon after breakfast and found a new place not far from camp. G was having a garden-planning morning. I left him tramping about on a flattish piece of ground near the creek, spade in hand and purposeful gleam in eye.

It was, to use a well-worn but apposite phrase, a dazzlingly beautiful day, but I had no time to dawdle about poetically. The tide was on the way out and would not be back in again before late evening. The time for fishing was now. We had a very thin day foodwise yesterday and I was anxious to pull in a meal as soon as possible. For bait I used the back of a small parrot fish head left over from last night's meal. It did not smell too good, but at that moment there was nothing else to be had. The tide was not yet far enough out for collecting "cucaracias," and it was just too far out for crabbing. If my smelly piece of parrot was totally disdained I could always crack a few winkles.

The new fishing rock I was trying is amazingly comfortable as regards rock furnishings. So much so that it is to be called Armchair Rock. Unfortunately the water around it is rather shallow at low tide and it cannot be reached when the tide is high, but this morning I managed to time it right. With the first cast I felt almost instantly the familiar tug of a parrot fish, but one so small it could not get its jaws properly round the bait. Either that or it was disgusted. I wound in the line and tidied up the bait. On an afterthought I added a juicy morsel of winkle to increase the allure. It did the trick. The same little parrot hooked himself on, no escape for him this time. But he really was embarrassingly small. I could imagine G's indulgent expression if I walked back to camp with only that to show. He would probably say, quite genuinely, "Well done, at least you caught something." To hell with that! Gambling on the offchance of something substantial passing by in pursuit of smaller fry, I used the whole head as bait, throwing it as far out as possible. Nothing to begin with. Then the line suddenly went slack. I did not know what was happening and started vaguely to pull in. All at once the thin line shot through my fingers, burning into the joints and I gave an involuntary yell. Luckily I had the stick handle of the line wedged between two rocks, otherwise the whole lot would have been lost. The taut line was zooming around all over the place. I picked it up and pulled experimentally. I knew the fish could not be all that big or the line would have snapped at once. Gradually I started to haul it closer. A fine black fin broke the surface, confirming my suspicions that it was a shark. Alerted by my first cry, G was making his way along the beach towards the rock. He arrived at just the right moment to help finish the thing off. I had landed it without difficulty but was having trouble getting the knife to penetrate its thick skin, as it thrashed about furiously. "Lie still while I kill you, you bugger," said G as he stabbed the little shark through the back of the neck. Fried steaks for lunch, poached "fillets" for supper. I was so pleased, and so was G.

*   *   *

Re-reading that piece from my diary, I cannot help smiling. What a song and dance to make over one little baby Black Tip. We were to become so blasé about such things. But I was crowing over something more than catching a shark. I had shown myself efficient as a hunter and provider of food. However I felt about the marriage, I still had my pride as a woman, and no woman likes to be caught out with an empty larder. As Mrs. Robinson Crusoe, I did not have a freezer and I could not go shopping. Money did not exist on Tuin, and, if it had, we could only have used the coins for weighting fishing lines. The provisions we had brought with us could only diminish. But there was the whole sea out there, an endless reservoir of excellent, nourishing food.

So far G and I had always been fishing together. I liked the way he taught me, by demonstration as opposed to lecture. "Well," he said, "I've taught my three boys to fish, haven't I?" True, and I was decidedly pleased when he conceded that I was "not a bad learner." To my delight and his surprise I found that fishing was an occupation I enjoyed. From the moment when we first took up our homemade handlines, his a smart, streamlined "Y" of wood with notches carved into it for the line, mine a much cruder copy but nonetheless effective, I was thoroughly caught up in the spirit of the hunt. I felt happier with G going fishing than at any other time, but still wanted to have a go alone. When he started on his garden, it was the perfect opportunity. More than that, it was necessary. If I did not catch a fish that morning, the cupboard would have been bare. The fact that G was working too added further zeal to my desire to prove myself productive. When the fire was made and I had cooked the fish I had caught and the moment came to call G in from his digging to where I served the meal under our homely camp tree, some quirky little womanly instinct was temporarily satisfied.

Fishing was a vital part of our existence; there were very few days before the start of the monsoon season when one or both of us did not go. Because we were slaves to the tide, all other activities had to fit in around our fishing times. It was by no means all fun and games. Failure to catch anything because of a slack tide, the wrong time of the moon, or G.B.P. (General Bad Planning) was not merely disappointing; it meant no supper. And if there was one thing that wiped all the joy out of a day on Tuin, it was the prospect of no supper. Rice was strictly rationed to once per day, usually breakfast.

We would have been sensible to have brought a great deal more in the way of fishing tackle with us, not that castaways can always rely on the chance to be sensible. Sophisticated equipment was not what we needed, only a great many more hooks and lines. Obviously we had expected to have to improvise, and we did, more and more as the two reels of line and two dozen hooks we had to begin with vanished or deteriorated. However, we did make them last as long as possible:

Diary
Yesterday we had to abandon two fishing lines at opposite ends of our long fishing beach. Both were caught on coral, and one was a length of G's best 100lb breaking strain. This happens frequently, and is exasperating, to put it mildly, when the fish are biting well and one is left with nothing on which to bring them in. We have found that it is fatal to take too much spare line; the same thing invariably happens again and one ends up leaving a sorry little trail of sticks marking the spot, where, hopefully, the lines may be retrieved at low tide next day. We are already reduced to using makeshift lines for repairs; one of G's sons' kitestrings, odd pieces of twine and unravelled rope. The latter has a horrible habit of kinking, and wraps itself around chunks of the seabed with maddening efficiency.

Today I went to the rocks to the right of camp (Armchair locale) and succeeded in finding one line more or less straight away. The other was in an area of F.F.R. (First Fishing Rock), a good trudge away across the now familiar expanse of moonscape stretching away to the water's edge at low tide. It was a trickier job to trace the lost line here. Rocks naturally look different when three-quarters submerged beneath waves, which was how they were at the time we were fishing. I enjoyed matching the tops of the formations as they stood at high water according to my memory, with the green and grey slime-covered mountains now exposed. Eventually, after much fruitless searching, I recovered the line from where it lay wedged securely down a crevice knotty with mussels. Alas, the hook was gone.

To catch a fish one obviously needs bait or a lure or a trap of some kind. In the early days, we concentrated on bait. On Cocos Island, where G had made one of his two previous attempts at the Robinson Crusoe year, he had been shown a useful little mollusc referred to as the "cucaracia." The fact that he was led to the discovery of this creature by others early on in his stay points to one of the reasons why it was impossible for him properly to continue the island project on Cocos. As in the case of the next island he tried, Juan Fernandez, off the coast of Chile, there were always other people there, which undermined the genuine "castaway" idea behind the venture. Tuin had no safety nets in the form of friendly coastguards with regularly delivered supplies and communications with the mainland; it was an entirely different situation, but some of the things he had learned on those other islands could be useful here. For instance, the cucaracia.

The "cuckoo," as we came to call it, having no more scientific tag at our disposal, is a strange, not altogether unappealing creature, rather like a giant leather-jacket grub to look at. Its outer carapace, between one and five inches long and oblong in shape, is divided into segments, which enable the muscular animal inside to curl itself into a ball like a hedgehog when alarmed. The shell is blackish-green with a frill of mossy fur in a paler shade round the edge. The live part underneath is a bright orange tongue of gristle surrounded by a thick suction pad which attaches it firmly to rocks. They are elusive, tending to crowd themselves into crevices, looking with their shield-shaped backs like cowardly members of some misplaced Roman phalanx. It was by a rare chance that on the occasion of our first fishing trip on Tuin, G saw and identified a stray "cuckoo" stranded on a flat boulder.

The art of prising out the tongue centre requires a little practice. A blade is slid under the shell to loosen it from the rock, and then as it comes away the point of the knife must be jabbed quickly into the muscle before it has a chance to squeeze up into a ball. One of the greatest advantages in using the "cuckoo" is that it stays firmly on the hook. A disadvantage is that it seems to appeal only to certain types of fish, whereas other forms of bait, although less convenient to use, attract almost anything that happens to be in the vicinity. We used winkles, mussels, oysters and other shell creatures for which we knew no name, and of course chunks of fish once we had caught the first one. But there is no doubt whatever that the best bait of all is crab.

Crocodile Bay was the place for crabs. This large, circular bay, fringed with dark green mangroves, always reminded me of a well-shaped set of upper dentures with spinach between the teeth; it had that same clean curving bite but was definitely in need of Polident at low tide. The water ran out muddily between the hooped feet of the mangroves leaving a thin bubbly slime bestrewn with green and black detached winkles and sorry little missed-the-tide crabs. I should perhaps mention here how Crocodile Bay acquired its name. It must have been less than a fortnight after our arrival. One afternoon when the sun was far enough past its peak to make walking out to our fishing rock bearable, G went on ahead to begin fishing while I stayed in camp for a few minutes sharpening a knife on a piece of carborundum. When I caught up with him, jumping goatishly from sandhill to sandhill as was my habit, he said quietly, "I don't want to alarm you, Lu, but I think I've just seen a croc."

"Eek! Where?"

"It came out from behind those rocks over there and went running all the way across here and then into those mangroves. I'm not kidding, Lu, it was about eight feet long."

It was quite probable that Tuin was frequented by crocodiles. We had been warned on Thursday Island that salt-water crocs, up to twenty feet long and notoriously aggressive, were common in the Torres Strait. It was possible, judging by the relatively small size of the animal G saw, that Tuin could be a nursery for young crocodiles. We did not know a great deal about the breeding habits of sea-going crocs, but we understood that when the female has laid her eggs she does not stay around to look after them. When the little ones hatch out about three months later, they are all set to take care of themselves. There is no need for mom or dad to come back. G and I sincerely hoped that we had our facts straight, for although we would have liked to observe and photograph crocodiles, preferably from the safety of a tree, having fully grown specimens sharing the island with us could make life rather uncomfortable. We had also to bear in mind that our creek might prove to be the only source of easily obtainable fresh water on the island, and if this were the case, we would not be the only creatures drinking from it. We were hardly in a position to be polite because they were here before us.

What was somewhat mysterious and did raise doubts in our minds was the way in which G described the thing he had seen: "It was holding its head up high and lifting its legs right up. Like a trotting pony."

Somehow I could not imagine a crocodile moving like that. The next day I was treated to a glimpse of the creature while making my way over the same piece of ground. An unusual shape on the top of a rock caught my attention. It was later in the day, and my eyes were not properly adjusted as a few seconds earlier I had been staring at the last white brilliances of the sun before it flared to sunset. But as it began to move I could see the outline of the reptile perfectly. It was certainly some kind of saurian, but exactly what kind I did not know. Again, sensing an alien presence, it made a dash for the mangroves. There was the elegant, high-stepping gait, the head, small for a crocodile I thought, held stiff and alert. This was surely the answer to the galloping mystery of the interior, and as long as it kept running away from rather than towards us, we would remain more interested than disturbed. Nevertheless, as a precaution, G asked me not to wander near the mangroves alone. As the year went on, further indications of life in the mangrove swamp made the name of Crocodile Bay stay with us, although "Crab Bay" would have been a name more indicative of its uses.

At the moment when the tide began to turn there was a grand exodus of crabs from where they had been biding their time in the cool shallows beneath the mangroves. They scuttled out as soon as the water began to recede and we learned that this was the best time for spearing them. There were always one or two which, for one reason or another, did not manage to keep up with the rest. At first they crouched from the heat in puddles beside the few rocks in the bay, but when these dried up and the shade moved, they were lost. All the moisture left their bodies and presumably when the tide came up fish ate them, because all that was left at the next low tide was the cleaned-out carapace and the odd claw, shield and sword of another small Ozymandias. Certainly we preyed on these loiterers whenever we managed to descry one in his hiding place, but our main harvesting was done actually in the water—man to man, so to speak. There was something valiant and touching about those crabs. When we stalked them mercilessly with a three-pronged spear they seldom ran away. Tiny fellows an inch and a half across would fearlessly fling down the gauntlet, raising stiffened pincers in outraged challenge. And with all three nails of the spear stuck right through the body they were still capable of pinching extremely hard when one went to pull off the claws. We had one resident green crab on First Fishing Rock who would succumb to neither persuasion nor violence. He had made his home in a well-protected citadel of rock and would creep out to watch us and wait for tidbits when we were fishing. If we were low on bait and wanted to use him, he would retreat smugly just beyond our reach and bang his pincers together menacingly, like a boxer fisting his own glove before a fight.

I am sure I invested the crabs with these human-sounding qualities, and found characters in fish and birds, for much the same reasons people give anthropomorphic personalities to pets. The human mind must impose. However, if it makes spearing crabs less tedious, or brings joy to the life of an old lady through her budgerigar, it is a harmless enough occupation. It is when the game-playing inventiveness of the human mind extends itself to its own kind that the simplistically termed "misunderstandings" occur. G and I were both to become victims and perpetrators in this field.

We always took the claws off the crabs because the holes they left made good places for threading the quartered body on to the hook. Had it been possible we would have used only crab bait every time we went fishing, but we could not always be sure to be there ready with spears at the precise moment when they ran out to sea. We were damned if we were going to go prodding about in the middle of the night with no flashlight and God-knows-what besides crocodiles lurking in the mangroves. Also there was one drawback to the crab as ideal bait: despite assiduous attention to threading on, it came off the hook far too easily. It was not so bad while we still had conventional barbed hooks of sensible sizes, but when we progressed to bent safety pins and bits of filed-down coat hanger, what used to be an occasional nuisance became a constant irritation. The subtle and cunning attentions of shoals of little zebra fish made matters worse; deceiving us as encouraging parrot fish enquiries they would calmly nibble away all the edible parts of the bait leaving nothing on the hook but an empty leg socket.

One day, when this had happened to us again and again and we were running out of crabs, tired, hot and above all hungry, G decided that he had been messed about enough. He snapped out of the heat-drugged apathy of a failed fishing trip and set his mind to devising a 100 per cent foolproof method of attaching crab to a homemade hook without zebra fish stealing it all. It meant traipsing all the way back to camp and then out to the rock again, but if it helped to furnish us with something for supper, it would be well worth the effort. G took a whole small orange crab, de-legged it and pushed the safety pin hook through two sockets. Then, with strands of nylon unravelled from the net around a glass float found on Long Beach, he tied the whole thing into the toe of one of my Dior stockings. These, incidentally, apart from having been the "something new" on my wedding day, were brought on the expedition with homemade goat's cheese in mind. Sadly, one of the stipulations on the Government permit allowing us to live on an uninhabited island in the Torres Strait forbade us to include any livestock in our baggage. Probably just as well, as we could not have afforded to share our fresh water with a goat.

The occasion of the crab in the stocking stands out as clearly in my mind as if it happened yesterday. The difference is that the conditions that made the episode poignant at the time could never be re-created yesterday or any other day. It is G's face that I see. He is excited as a boy because he has invented something; he is wily as a hunter because his blood is up; he is determined as a man because he and his woman are very hungry. When he is tired or hurt, afraid or on the defensive, his eyes are cold little unreachable marbles; now they are bright with life and anticipation. There is almost a hint of a jaunt in his pace as we head out towards the rock once more. But the tide is coming in fast, there is very little time left before the rock is cut off from our home beach. We sit side by side on the rock while G makes the final adjustments to his line. I am merely an observer on this occasion, having disgraced myself and punctured my confidence by losing not one, but two lines earlier. My enthusiasm is all with G, willing him to succeed.

He stands up to swing the strange lure in a long arc over the water. He has damn good aim. It lands right where the coral cod lie just in front of a deep coral shelf.

"That'll get the buggers."

We wait. The sea, rising higher with each inward wash, makes sounds around us, but the tension of waiting creates a sensation of silence. G's eyes and the sky and the winking sea are blue, blue, blue. The faded string line hangs below the surface of the water. The bait has sunk out of sight. The fingers of G's right hand, still, incongruously, bearing the traces of a nicotine stain, twitch on the line. Waiting.

"You watch, he'll be around in a minute, Lu."

G always had a very personal relationship with the fish he was about to catch. If it stole the bait, refused to bite properly on the hook or played sly, tantalising games with his patience, he would become very cross and very determined.

Suddenly the line is moving. Clack clack as the wood it is wound onto turns over and over on the rock. G is letting out line rapidly.

"He's big, Lulu, bloody big."

I move back to give him plenty of space for landing. He is gripping the line with both hands and holding down the wooden end with one foot, back braced against the sloping rock.

"Bugger it!"

Something has happened. The line is taut but not moving.

"The bastard's wound it round a bloody great rock. Wait a minute, he's off again—*shit*! He's gone, Lu, bastard's gone."

An "Ohh—" from me.

There is a long, glum silence while the sea continues to rise impassively. The slack line dangles from G's hands.

"I suppose he took the lot, did he?" I ask.

G pulls up the hook, at least that is still on. All the crab has gone, one wispy thread of Dior remains.

"What's for supper if we don't get any fish?"

"Tea."

"And a bit of rice?"

"I'm afraid not."

I have one minuscule ace up my sleeve. If it is to be tea only, I am going to slip a little surprise into G's cup. A few days ago I made a wonderful discovery. Two airline sachets of sugar had been floating about all this time in the carrier bag I had brought my film in. To think they might have been eaten by lizards. I did not say anything because I wanted to watch his face when he tasted the sweet tea. But he has not given up yet.

"Right, let's have that machete."

He clambers down to a rock below now half submerged beneath the incoming waters. Three small volcanic-looking oysters offer a final chance. They refuse to come off the rock so he smashes them open where they are and digs out the slippery flesh with his fingers. He jabs all three of them onto the pin. As he throws the line two fly off. Curses. The third gets a bite.

"Quick, get me some more, Lu."

There have to be some more. I climb gingerly down the rock and peer under the water. There is one. I bash it with the machete as it is left uncovered by the water for a second, ragging the ends of my fingers as I gouge out the body.

"Ta, that the lot?"

It is.

"Right, this is it. I'm going to get him."

I come back up. As I turn back to the sea there is light sparkling on splashing green silver as a fish breaks the surface. G has done it.

"Well done, oh well done. Well done!"

"Little git, look at the size of him."

"Never mind! It's supper."

It is a parrot fish, and although it is small, a hell of a lot better than nothing. I know that G would like to stay and chop this one up for bait, but we have to go. Already the sea is up to our necks on the way back and we have to walk inside a wall of stones under the water because of the danger of being swept away by the current.

Back home at last, and dry—G commenting, "First bloody bath I've had in months"—I poached the little fish in seawater. We had half each, but I cheated. When G was not looking I slipped some of mine onto his plate. Woman to man.

Every day during this period, roughly within the first three months, I was learning, exploring, making fresh discoveries all the time. On a practical level I was learning what Tuin had to offer, how big it was in some ways, how small in others, and what its requirements were of us. G was learning too, but the joys of novelty were fewer for him. He had been to hot places with palm trees and golden sands before. He had caught shark, made camp fires, lived in a tent and planted vegetable gardens on other islands. He reached the conclusion very swiftly that Tuin certainly fit the bill as a survival project base, but had not much else to recommend it. I was more hesitant in my assessment, still feeling my way, and privately sensing that Tuin had already begun to give me something I could not name and so far had not been able to share with G. The only real novelty for G lay in the fact that, one, this island really was isolated and uninhabited and had less in the way of natural resources than anywhere else he had been, and two, his companion here was the new woman in his life.

Some things we did learn together; for example, where the best places were for fishing and what the Torres Strait had to offer in the way of seafood. It was not always easy to identify the fish we caught by matching them up with the drawings in our reference book, but it was fun to try, and each new fish represented a potential variation on our menu. Our main concern was to weed out the poisonous specimens, of which there seemed to be comfortingly few, although some of the things we brought in did not appear to be anywhere in the book, and these we threw back or risked according to how repulsive they were. One felt that permanently hungry as we were, if the sight of a peculiar fish actually put us off, there must be something sinister about it.

During this period we were catching more parrot fish and shark than anything else. We originally misidentified the parrot as blue-boned coral cod; it was only on pulling in a real coral cod one day that we realised our mistake. Parrot fish grow up to a foot or more in length, but there are a great many tiddlers. They are of a green somewhere near olive with silvery tints, have large scales and needle-sharp spines on their fins. G gave me my first lesson in gutting and scaling on one of these. We both received painful little pricks in our hands which came up filled with pus the next day. A warning of things to come. Other fish we caught on handlines were: snapper or sea-perch, coral cod and coral trout, a member of the tuna family, the occasional queen-fish, or "wahoo," as our book called it, bluefish and barracuda. Several times when we were after shark one of their sucker fish would come onto the line, if it did not hitch a free ride with its host, but there was not much good eating on them, so we generally threw them back.

Just a few days after our arrival, G had remarkable success with a homemade spear. I had found a long, slender bamboo washed up on the eastern shore. To the end of this G bound three old six-inch nails which he had brought along with this purpose in mind. I was later to learn that the inhabitants of other Torres Strait islands have been trading various commodities for iron to make their spears since the early nineteenth century. Before this they picked up what they could from the many shipwrecks in the area, but prior to the arrival of ships one wonders how they managed. There is evidence that the eastern islanders employed all-wood harpoons when hunting dugong, or manatee, and it is notable that they caught far fewer than their western neighbours who latched on to the usefulness of iron at an earlier stage and became well known for their production of efficient, iron-tipped harpoons. Whatever, in the twentieth century the inhabitants of Tuin were very glad of three rusty nails.

G and I had both noticed that besides blue-spotted stingrays moving around in the shallows, there were small brown sand shark, otherwise known as shovel-nosed ray. These, we gleaned from our fish book, made "excellent eating." That day, as I was making the breakfast, the sandspit in front of camp was just beginning to be covered by the tide. This seemed a good moment to experiment with the spear as there were always some shovel-noses near the edge of the spit at this time of the tide. It was the cool of the morning, so G had not yet covered his body against the sun. I watched him stroll down to the spit, the long spear balanced lightly on his shoulder. He walked without any self-con-sciousness. I recall with absolute clarity the precise thought that went through my head: There's hope for the old bugger yet.

He moved slowly along the spit, scanning the water patiently for the telltale clouding of sand which marked the movement of a ray. Where there was one there were usually others not far away. Once he lifted the spear as though to throw it and then evidently changed his mind, but kept it held ready, pointing down towards the water like a long, questing antenna. Suddenly he took one quick step forward and thrust the spear straight down and then out of the water in a scooping movement giving the victim no chance to wriggle off the prongs. He saw me watching and waved the spear triumphantly, a lively little shovel-nose firmly impaled on the end. It did prove to be good eating, and we thought we had found a relatively easy way of securing a meal, but ironically, try as we might, neither of us caught another shovel-nose for months.

Another thing that we learned together was that it had been a grave mistake to pitch the tent on the sand. It is true that on the day we arrived we had no way of knowing what possible dangers awaited us should we set up camp on the edge of the unexplored interior. Had we known the misery our initial error would cause, we might have taken the risk. Those annoying little sandflies which disturbed our first night on Tuin turned out to be a great deal more than just a nuisance. They were the triggering cause of an ailment that was to amount to a disability and blight all the first months for G. All we knew as the nights went by was that the sandflies made sleeping on the beach uncomfortable. Therefore as soon as we had established that the interior was not alive with snakes or other undesirables, we prepared a flat square of ground under a shady tree and repitched the tent there. G put in a stint of heavy labour, pulling up the grass and chopping out its tough knobbly roots with the spade. He then levelled the ground and removed all stray twigs and stones from the area. Meanwhile I cut sheaves of soft grass to make a mattress. Criss-crossed into three layers and held in place by the groundsheet, the effect was refreshingly soft after the hard-packed ungivingness of sand. Not surprisingly, it did not take long for our bodies to mash the grass mattress into the earth so that soon the bed was as hard as before. However, the sandflies troubled us less. We were not to know that the damage had already been done, and soon the effects would make themselves known.

At the same time as I was learning where to go to gather passion fruit or meat coconuts, how to cope with a shark and handle a machete, I was also beginning to understand a little about our very different characters. It took me a long time to accept that when G announced he was going to do something, e.g., build a raft, start on the shelter, dig a trench from the pool on Long Beach, it did not necessarily mean that the intention had reached the stage of decision in his mind. I remember being quite shocked over the matter of the digging of the trench. He said at the time we found the pool that we should go back the next day with a spade. The next day came and we did not go. I brought the subject up and was shushed with a: "Oh, not today, Lu, I don't feel like it." Don't feel like it? Since when have feelings had anything to do with a decision to do something? I kept quiet and restrained myself from going alone as I was aware that this would cause an uncomfortable atmosphere. Besides, we would make a much better job of it together. And we did, several days later, when G felt more like it. My strict disciplinarian attitude was going to have to loosen up a lot as far as he was concerned.

It was clear from the start that I was not going to get away lightly with having committed the sin of falling in love with the idea of an island, and not with G. Although in some ways I did behave as my bachelor self, creating my own routines, designating certain tasks as my duty, there was no escaping the fact that G was not going to acquiesce quietly to being one of a two-man team. Whatever the reasons, we were married, and G accused me of "welching on a deal," an expression I found peculiarly repugnant. Playing the conjugal role in the tent was not one of the duties I felt to be imperative for survival, and if my values were being revised in other areas, this was the one sensitive spot I could not allow to be violated. Sex was something too valuable to be misused. But the pain and resentment my coldness caused had a wretched effect on the quality of our daily life. During the early months G covered his hurt and anger with an air of noncomprehension and irritable resignation—there was evidently something wrong with me as a woman. He also slept a great deal, perhaps partly as a means of escape. For my part I was just beginning to discover that there were two entirely separate lives for me on Tuin, and G featured in only one of them. But it was a while before I fully recognised the importance of the "other life" for me. For the time being, the everyday business of survival dominated both our lives.

At night, before we had moved the tent off the beach, I would lie for hours, hands behind my head, eyes open, listening to the strange noises that came from the creek. G would be asleep, turned away from me on his side. When the tide came up, it would run into the lower pool of the creek, gurgling and splashing and making curious thumps and sudden swishes as though a large beast were taking a bath. I thought of the long, heavy bodies of salt-water crocodiles sliding down the bank to drink, or coming in with the sea and swimming right into the pool where that swishing sound could be a huge tail stirring up the water. I wondered how silently they were capable of moving on land, and whether anything about the tent might attract them.

It is curious for me now to recall the matter-of-fact nature of my fears; if a croc walked into the tent by the front flap, I would attempt to cut my way out of the back and collapse the tent over the beast to confuse him as I went. My knife was never far from my side. G slept deeply, it could be difficult to rouse him in time. I might have to drag him out by the hair. When I had exhausted the possibilities of a crocodile invasion, my thoughts would usually drift to such banal subjects as food, or how long it would be before there was enough fresh water to wash my hair, and was there a different way to cook parrot fish without using oil, fresh water, or any other ingredients?

CRAB WITH RAISED PINCERS

3

TEMPO AND PATTERNS

"How do you fancy a nice cool cucumber salad to go with your smoked shark, Lu?"

"Good idea. I don't suppose lettuce would grow very well in the Tropics, would it?"

"Have a read of the packets, we could try one of those hardy Oriental types."

We were in the Gardening and Household department of Woolworths in Townsville, one of our stop-off points on the way up the Cape York coast from Brisbane. The Yates seeds rack offered a wide selection of vegetables, quite a few of which, it informed us on the packet blurb, would flourish in a hot climate. We thought we were being neither too ambitious nor too conservative when we came away with our final choice: two kinds of tomato, sweetcorn, rock melon, Queensland blue and butternut pumpkins, Chinese cabbage and spinach, cucumber, cour-gettes (zucchini), capsicums (peppers), kohlrabi and a couple of types of bean.

Then I wandered among the stacks of picnic beakers and camper's metal dishes. I had had enormous difficulty in England finding a good quality metal plate for G. I wanted to have his initials inscribed on one for his birthday. I was assured by a cocky assistant in the Camping department at Bentalls that he had just the thing for me. "Look, solid as iron," he said, tapping the plate with his knuckles. Three distinct dents showed up when he took his hand away. In the end I rather boringly bought G a stainless-steel goblet, and had his initials put on that. But we still wanted a plate each. Finally we chose metal soup dishes that would do just as well for porridge or fish, a tin mug each and a bright green plastic bucket. We already had a knife, a fork and a spoon each, part of a set my mother had given me when she thought I was finally settling down to become a civil servant. I left the rest of the set with an elderly disabled friend in Kew; she said she would think about me eating tropical fruit while she ate her meals-on-wheels. I brought my old fish-slice and G put in two good kitchen knives.

The contents of our provisions box were bought in a big supermarket and the rest of the *batterie de cuisine* and tools in a grey, dust-covered shop in Cairns, full of army-surplus-looking fish kettles. Here we added to our baggage a metal washing-up bowl, one large frying-pan, a medium-sized and a small billycan and a useful object called a dipper which was like a tin mug big enough to cook in if necessary. In the same shop we found the wonderful all-purpose machete, fish hooks and line, and waterproof matches. A spade, an axe and 1,000 blank sheets of paper completed our purchases.

When the white population on Thursday Island heard about our project, there was a mixed response. Curiosity mixed with skepticism. After two nights at the notorious "Grand Hotel," a place where bed-bugs and the last vestiges of crumbled Colonialism co-exist under creaking electric punkahs (ceiling fans) with an all-night blacks' drinking dive, we were taken into the home of a young couple posted to Thursday Island on overseas telecommunications work. They took us to tea with other couples, and advice and opinion flooded in from all sides. One practical-minded Dutch lady, who had been a POW with the Japanese, pressed mung beans, lemongrass roots and a dried guava on me. In a workshop room in the OTC station we picked up some packing foam and string to parcel up our CB radio, and the manager kindly gave us an aerial for it. Alas this piece of equipment was never to be used. During the crossing from Thursday Island to Badu Island an excitable member of the islander crew accidentally picked up the aerial, which had been stowed among a heap of spears, and flung it overboard at a fish. I noticed an old refrigerator outside the OTC station and was eyeing the metal shelfgrids covetously when the manager's wife said, "Yes, they're great for barbecues," and thrust two into my hands. A young man from the Post Office gave us four ancient distress flares— "Well, one of them might work"—and several empty wine flagons to hold drinking water. We later discovered that a small lottery was held as to how long it was reckoned we would stick it out on the island. No one gave us longer than a couple of months; most, considerably less. I do not know who raked in the winnings, as not one person thought we would last the year—with each other, never mind the conditions on the island.

We rated the success of the vegetable garden high on the list of survival necessities. If we planted more or less straight away, there should be some produce before the end of three months. By that time we knew our stores would be finished; we would have to rely on sweetcorn and beans for bulk. My knowledge of gardening was limited. I had picked and planted herbs in English country gardens and I knew how to grow turnips in the north of Scotland. I was also a dab hand with mustard and cress in bed-sitting rooms. G was not quite so ignorant. He had been brought up around farms and had worked on the land. After a spell in journalism and then success in the publishing business, he still had agricultural leanings. He took a farmhouse in Wales and later a villa on an estate in Italy. In both these places he grew vegetables successfully. If the grapes in his vineyards had been as successful as the tomatoes in his backyard, he would probably still have been there. But it was in Italy that the idea of going to an island first came to G. Two wet seasons had ruined the grape harvest, his business in London had collapsed and his relationship with the mother of his three sons was falling apart. He sat overlooking the hills at Lucca, in his own words, "pissed as a fart," and thought: There's got to be something better than this. There must be somewhere, somewhere I can go . . . an island . . .

Eight thousand pounds ploughed over a period of three years into the two island ventures previously mentioned were lost. There was nothing left to plough into Tuin but a few packets of Woolworths seeds and a lot of hope.

In camp, G mused over the packets of seed. He looked inland towards the grey-green plain and up to the northern hill, where the trees and undergrowth obscured all view of the ground. "I always enjoy planning my gardens," he said. "I think I'll get in a couple of tomatoes first, there's a lot in a tomato, you know . . ."

He extolled the virtues of the tomato frequently. I had visions of a magnificent bumper crop and hoped they would preserve all right without pickle vinegar. We planned to dry seeds from the first crop for continuous planting.

G began by digging into three or four patches of soil on either side of the creek. There was only water in the lower part. Higher up, long grass was growing in stiff clumps in the dry bed where the stream would have been. The soil varied in each new patch G dug. On the banks of the creek it was sandy and dry, further along it became greyer but was still loose and dry like sand. After a fair amount of experimentation we decided to concentrate on one area where the grass seemed to be reasonably well nourished. We set to work in the early morning. I pulled up what I could with my hands and G dug out the stubborn roots. The soil was quite dark here and even felt very slightly moist.

It had seemed pleasantly warm when we began, but in a very short time we were both striped with muddy runnels of sweat. "Here, Lu, come and drip over here, this ground could do with a good wetting." I rubbed the back of my hand over my face and G chortled. He described in detail the assortment of smears I had left on cheeks, nose and forehead. We sat down for a few minutes on the edge of the patch we had been working. An outsize grey ant ambled across the clods of dirt. "Have to watch those buggers, they'll have all our seeds." We started to dig and pull again but the heat seemed to grind down our energy like a huge stone.

When the sun climbed above us we had no choice but to stop. The "cool of the morning" lasted no longer than an hour. We had managed to clear and level a handkerchief of earth no more than four foot square.

"I'll drop some seeds in tonight," said G as we slumped, worn out, under our camp tree. It was not very comfortable, but G managed to doze.

Soon I padded down to the beach to wash out the breakfast billy. Small fish with almost transparent bodies came after a dribble of porridge crusted on to the side. The sun struck long fingers of light on the wide, rippling sea. I felt small and happy scrubbing away with a coconut husk, squatting at the edge of all that sea. After this I felt ready for a walk.

Along towards the northern end of the island I had noticed some long purple grasses. I thought these might make a better cushioning layer on the ground than the spiky green stuff around camp. The heat was bearable if one moved slowly. I thought of race-horses being walked around the paddocks after sweating through a race and wondered if our bodies would eventually acclimatise, enabling us to work on when the sun was high, but I doubted it. Even the little darting lizards slowed down in the middle of the day. I was thinking about the lizards, browsing along in a vague dream, when a thick brown log, fallen across the rock I was about to step on to, winked at me. I froze. The foot raised to step on to the rock stayed in the air. There was a sudden clatter as shards of loose stone were flicked up in a clumsy flurry of movement. My eyes followed the trail of flattened grass which led into a dense group of tee and gum trees. I had startled a large goanna taking his midday nap. I just had time to notice, before he disappeared, that his dark body was sprinkled from head to tail with yellowish spots.

It took me some time to relocate the purple grasses. They were hidden in a deep copse behind a wall of trees. It was very hot and still in there. I sat down cross-legged by a clump of grass and took out my knife. It was one of the kitchen knives G had brought and far more efficient than the special angler's knife we had been given which snapped the first time I tried to prise open an oyster with it. Taking hold of a good handful of grass near the base of the stems, I hacked experimentally. They were very tough. There was no way I could tear them out or break them with my bare hands. It was going to be a long job. I settled patiently to the task, tackling no more than four or five stems at a time. The heat lulled me and I felt totally absorbed. I had it in mind to make a daybed for G.

I made my way back through the interior, cuddling a big bundle of grass. The sand was uncomfortably hot to walk on at the top of the beach. G had been digging again. He had prepared another square patch, this time a little closer to camp. "Soil doesn't look bad at all there, Lu. I'm going to get some sweetcorn in. If only these bloody legs of mine didn't keep giving me pain."

The legs were becoming a worry. There was not much to see on them at this stage, just small red spots where he had scratched his sandfly bites, but they swelled up alarmingly if he stayed for any length of time in the sun, or did anything strenuous. Also he felt nauseous quite often, which we could not attribute to anything we were eating. I heaped up the grasses for him under our camp tree.

We fished in the afternoon and when the sun began to go down and I was cooking the meal, G put his seeds in. He lay full-length on the ground to ease his legs and tenderly poked little holes for each seed. He had dampened the soil lightly beforehand. I flung in a few melon seeds but G was the one who took the time and trouble over the garden. It became a ritual with him. Every morning, before breakfast, while I was seeing to the fire, G would make his rounds of inspection. When the first green shoots began to show, he got to know them individually. They were his little green soldiers, and every one that succumbed to sunstroke or a grey ant was mourned. He was very assiduous in his attentions to the garden, working in it every morning and evening and occasionally, perhaps unwisely, in the middle of the day. He dug more small beds in all directions to test out the soil, trying out a row of seeds from each packet. For the pumpkins and melons he made tidy circular mounds spaced about a man's length apart, and for the cucumbers he dug a neat rectangular trench, in the hope that the soil deeper down would hold more moisture.

Even right at the beginning, use of fresh water was severely restricted. G would rinse out his tea mug after breakfast each day and fill it carefully with water from the muddier creek pool. We kept the lower pool as clear and undisturbed as possible, skimming the water gently off the surface with a mug, never dipping in the billy or allowing fish-tainted hands to go in. As the pool shrank gradually to a puddle we used the shallow lid of the billy to skim up the water. At first G watered each shoot individually with a spoon, concentrating it where it seemed to be most needed. Then the opportunity to make a little sprinkler presented itself. One of the billycans I had bought rusted up after the first time I had boiled water in it. Unlike the larger one, which was subsequently used for everything except winkles, which made it stink, the small one was evidently not designed for the outdoor life. Using a bradawl I had thrown in at the last minute in Kew, G punched holes through the bottom, making an efficient spray, which he waved pontifically over the patchwork of vegetable beds.

I was delighted and impressed that G was so absorbed in the work of the garden. As the condition of his legs worsened, confining him to camp except for vital fishing trips, the vegetables became more and more his province. We were both prepared to share in all the chores, but as the days went on, certain jobs began to fall more particularly to one or other of us.

The task of collecting, chopping and storing firewood devolved upon me. I did most of the collecting in Coconut Alley or along the beach north of camp where there was plenty of light kindling readily available. Snapping or twisting off the twiggy branches near the trunk, I formed them into manageable heaps on the ground and then dragged them back to camp. Dry, silvery mangrove sticks made excellent first-layer-after-kindling fuel, but it was impossible not to be scraped and torn while gathering them. Although brittle, the branches were surprisingly springy in parts. Reaching forward to break off one piece, I would inadvertently exert pressure on another, which would then bounce back and claw my bare skin.

There was an even better type of light wood than the silvery mangrove. It was hopeless in the trunk, being too full of sap and spongy when dried, but very good if just the thinnest branches were used. These grew high up, and to reach them, the whole tree had to be brought down. Uprooting was a labour and a game in which I became thoroughly immersed. While I still had plenty of strength and my biceps were improving steadily, I made it almost a ritual to tear down one tree a day. First I would choose a tallish specimen with an abundance of good burning material on it and not too sturdy a trunk. Then, if it was positioned among a tight group, I would climb up a tree beside it and find the place in its trunk where it just began to be supple. Leaning across, I would push it backwards and forwards with all my strength until something near the root began to give. The noise it made, creaking and heaving in the quiet of Tuin, impressed me deeply. If the tree stood alone in a clearing, I would have to charge it to achieve the initial loosening effect. Occasionally this worked remarkably well, particularly with lightning-blasted Melaleucas, but often my charge would do absolutely nothing, and I would end up with a sore arm and a red face. Once I tried slinging a rope of what I thought were unbreakable lianas over a high branch and hauling with all my might. The trunk bent and the whole tree moaned and rustled as though swept by a gale. I thought I was doing rather well until, with sickening abruptness, the liana snapped and I was flung onto my back with great force and no dignity. When I told G about this he laughed and said I was wasting my energy, and that he would chop down plenty of trees when he was ready. Too impatient to wait, I carried on in my own way.

I quickly discovered which types of wood were best for different kinds of fire. If it was just a case of boiling a billy for a cup of tea, a handful of brightly burning plum-tree twigs was ideal. Our camp tree yielded but one small purple fruit per day, so we called it One-Plum-a-Day tree. Sometimes I cut this plum in half and decorated the morning porridge with it, but usually we ate it straight away. If the tree failed to produce its statutory yield, G would look at me most suspiciously, but I swear I never guzzled our daily plum.

Mangrove wood and the trees from Coconut Alley were good for cooking rice, split red mangrove the best for roasting fish. To start all fires I used paperbark and a match. G and I had discussed the possibilities of rubbing sticks together, flints and tinder-boxes and so forth. We decided that as modern castaways we would have saved one carton of matches from the wreck or whatever. Robinson Crusoe had gunpowder, rum, herds of goats and wheels of cheese. We would at least be allowed the luxury of a match. However, twelve boxes of matches containing forty-seven matches each do not last very long, and I was anxious to save most of them for the rainy season. So the system was to try to light just one fire per day. The labour of keeping the fire smouldering was easier to come by than a box of matches.

Paperbark, the loose, tissue-like bark of the Melaleuca, or tee tree, was perfect for getting the fire alight. Even in a high wind, a strategically placed funnel of the thinnest outer layers would almost always light in the end. I had discovered two sizable "plantations" of these trees at an easy distance for carrying armfuls back to camp. From some trees the "paper" came away in long strips. With these I bound the smaller pieces to make compact parcels. If there was any moisture retained in the bark from dew or rain I spread it out to dry in the sunshine on a lattice of branches. I was not to know then that later in the year the "plantations" would become black swamps, the layers of paperbark soaking up moisture like a sponge.

Because I became so much more impatient watching G's efforts at fire-lighting than struggling with my own, it seemed simpler all round if fires became my job, along with gathering in the wood. Before this there had been one or two unpleasant little tiffs, particularly where chopping was concerned. During the first month I had hopefully dragged in a large pile of heavy wood and left the axe beside it in what was, I suppose, a rather hinting fashion. This irritated G to a degree. I had even found a large, smooth stone which I thought would be good to lay the logs across for easy chopping, and positioned this on a flat space of clear ground near the woodpile. Nothing happened. It sat there between us, an unswallowed bone of contention. I blithely marched off to fetch wood, flinging over my shoulder the words: "If I bring in a few mangroves, you'll chop them up for me, won't you? I think we ought to start laying in a store of wood." I should have taken G's silence as a warning of things to come. When I returned some time later dragging three fine logs, he was in precisely the same position as when I had left, recumbent in the shade of One-Plum-a-Day tree. "Darling," I chirruped as I approached, "look what I've got. And there's plenty more where these came from. If we bring in half a dozen a day and chop them up, we'll soon have a good lot in store. There are some lovely straight trunks, too, that could be just right for the shelter. We ought to get started on that before long."

"Daar-ling," he replied, mocking both the endearment and my accent, "that is a horrible habit you've got. You call out when you're halfway down the bloody beach and I can't hear what the hell you're rabbiting on about. And another thing, in future shut up about this 'we' business. If you want to do something, you get on and do it. If I want to chop some wood, I'll do it in my own bloody time. You're so fucking dictatorial, Lu.''

This was dangerous ground. Because I knew basically why G was so fed up, I did not have a leg to stand on. ''I'm sorry if it seems that way. I really don't mean to be. How about some tea?''

''All right,'' he said belligerently. ''I'll make it. I've had enough of your smoky shit.''

My hackles rose. It is true that there had been one or two decidedly ''smoked'' cups of tea. Not like Lapsang Souchong at all. However, it was not always easy to avoid this. The lid of the billy did not fit properly and when the wind suddenly lifted up and blew out the fire at the same time, smoky tea was the result. There was not enough water to chuck it out and start again.

G got to his feet and shambled over to the fire. I would have coaxed a spark from the heat already in it but G built a neat little nest of paperbark and twigs and used a match. I made no comment and felt virtuously tolerant. G piled on the small pieces of mangrove I had been able to break up with my hands and feet. That irritated me too. He had not even filled the billy yet, so he was wasting my hardwon wood for nothing.

''Shall I put some water in the billy?'' I asked.

''You just sit still and do nothing for a change. *I'm* making the tea this time. Now, where do you keep the mugs?''

''Hanging in the tree right in front of you.''

''Ah.''

He shoved on another four pieces of wood and wandered off down to the creek with billy and ladling mug. He was wearing a filthy old denim shirt and nothing else. The tail slipped out from between his buttocks as he moved off. I could not sit still anymore, so I walked down the beach. Might as well have a bath while I'm here. G will probably be about three days making the tea, I thought nastily. By the time I was back up in camp G had the billy on the fire, loaded up with yet more unnecessary wood—my bath had not mellowed my mood—and was hovering about with our one packet of tea in his hand. He stood poised over the billy, ready to shake it in. That was too much for me. I could just see it spilling all over the ground.

"Hold on," I said, "use a spoon."

"Oh, Madam is back, is she? Where's the spoon?"

I gave it to him, he used it and then put down the tea, still open, beside the fire. In my camera bag I had a plastic container full of sachets of silica gel. I emptied these out, placing them carefully among the parts of the camera and took the container to where G was standing. I put the packet of tea in it and closed the lid firmly. "There, that should keep it safe."

"Tea's ready," said G and lifted the billy over to our place in the shade. "Now, there's a decent cup of tea. None of that foul brew that old cow makes."

I could feel my face go tight and pinched. "Hardly surprising it turned out well considering you used up all the best wood for it."

"Oh, not that again. I'll chop some bloody wood for you."

"Great. When?"

'Jesus Christ, Lu, I've said I'll chop you some wood. Now shut up about it."

I cringe inwardly when I recall my own behaviour sometimes.

G did chop some wood. He would wait until we had caught a fish and were ready to cook it. Then he would take the axe and chop just enough wood for one fire. Often it was late and there was a rush to get the meal over before the mosquitoes came out. He complained that much of the wood I had been bringing in was too hard to chop. After a week of this I had had enough. I picked up the axe one morning and set about learning to use it myself. G was quite right about most of the wood, it was impossibly hard. So I learned to recognise which branches were good and in future brought in only those. After observing my ineptitude for a few days G taught me how to wield an axe properly, and he did it with kindness and love.

I had been swinging the axe high into the air and bringing it down with an ungainly crash on to a branch laid across the chopping stone. Often, blind with sweat and determination, I would miss. G was lying watching me one day when this was going on. His voice came suddenly, very gently, from under the tree: "Lu, you're going to cut your fucking foot off in a minute. Come on, let me show you."

He taught me how to use the weight of the axe, to do the job calmly and not to waste energy. So, the woodpile became my responsibility. I built it up steadily, adding a little to it every day. It was an enjoyable exercise and gave me much satisfaction. Occasionally, if we caught an especially large fish and wanted to roast it whole, G would split enough tough mangrove for the cooking fire. Without being nagged.

Many months later, when some of the tensions between us had either dissipated or been accepted as permanent impasses, we talked about G's reluctance to help initially with the wooding. A combination of factors had built up a resistance in him against having anything to do with a regular routine task that was not self-imposed. At first I thought he was simply idle. Then it became increasingly apparent that when he set his mind to a job that interested him, he would work at it with great diligence, as with the garden. But the everyday chore of wood-chopping did not attract him at all. Also, he did not want to be told what to do. He had had enough of carrying out orders in the army. He particularly did not want to be told what to do by a woman twenty-six years younger than himself and cold in bed to boot. My jolly-hockey-sticks sergeant-majorishness was anathema to G. His lackadaisical attitude to getting our everyday life organised on Tuin appalled me. The law of opposites attracting did not work for us. Our differences goaded us frequently to a display of our least desirable traits and yet there were unspoken areas of understanding. One afternoon, when his legs seemed to be on the mend, G came to me to gather in a load of wood I had stacked into a number of piles in the interior. He was full of enthusiasm and good intention and I warmed to his mood. It must have come as a horrid shock to him to realise that he was no longer physically capable of lifting up and carrying a piece of wood which in better days he could easily have managed with one arm. He had lost weight by then, we both had, but neither of us fully realised what a toll the leg problem and his depression had taken of his strength.

I remember him struggling to balance the wood on his shoulder, bits falling off, getting in the way of his legs. He walked a little way and then stopped and let the logs roll to the ground. "Think I must have had too much sun today, Lulu," he said, swaying and wiping at his forehead with a bark-stained wrist. There was something in his voice that made me want to put my arms around him. I wish I had. We both knew he could have taken a small load at a time, but that was not the point. I never asked him to help with the wooding again.

*　　*　　*

Food was, second to none, our greatest mutual preoccupation on the island. As what we were to eat could make or mar each day, I tried to vary it as much as possible and make it interesting:

Reef Pilau
Take the frill and flesh from one large blue-lipped clam. Chop finely and mix with the hinge muscles of one dozen mud oysters.
    Allow to marinate in own juice in shade.
    Boil 2 dessertspns. of brown rice in one mug of mixed fresh and sea-water. Drain swiftly before salt impregnates rice. Using half a teaspn. oil grease bottom of frying pan. Heat over steady mangrove flame until a piece of clam-lip shrivels on contact with pan.
    Seal marinated mixture briskly, shaking pan.
    Add rice and lower flame with peepa husk. Heat gently.
    Meanwhile have your man open 12 small purple rock oysters for garnish.
    Serve on a bed of chopped snake-bean leaves when in season.

Barracuda Vinaigrette
Poach 2 large barracuda steaks lightly in sea-water.
    Drain well. While still warm, pour 1 teaspn mixed oil and vinegar and pepper over each.
    When cool, flake up and stir in half a mug of 3-days-old mung shoots. Add pinch of salt if necessary.

Open Roast Blue
Gut one medium-sized bluefish. Do not scale.
    Roast slowly over hot embers until completely black.
    Turn over once. Press with stick on fattest part of fish to test. Flesh should feel firm and stream of boiling bubbles shoot out if cooked.
    Crack off blackened scales neatly.
    Serve one side of fish per person.
    Save head for picking between meals.

Parrot Rissoles
Peel and chop 2 large cassava.
    Boil in fresh water until soft. Mash.
    Scale and gut one parrot fish.
    Poach well. Remove flesh from bones.
    Mix with cassava.

Add pepper if available.
Form into balls. Flatten each slightly.
Fry in one dessertspn oil.
Serve at once.
N.B. Sweet potato (or yam) can be substituted for cassava, or, if neither is available, use 2 parrot fish and half a cup of cooked white rice.

Black-Tip and Bean Stew

Soak ¼ mug of red kidney beans overnight.
    Chop 4 strips of wind-dried black tip shark into cubes.
    Cook with beans in fresh water with a dash of sea.
    Add 2 dessertspns white rice when partly cooked.
    Drain and serve.

Coconut Snapper

Gut, scale and fillet one large snapper.
    Simmer in billy with juice and grated meat of one coconut, preferably Long Beach type.
    If required, use a second coconut for more juice and save grated meat for morning rice.

Palm Beach Pâté

Boil 8 small or 4 large turtle eggs.
    Boil and mash 5 yellow sweet potatoes (or yam).
    Mix together to a perfectly smooth pâté.
    Serve for lunch with slices of cold poached shark or on its own.

An ideal accompaniment to the above dishes is young passion fruit nectar, simmered in top-of-the-pool water and strained through 3 layers of Lucy's sari. Serve at rock pool temperature.

The recipes here are listed more or less in order of the availability of ingredients during the first six months or so. Use of items from the stores box on a daily basis was limited to half a cup of rolled oats between us for breakfast and when these ran out, one fifth of a cup of rice cooked to a porridgy consistency. Where rice, beans or condiments were included in a meal it was somewhat in the nature of a treat, or because our catch had been so inadequate that it required bulking out. Our standard fare was plain fish poached or roasted as these methods of cooking needed no other ingredients.

At the very beginning G and I took turns with the cooking. On Cocos Island he had prepared most of the meals for his three boys, who spent some months there with him. But like a lot of men who tend to be extravagant when let loose in the kitchen, G found it hard to temper his zeal to produce something good with the knowledge that the stores could not be dipped into every time a meal was being made. Although his lifestyle over the past five years had been far from lavish, he had nonetheless retained the habit from his wealthy days of using whatever he had without a great deal of thought for the future. Economising had never been his forte. Once we were castaway and I had emphasised the necessity of eking out the stores as long as possible, he began to appreciate the traits of discipline and denial in me that so oppressed him in other ways. After a short time on Tuin, management and rationing of stores fell automatically into my hands. It followed that I should take over the cooking entirely as well. This arrangement suited us both, although later I was to feel the same pressures as Captain Bligh must have felt, being forced meanly to dole out smaller and smaller portions as time went on.

I worked to a system that was in fact extremely flexible, but guided by one or two hard and fast principles that made it into at least a partial routine. I believed in starting the day with something in our stomachs; therefore breakfast, however tiny the portions became, was absolutely regular. From time to time the position of the tide necessitated our going fishing the moment it was light enough for us to see. We both found that our energy and enthusiasm on these dawn trips flagged very quickly if we went on a completely empty stomach, and as we grew thinner the mild morning cool seemed to bite right into our bones, weakening and demoralising us. So even if it meant stumbling around in the dark, I made sure that the least we had was half a mug of hot tea inside us before we went. The mere heat and ritual of this seemed to improve our spirits, for there cannot be much energy value in sugarless black tea.

The time and content of the next meal of the day depended entirely on our luck fishing. If, for instance, we caught shark or a big queenfish or tuna in the morning, we would have enough for a lunch and a supper. I would poach a couple of steaks at midday and preserve another two servings by rubbing salt and vinegar over the pieces of fish which were then left in the shade, to be cooked later on. As the weather became hotter, we could not risk keeping the fish even for a few hours, so we either dried what was left over or used it for bait. If we had no luck at all with fishing, we would return to camp for a rest and cup of tea in the shade, and then transfer our attentions to gathering the main ingredients for a meal from the beaches.

It did not take many days of the statutory one dozen oysters each for us to become heartily sick of such a frustrating luxury. Our bellies spent a great deal of time informing us that what they wanted was something substantial. However delicious an oyster may be, and some of them were exquisite, it cannot be described as filling. So after a while, if oysters were to make up the main part of a meal, I tended to mix them with other things and even cook them to make them seem more solid. An example of the sort of thing I experimented with is given in the first recipe listed. That particular dish earned me a terrific compliment from G. He said, "You produce better things out of a blackened billycan than most women do using a full range of equipment."

That may have been the grateful voice of an extremely hungry man speaking, but whatever, I was very pleased and proud. The production of that type of meal took a whole morning or afternoon. This was due to the fact that the best oysters, and the clams, were on the other side of Tuin. While G was still able to come with me, these expeditions were very enjoyable.

First of all we would do the best we could to ensure that G did not suffer any further punctures or lacerations to his legs on the way over. He would don his barely-holding-together "Robinson Crusoe" trousers, authentically frayed at the bottom where the ankles had been cut off to make oven gloves, and bind what remained of the soles of his thongs on to his feet with bandages. I was so glad I had included plenty of bandages in the medical kit, materials for tying and binding were something we were always wanting. I did experiment with various vines, plaiting, chewing, soaking and drying them, but none of them proved reliable. One variety, which I found near the purple grasses in the north, was at least strong, if not very supple. I found that if I bashed it patiently all along its length with the back of a knife, and then hung it up to dry, it would serve as a temporary washing or fish-drying line when our precious rope was being used for some other purpose.

We crossed to Long Beach through the least hazardous area. By now a path through the thick reeds on the other side was well established. I had dragged a log behind me several times to flatten some of the reeds permanently. On stepping out onto the windy shore, we turned left and made our way via the black rocks to the brownish slime of the

Starting out: the sum total of our worldly goods stacked on the beach at Badu.

A fine catch in the early days, when it was still cool enough – and I was still 'civilised' enough to be wearing clothes.

Strips of shark drying in the sun and wind. The view shows Tuin's face at low tide.

PHOTO: GARY STEER

Getting down to the business of being an island woman.

Cray!

Tying crossbeams into uprights on the first shelter.

Camp. G takes a turn in the 'open plan' kitchen.

coral revealed at low tide. Here G stopped and settled himself with bucket and knife on a comfortable rock. I would take the machete and work slowly northwards, whacking mud oysters off the rocks as I went. We needed two dozen or more to make an adequate meal, less if I could find a clam or some big flat black-bearded oysters to go with them. Little purple rock oysters were ubiquitous. We could pick up a dozen or so of these on the way back. It took some time to find the mud oysters, because they were well camouflaged under a uniform layer of coral slime. I identified them by the small, bulging shape they made on top of a stone or piece of coral. When I had four or five I would lay them in a row along the blade of the machete and carry them carefully to where G was waiting. He smashed them and cleaned the innards while I went back for more. Team efforts of this kind gave us both satisfaction. Later, when G was busy in the garden, or confined to the camp area because of his legs, I would go over and fetch the oysters alone, bringing them back to be cleaned in camp. Although I loved to be alone on walks, I missed G's presence on the oyster missions.

Designing and improving my cooking fires was fun. I graduated from a scruffy little pile of twigs on the ground to an efficient split-level range plus special separate roasting section. The transition was gradual. The rusty twenty-litre petrol drum I had found on the day we arrived was in such poor shape that it fell apart after being used two or three times as a fireplace. But I had seen its potential. In the course of my travels around the island I came across several washed up petrol cans in various states of usability. I saved the best ones to go towards forming the base of a raft G had in mind. Those with badly damaged sides were cut in half length-ways with the machete and used as seed trays. The two that were left in moderately good condition went to make my first double range. Before I had become adept at the art of cutting tin with an axe, the sight of my crude hacking drove G to cut the tops out of the drums for me. I then told him where I would like air vents and he made neat, square openings with the cut out piece of tin folded back to help prevent the wood falling out. When these tins wore out I had learned enough to make the next two more manageable. I left one of the tops on, asked G to cut one large vent in the side, through which fuel could also be fed, and a smaller one near the top. I then laboriously cut a circle of small slashes in the top. This was my slow burner, ideal for simmering rice. The other one, with the whole top cut away, was for fast frying, rapid boiling and with a small low fire and a refrigerator grid on top, for roasting small parrot fish or snapper.

The separate roaster was situated in front of a thick hedge of bush that afforded some protection whichever direction the wind was coming from. Making numerous trips to the beach, I collected a pile of suitably proportioned squarish stones and arranged them in a rectangle that could be made smaller or larger depending on the size of fire required. A few big flat stones placed nearby served as safe surfaces for a hot billy or frying pan. A refrigerator grid laid at the required height across the stones was perfect for roasting the larger fish. A couple of conch shells set upright in the ground on either side satisfied my decorative urges, and the handy branches of a tree above held mugs, oven gloves and billy lid. I was always happy pottering about in my kitchen under the sky.

Gradually, within and beyond the banalities of routine, the rhythm of Tuin established itself. Sun, moon and tide wielded an implacable baton, conducting our every move, dictating to us when it was time to fish, time to labour and time to rest. And yet within the metronomic strictures of heat and night and day, we were free to flounder or flourish. To survive one must conform. When the pattern of conformity is set, then you can see where your freedoms lie.

Diary
It has taken me months to adjust to the pace insisted upon by Tuin. I mean the external pace, the speed at which one lifts a foot and puts it down to make a step. The complex emotional gear-changes come afterwards. Tuin is not cleared ground made meek for the convenience of human feet, to be ignored and charged over. The in-between part of A to B is a palpable reality as large in relevance as the destination. The unsteamrollered demands a certain deference. Walk on me, says Tuin, I am only an excrescence on a coral reef in an almost forgotten corner of the world, but if you refuse to acknowledge my nature you will suffer.

Acknowledgement was a necessity and awoke animal responses and animal adjustments. Appreciation was a long step further on, very human.

The walk from camp to First Fishing Rock was excellent teaching ground for beginners in the art of Tuintime. Depending on the position of the sun the first one hundred yards was a straightforward matter of padding over loose coral sand. If the sun stood high, and the sand scalded the soles of our feet, it was less a question of pad than skim. Down the beach was no problem, up and along another matter. The depth of the sand made it impossible to walk with a loose stride. Both G and I noticed the peculiar waddling quality of movement we were forced to use. There was something very elderly about it.

Crossing Crocodile Bay at low tide was easy enough, hill-hopping and puddle-jumping. The pace teacher really began after this. Over a firm breast of sand, then the rocks. On one side was the false beach of Coconut Alley, the heads of the taller palms standing out in elegant incongruity behind the broad forest of encroaching mangroves dividing them from the beach. On the other side, all blueness and heat dazzle, the hovering brilliance of sun and endless rippling sea. But one can look neither to left nor right. All attention must be on each footfall. Over the split and crumbled rocks there is a slippery coating of mossy slime. It is the colour of verdigris and on the smoother boulders has a soft bloom like a sloe. The lifted foot sucks up skeins of this, leaving quiffs and peaks in the footprint. Between the outcrops of rock the coral slime loses its woolly quality and is just grey mud. But the soft blanket of ooze is misleading. It barely covers thousands of razor sharp mussels and coral fragments. It is not difficult to learn to test each step with graduated weight. It only takes time. Impatience earns instant reprimand; a toe stubbed on a hidden mussel, split open at the end; a tender instep bruised and torn; sucked in breath, curses, sickness in the throat. The rocks, palms and sea impassive. Calm down and continue with care. Slowly.

I have a vivid recollection of one small accident caused by imprudent hurrying. G and I were going fishing on Prize Parrot Rock. I was away out in front carrying bucket and fishing lines. There had been rain and the rocks were cold and slippery. It was very early morning and we were anxious for a good catch, having eaten nothing but coconut and winkles the day before. I saw a crab and made a hasty lunge for him with the machete. The sharply protruding bone on my right ankle caught the edge of an oyster encrusted with coral. I lurched, gasping, and lost my footing, bones seemed to be crashing into rocks in all directions. Everywhere I put a hand to try to save my fall I was cut. Finally I landed, hip-bones first, in a jaggedly ridged trough between two rocks. Elbows, shoulders and neck were grazed. None of the damage was serious. It was just a horrid reminder of one's fragility in an unyielding environment.

It was not only the abrasive qualities of the island that commanded one's pace. The sun itself made a mockery of rushing. I learned to walk on Tuin. Within weeks I lost the brisk, brittle city stride, the jolting, stiff-legged crossing-a-road pace. The sun melted the resistance in my limbs and throughout my body, from the soles of my bare feet, conscious of the texture of every footfall, to the crown of my uncovered head, protected from burning by a coiled plait of hair and loose tufts shading sensitive ears.

Diary
Long Beach. For most of the year on this side the sea breaks in low, long white lines of surf over gently shelving sand. When the wind changes to the north west, and Palm Beach and Crocodile Bay are stormed and buffeted, the water here is suddenly stilled. It becomes calmer than a loch on a summer's day. Squat bush trees at the edge of the interior, their long, ghoulish arms stretching inland, are petrified. Frozen in motionless heat. I stand beneath Lone Pine tree, whose slender branches create a thin web of shade, and flex my toes in the warm sand. A translucent spider crab, legs fragile as rolled Chinese wafers, scuttles rashly from the shade of its cool hole. The clatter its delicate movement makes is shockingly loud in the stillness. Shall I go to the left or to the right? My feet take me right. There are tramlines of footprints in both directions. The tide has not come high enough to cover them for a long time. Every one of those footprints is mine. What long big toes. I don't seem to walk in very straight lines. Sundrunk perhaps.

How many days and days I spent walking on that beach. Every part of me reacted to the sun, which slowly burned away the division between mind and body and rolled me into one sun-undulating being. Heel going down into soft sand rocking through calf and thigh to bowl of pelvis, up spine to skull, down through hollows of collarbone to fingertips, round again. Mind following feet following feet following mind finally just walking.

I used to go to a special rock under the tall Long Beach mangroves to scribble down bits of diary. At the far end of the beach I had to pick my way over hundreds of bony red mangrove roots, curved one over the other like untidy croquet hoops pushed at random in to the wet sand. The rock itself lay right at the edge of the interior, its rounded bulk framed by long, trailing branches. Before climbing up into the couch-shaped dip in the top of the rock, which came just above my head when I was standing beside it, I would untie the strip of orange *crêpe-de-chine* from around my hips and throw it up to where I was about to recline. Knife and sheath belt would follow and finally the small bag containing pen, paper and one volume of Robert Graves' *Greek Myths*. The few seconds this little preparatory ritual took gave me extraordinary pleasure. Using convenient rocks as steps, I would scramble up and carefully arrange the sari strip, folding it exactly where the bony base of my spine was about to go. The moment of actually sitting down was perhaps the most delicious of all.

It is amazing how comfortable a body can make itself upon a hard rock. The secret lies in complete mental and physical acceptance and surrender. If one holds the body taut, repulsing the rock for its ungivingness, comfort can never be achieved. The sari was unnecessary as padding, a nicety demanded by the mind, like taking paper plates on a picnic instead of eating off leaves. It was not long before I abandoned that and the knife as well. Book and writing gear were more difficult to cast aside, representing one of man's most essential and seductive powers, communication, but in the end they went too.

Somewhere around August, September or October we completely lost track of the date. Neither of us had made entries in our small printed diaries for some time. G asked me, out of the blue, what day it was. I had no idea.

"Well, what month is it?"

"August?"

"No, no, way past that. Probably nearer October."

"It can't be, surely, it doesn't seem that long . . ."

Tuintime had quietly taken over. It became a matter of day—dawn, morning cool, heat-of-the-day, sun-over-the-yard-arm, sun-over-Tukupai, sunset—and night—sandflies out, "Oh Dear" bird, moon, scrubfowl sounds—and then dawn again. We had the biggest water clock in the world, the whole of Camp Bay, to tell us when it was time to go fishing. When the water fell below a certain rock, we had to go, or wait until the tide had been right out and was coming in again.

We learned that fish seem to have "periods." They tend to bite well when the moon is in its first quarter, go off around the full moon and start to come around again in the second quarter. Fishing at other times can be lucky but is far less reliable. The tides were something of a mystery. We were both fairly confident that the tide ought to be approximately an hour later each day. We were baffled by its inconsistency, reluctantly concluding, after many months' observation, that it had as little regard for what it ought to be doing as we did. Over a year later I was to find an answer to the mysteries of the tide in the Herbarium Library at Kew. According to notes by J. N. Jennings the reason for the inconsistency is as follows: the tide in the Indian Ocean is dominantly diurnal, whereas in the Pacific it is semi-diurnal, resulting in mixed tides in the Torres Strait. Although the diurnal components match in range and time, the semi-diurnal are out of phase. Marked differences in level result, accentuating the normal effects of significant tidal range in restricted channels, to produce strong tidal currents. In other words it is a mixed up little area of sea. We were to find out more about currents later on in the Tuin year.

So the sun continued to make its arc over us with the regularity of a mono-directional pendulum. The roughly cut pieces that overlapped and divided our lives fell into a vague shape. I was much preoccupied with wooding and the gathering of fruit and coconuts; G with the garden. Large projects, such as the building of the shelter, loomed in rather a threatening way. G knew how anxious I was to start on it and predictably reacted negatively against any form of nagging. I could not tell how much of his reluctance to get started was due to the condition of his legs or a general inertia. At first I minded "on principle," because he had said we would be out of the tent within three weeks and living in some kind of a house. But this was prearrival-on-Tuin talk, theoretical and archaic as my "principle."

The only thing that continued to irk me was the presence of our bags and boxes in the islander's corrugated iron shed. Somehow it just seemed very unenterprising to dump all our gear in it and indefinitely postpone building somewhere of our own. After a while the subject of the shelter became almost taboo. I secretly hoped that if I behaved as though I had completely forgotten about it, G would one day make a start of his own accord. However, I had made it clear that I would willingly drop whatever I was doing and help in any way possible as soon as he got the building urge. This over-eagerness on my behalf probably set him back another month.

Finally the day came when I returned from a walk to find G measuring out a piece of ground with the rope.

"We'll need to get the uprights in first, Lu."

"Right-o, anything I can do?"

"I thought I might go over and see if there are any straight trunks near that hill, bring the axe, would you?"

He was gesturing in the direction of the northern hill. As I leapt over the creek to join him I could not suppress a small "Yippee!"

"Do you reckon there's any nasties up that way, Lu?"

I knew damn well the place was hotching with green ants but I was not going to put him off. "Well, there might be the odd ant. Tell you what, I'll get your trousers."

On the way G outlined his plan for the shelter. He explained that we would need to find six sturdy uprights to begin with. The idea was to have a simple sloping roof supported by a structure of beams and rafters. The shelter would face the sea, its back to the wind, and be closed in on three sides. We were not aware at that stage of the dramatic about turn the wind would take during the three months of the rainy season.

We marked two good straight gum trunks that would do for the shortest uprights, at the back of the shelter. Finding the next two, and the tallest pair that would go at the front, presented more of a challenge. We would see ahead of us a beautifully proportioned, mast-high tree and then find as we drew nearer that it was spoilt by a kink half way up or deformed by some huge carunculation. We reached the base of the small foothill that preceded the northern hill.

"Plenty of good beams here," said G, "but nothing tall enough . . ." He stood for a moment, rubbing his wiry beard thoughtfully then quite suddenly he began to yell, "Fucking hell, get them off me, Lu! Shitting bloody Jesus they're everywhere . . ." And they were. G had unwittingly been standing directly beneath a branch where a legion of green ants were in the process of building one of their leaf traps. He had absently put a hand on the tree trunk and columns of ants had immediately run up his arm. Green ants have a vicious bite that feels like a sharp sting combined with a swift injection. G was being bitten on his hand, arm, neck, ear and now they were crawling all over his head and falling down the front and back of his shirt. He was performing an insane sort of one-man Scottish reel. I rushed in to help, tugging his shirt off and swiping the ants away with my hands.

"Don't brush them off, kill the buggers, kill as many of the little sods as you can!"

Slapping did not kill them, it only made them panic, whereupon they would bite immediately. They had to be individually pinched or squashed to death. A few had escaped my brushing motions by running down G's trousers, which he promptly tore off and hurled away into the bush. The ants that had fallen to the ground were now running up my legs. I executed a series of lightning *pas de chats*. G was raking away the last of the tormentors from his head and neck. Then, as suddenly as they had come, they were all gone. It was as if a general had given the command to retreat. We wiped off dead bodies and I retrieved G's trousers. All the ants had left them too.

"Bloody hell, Lu," said G, weakly. "I bet those woods are full of the bastards."

He was right, but we still had to get our uprights. On that first occasion we found four altogether, enough for a start.

In the cool of the morning next day we retraced our steps, only leaving our path to give a wide berth to the green-ant tree. I noticed that they had industriously completed their leaf trap, which now hung in the tree like a forgotten Christmas decoration, webbed with sticky-looking white threads. I observed all this through the zoom lens of my camera, not wanting a repeat of yesterday's performance.

G spat on his fingers and set to with the axe. The gum trunks were hard and the blade none too sharp, but he managed to make a deep bite into one side with just a few blows.

"Now get yourself out of the bloody road, Lu, it's going to fall that way."

He chopped into it on the other side and the tree toppled neatly into a clearing.

By the time he had felled the fourth tree G was dripping with sweat and his feet were beginning to swell. I gathered armfuls of light wood from the tops of the felled trees and we made our way back to camp, saving the work of lugging in the trunks for the evening cool. Later in the day G put in markers where the holes for the uprights were to be dug.

We went back to fetch the trunks well armed with shoulder pads and rope for dragging. I remember feeling most peculiar wearing a bra and pants for a photograph and thinking what a stranger G looked in bathing trunks. It was a relief to both of us when I hung the camera in a tree and we took off our clothes once more and got on with the work. It was odd how G's old shirt and filthy trousers, worn for protection against sun and bites, seemed to fit in naturally, whereas the bathing trunks and my undies seemed oddly embarrassing. In the first weeks I had occasionally worn clothes in the morning, before the sun began its ascent, but very soon I abandoned this habit, and the only bit of material I ever wore was the strip of sari cloth around my hips, which was so useful for making into a bag to collect coconuts on walks. For some obscure reason I have never yet fathomed, G had brought with him a pale pink satin and chiffon jumpsuit, a relic from the model box used in his magazine publishing days. It came in very useful for evening fishing sessions when the sandflies were out, although the deep decolletage did not afford him any protection on the chest. It was last seen floating off in the direction of Papua New Guinea, an intriguing catch for some fisherman up that way.

G lopped off the top branches of the trees and neatened the ends. He left convenient forks into which crossbeams could be securely lashed. We carried the heaviest trunks together, one at each end, our shoulders well padded with trousers and sari. I did not admit it to G but I thought at one point that the wood was going to mash straight through my collarbone. In spite of his weight loss G still had plenty of power left in his muscles at that stage. When we went back for the next load I helped him balance one on his shoulder and then lashed myself to the other with the rope and dragged it in his wake. Digging the holes was fun. We wanted to be sure that the shelter would be solid so we planned on burying at least one third of each upright in the ground. The two middle trunks were about twelve foot high, so this meant holes four foot deep. The type of soil we had to deal with did not lend itself well to hole-digging operations. I had had problems the first time I tried to dig a "bassura" pit. We needed somewhere to dispose safely of fallen apart "ovens" and seed drums rusted beyond redemption. It was a stone of Sisyphus situation: every time I succeeded in digging out a good space, one of the sides would suddenly cave in and fill up the pit. After two or three attempts my common sense woke up. I chopped down a corky pandanus, hacked it into lengths and shored up the pit as I dug. It was not so simple to apply this trick to the holes for the uprights, which needed to be deep and narrow. Luckily there was a greater quantity of earth than sand on the site chosen for our house.

G began by sharpening the end of the upright and then driving it into the ground as far as he could. He would then whip it out and start digging furiously. When he had gone down as far as he could with the spade, it was my turn. I lay down flat on my belly, and using the billycan as a scoop, stuck head and arms down the hole and threw out clods of sandy earth in all directions. When I could reach no further without falling in, G held on to my ankles. I finally emerged, glistening with sweat, hair matt-black, like some giant witchetty grub.

Next I went down to the beach with our green bucket and filled it up with small rocks. These I poured around the upright which G held in place in the hole. He had made a plumb-line out of a stone, and a piece of packing string. We were amazed at how bent our straight trunks turned out to be. I sweated off every trace of earth on the trips up and down from the beach. It was a good moment when at last the hole was filled in, the earth tamped down and the pole deemed perfectly upright. It was better still when all six of the uprights were in position, with supporting poles in between, but there was to be a long gap before the next spell of labour.

CORAL TROUT AND PARROT FISH

4

EXCURSIONS

When the top puddle of the creek ran dry my beauty routine lost its mainstay. I had been in the habit of passing the palm of my hand, wetted with fresh water, over my face each morning. Loath to abandon the luxury of a matinal rinse altogether, I shrugged my shoulders and switched to sea water. If the sun was drying out my skin I was not aware of it. I did not seem to burn easily. If there was ever any soreness on my face and shoulders after a long fishing session in the sun, I would rub the oily inside of a meat coconut over the skin. However, we all have our little vanities. For the first couple of months, when I was not actively engaged in some aspect of our survival or lost in the arms of Tuintime, I would occasionally have a twinge of concern over the condition of my hair and rapidly shrinking breasts. It had been suggested by several people that I should have my hair cut short before leaving civilisation. Vidal Sassoon's in London, which generously did my hair for our wedding, offered to cut it, but I preferred to risk leaving it long. I took a pair of scissors to the island just in case. At Sassoon's they also kindly presented me with a large crate of haircare products: elegant brown cylinders containing shampoo, moisturiser, Finishing Rinse, sachets of Protein Pack and tubes of Hair-In-The-Sun. It weighed a ton and alas every one of the potions required quantities of fresh water for its use and would not lather in the sea. I knew that salt water is not good for hair, but I refused to breast-stroke carefully around our desert island bay like one of the permed heads in Majorca, so very soon my hair became salty, sun-bleached, dried-out and split. I was glad though that I kept it long, as it protected my head well from the sun and until nutritional deficiency had a dismal effect I was not unduly worried about its condition. G's mother, who sounded a lovely, cuddly person full of country lore and wisdom, had, he told me, sworn by the benefits of tea on hair. After I had heard this I religiously dipped the end of my plait in my mug of tea every night, and then sucked it "to remove the excess moisture" . . .

There was nothing I could do about the pair of wizened little mandarins on my chest. Their demise was gradual. For a while, when I was slim and fit, I felt in prime condition all over, and my breasts, although slowly diminishing in size, remained firm and in the right position. It was later when my skin began to hang loosely like an old woman's where muscle and fat had been before that my breasts went slack and virtually disappeared. It would have been interesting to see what effect a mirror would have had on our morale at that stage.

Men have the same conceits with regard to appearance as women and G was no exception. He had brought a little hand mirror on the expedition and when he was feeling very low he would bring this out and contemplate what he could see of his face lugubriously. "People have always said I look young for my age. What do you think, Lu?"

Depending on my mood I would either make vaguely soothing, non-committal noises, or else I would answer, "I think you look four hundred and ninety-five, or even six, and here's me only one hundred and two. Let me have a look in that thing."

I suppose, in the course of the first eleven months on Tuin, I must have seen the few inches of my face that mirror revealed four or five times. But on each occasion I put it away quickly. The person I saw in the glass was a stranger, someone I found easier to live inside than look at. The fact that the size of the mirror allowed only one curious eye or a section of brown cheek or nose to be examined at one time perhaps distorted matters.

Reflection on the meaning of the worsening water situation gave us common ground for anxiety. There was one period, lasting about six weeks, when large grey clouds passed over the island daily. The shooting vegetables in the garden were at a stage when regular watering was crucial to their well-being. I would see G every morning from my place at the fire, emerge from the tent and look straight up at the sky.

"Big one over there," he would call, pointing out beyond Tuin's hills. "Could have a shower today."

And all through the day, no longer able to sprinkle the green soldiers, he would look up and hope. We agreed that it would have been better to have no cloud at all than the unkind tantalisation of those elusive grey phantoms that shied across the sky above us.

If there can be said to be a winter in that part of the world, it was happening when we arrived on Tuin. Although it was hot during the day, at night it became sufficiently cool for G always to make use of the maternity gown as a sheet and for me to drape the muslin evening dress over me. We always hoped that the drop in temperature, if it coincided with an approaching cloud, meant that rain was on its way.

Diary
We lie awake for hours sometimes in the long night, close together and yet wrapped in our own private cocoons of thought; intimately linked in a way that can surely only be experienced by two individuals who so ardently long to hear in the silence just one thing: rain.

That is perhaps rather romantically put, although essentially it speaks the truth. It covers up for the fact that during that period it was the only way in which we were "intimately linked." The days were short and the nights were long; twelve hours of darkness, mosquitoes, sand-flies and two people in a small tent who neither trusted nor liked each other very much. The longing for rain became precious in that it cut between the other tensions and brought us together at least on one level.

Before this there had been one or two thoroughly opprobrious nights, when we had spat and snarled and recriminated for hours, G finally folding himself over with some bitter Parthian shot while I lay rigid and burning with loathing and confusion. Should any part of his anatomy, albeit inadvertently and in the innocence of sleep, stray over to my side of the tent and touch me, I would recoil instantly like a stabbed cucaracia.

It was after one such night that I committed an unforgivable sin. In the supermarket in Townsville I had been torn between spending the last of the money I had kept for provisions on an extra bag of rice or some dried fruit. In the end I settled for the fruit as I did not know what would be growing wild on the island and there was nothing else among the provisions that would give us any vitamin C until our vegetables started coming through. I bought two half kilo packets. G and I had a measured few sprinkled on our porridge or rice each morning.

Still smarting from the wretchedness of a foul and pointless row, I got up as usual at first light, prepared the breakfast fire, made the porridge and waited for G to appear. Habitually seeking comfort and oblivion in the refuge of sleep, he was a long time coming. I decided to have my breakfast and go straight out wooding. I shook out my allotted sprinkle from the fruit packet and then in a blind moment of reckless misery thrust my hand deep into the packet, dug out a huge clod of fruit and rammed it shamelessly into my mouth. A bit of green chopped glacé fruit and a sultana fell into the sand. A small lizard, witnessing my crime with flat eyes, made as if to approach these dropped gems. I kicked a cloud of sand over him and picked them out of the dirt myself, adding them to the half-chewed peat-like gob in my mouth. Again my hand went into the packet and scooped up another load. There were only enough pieces of fruit left in the bottom to put on G's breakfast. Hearing movements from the tent, I nearly retched swallowing whole the mass that was still in my mouth.

The moments that followed were so filled with suspense I thought I would burst. The full significance of my deed hit me and I was waiting to confess to G. How could I? How could *I*, of all people, have let myself do it? I who was so strict, so disciplined, so ascetic? I did not have to confess verbally to G. Apparently my face told it all—and then when I did finally open my mouth to say something, an appalling smile spread over his features. "Well, well," he said. "I see you've had your breakfast." My teeth, of course, were a mass of black fruit skins.

The guilt of that episode stayed with me for the entire year. Even now I squirm when I think of it. The fact that I did penance and absurdly overcompensated by giving G the whole of the second packet and refusing to touch any more was irrelevant. You see, if I had been in charge of a group of people on severe rations, and somebody had done what I did, I would have had them taken out and shot.

After initial blanks and painful patches, the nights in the tent began to form a separate little world of their own on Tuin. With eyes closed, safe in that small Terylene rectangle, we travelled with each other on voyages of memory and hazy dreams of the future. I loved to hear stories of G's childhood. He told me that in many ways his life as the son of a chauffeur on the estate of Lord and Lady Duthie had been idyllic. As a small boy he would play about the farmyard and roam on the estate as if he owned it. With his mother, who occasionally went up to the "big house" to cook when it was Cook's night off, he would go into the kitchen and be fussed over by all the maids. When the staff sat down at the kitchen table to have their meals, he would quietly position himself, casually playing with a toy car, where he was able to catch fascinating glimpses of white thigh and suspenders above the maid's black stockings. At home, when he was sure no one was around, he would riffle through his mother's mail order catalogues, stopping enthralled when he came to the corset and lingerie page. When he was not diverting himself in this way he would be out with his brothers, potting pigeons with a homemade catapult and later graduating to an air rifle with which he shot rabbits and the odd stray game bird. He had a pet magpie, which grew so attached to him that it disturbed the classes at the village school by tapping on the window waiting for him to come out. He also had a ferret called Charlie, which horrified his warm-hearted mother by biting clean through the cheek of a little boy who had come to tea. G said it was the boy's fault, he had told him not to wriggle when he put Charlie on his neck.

It was the warm, country homeliness of it all that fascinated me. "Go on," I would say as we lay in the tent so far from any other world. "Tell me some more, tell me what you did at weekends." He described the family gatherings on a Sunday: first the big traditional lunch after church, which he hated and gave up attending as soon as possible, and then the institution of the week, Sunday tea. Either all the Aunties and Uncles would come over to his house or the whole family would troop over to one of theirs. There was always a gigantic spread, each sister or in-law trying to out-do the others. Ham, cucumbers and tomatoes from the garden, homemade cakes, jellies and trifle, the lot. G would go into minute detail over the food, and in my imagination I had two helpings of everything.

His older brother became the hero of the family when he went into the Forces straight after leaving school. When he came home on leave from some far-flung, romantic-sounding country, he received a hero's welcome. It made G think seriously of joining up the minute he left school, but he worked for a while on the land before he finally made the decision. By then the Duthies had gone and G's family had moved into the town of Aylesbury. He said his father was never quite the same after the estate packed up, but his mother, always busy, devoted herself to the home and comfort of her three sons, whenever they should be there.

G told me that there had still been a great deal of superstition and fears of dark or unknown forces around small villages in those days. Knives were laid across doorsteps, blade outwards, to ward off evil when a strange gipsy woman came through the village; a bird in the house meant imminent death of someone in the family. G got into terrible trouble for bringing two baby owls into his mother's kitchen one day, though perhaps more because of the mess of feathers than fear of evil retribution. There was also apparently a tremendous preoccupation with death and the rituals surrounding it. Unlike the "upper" classes who whisked their dead into the family vault almost the instant after they had breathed their last, it was the custom among G's parents' stock to lay out their corpses in the parlour. There they would lie, faces often uncovered, for all the relatives to look upon one last time. As a little boy, G dreaded these "last respects" sessions more than anything else, and because so much to do with death was dealt with through the Church, he soon acquired an abiding dislike of all ritualistic religious practices.

But what came across mostly from G's descriptions of his childhood and youth was a fullness and simplicity of life that had its foundations firmly rooted in the class system. There was no one more despised by G's mother and her friends than someone who tried to act "above his/her station."

It all seemed a far cry from my childhood memories of piano practice, cheese-on-toast or sardines after school, riding lessons on Saturday morning in Bushy Park and watching Daddy take "interesting" photographs of the *au pair*. Nobody seemed to know their stations very well in my day.

G's childhood stories evoked for me a wonderful visual combination of all the best of Laurie Lee and H. E. Bates. I never tired of hearing them. Equally entertaining and interesting was the world of army life that G unfolded for me with his anecdotes of the five years he spent in the Forces. He was in Korea for a sizable chunk of that time. It was the first time he had been abroad, a muscle-bound young farm hand with a distinct Buckinghamshire burr and a predilection for silk underwear, which he never lost.

It was in the army that G began to read and take an interest in all sorts of things not covered by the scope of his village upbringing. He was sent on a technical course and qualified as an instructor in electronics. He mixed with university graduates and people who wrote as well as the cronies with whom he went whoring in Singapore and Tokyo. He told me of endless nights crawling about in the cold darkness tracing wires when he was on Forward Observation Post duties, and of his days in Germany with the Parachute Regiment. When he left the army he took a course in shorthand and typing at Slough College and it was after this that he entered the world of journalism, starting off on small country papers and gradually working himself towards a job in Fleet Street.

I was far less interested in the stories that began with the phrase: "When I had money . . ." or "When I had my Jaguar . . ."

All our talks and reminiscences were journeys off the island. Escapes from our escape. Sometimes we would play a word game, "Botticelli," before we went to sleep, which consisted of thinking of a well-known figure and having the other person guess who you are by a process of questions eliminating other famous characters with names beginning with the same letter. But there were still many many hours in those nights, even when there was no animosity between us, when sleep just would not come to me:

Diary
The moon has been high these last nights, riding wind-tossed clouds that obscure pale stars dotted in the velvet black beyond. The strange light, throwing swift, jagged shadows across the flysheet makes me restless. I crawl out and squat beneath a tree. Silhouettes of shock-headed screwpines lash their sharp leaves about like the spokes of so many broken umbrellas. The mosquitoes are biting. It is too dark to read. I can only return to the tent, lie down and wait and hope for sleep and rain.

In the daytime we had a few other distractions not directly concerned with physical survival. There was my flute. From time to time the tender strains of Satie's "Trois Gymnopédies" could be heard, breathed haltingly into the quiet of the interior, a wistful harkback to old times and other people. Around camp I laboriously churned out practice pieces of "Frère Jacques" and "The Christmas Tree," but dedication waned as my skinny body struggled to control the breathing I had never properly grasped, and my poor flute succumbed to green mould and humidity. I had hoped to teach myself enough to make up a few Tuintunes, but I never got that far. There was a morning when the tide was going out fast and I was puffing my way through a new scale. Fishing had to take first place. After a couple of months I stopped playing altogether but sometimes, on lone wanders, I would sing.

G liked singing. I quickly swallowed my former dislike of "popular" tunes and soon picked up the words of all the songs he had learned in the army as well as the saccharine mournfulness of some Country and

Western ballads. A modern Captain Bligh, set adrift in the waters of the Strait, might have been entertained by lively renditions of "Lilli Marlene" and "The Lavender Cowboy" as he floated past our island in the tropical night.

We did have a book box. In England I had cleared the shelves of the room I vacated and carted all my books around local second-hand shops until I had got rid of them all at about 10p a throw. It felt like rather a callous way of disposing of so many old friends, but should I ever want them again badly enough, they would not be impossible to replace. I only kept a small French/English dictionary and the two volumes of Graves' *Greek Myths*. Unexpectedly, we were presented with about twenty books in Brisbane, a rather random selection ranging from a *Dictionary of Physical Science* to an anthology of poems. There were several books on fish, bird and plant identification, but on the whole we found these disappointing, always remaining doubtful as to whether the drawings and colour plates really did resemble the creatures or plants we were trying to identify. I galloped my way through the few novels on days when antipathy polluted the air of Tuin. They provided a temporary flight away from G and off the island, but I found I did not hanker for more when they were finished. We had a Bible, but neither of us fell prey to the Bible-thumping sessions that Defoe gave his hero.

On the days when G's legs prevented him from doing anything more active than a very little gardening and he lay slumped for hours in the shade, he would try occasionally to relieve the tedium of immobility by dipping into a book but, as is common in an apathetic state, he found himself unable to concentrate for any length of time. I amused him on one or two occasions by relating the stories I had read from Beckett's *More Pricks Than Kicks* in my own words, also tales from Maupassant like "Boule de Suif." In return he related for me in grisly detail the plot from the film *Jaws* and Ira Levin's *The Stepford Wives*.

As the weeks went by the book box lost its attraction for me, although from time to time I still thought I wanted a little "escape":

Diary
After our lunch of coconut meat and peepa juice I had planned to spend a while "off" the island, temporarily rejoining the world of other men through the pages of a book. I have a favourite shady bower for this purpose. I chose a futuristic work based on scientific fact.

One of those large paperback tomes with a message for mankind implicit in every page. I read the introductory pages with interest, it was far from being rubbish, but the problems being discussed did not exist on Tuin. Overpopulation, armaments, media . . . Soon the island was once more invading me physically and mentally, claiming all my attention. I had to explore, to wander, to be naked and timeless and warm, to search the sky for signs of rain, the trees and ground for things to fill our bellies, to look ever outwards abandoning introspection and speculation, taking notice only of all that is immediately around me.

I walked to a part of Tuin not yet thoroughly explored. Here the trees grow close together and high, on rough, rocky terrain thick with creepers and flesh-tearing undergrowth. I came upon three Cottonplant trees covered with bright yellow flowers. I had to push and scramble to draw close enough to test the blooms for scent, an infinitely elusive perfume almost lost on the salt air. Further on my path was blocked by a vast, storm-felled tree, spreading stalwart roots in all directions, the life urge refusing to surrender in this prone monster. Although bound and choked by hundreds of twisting vines, invaded by lizards, eaten into and used as a home by wasps, ants and all manner of destructive parasites, the tree lives and fresh new leaves have come through on slender branches fighting their way up towards the light.

I climbed down out of the woods on to the beach. The sea-sounds, familiar now as the wind, the sun and the view of other distant islands sang within me, keeping mind, body, all one, on Tuin. I shall not try to "escape" again today.

At one point G did take up one major distracting occupation. Years ago, in Italy, he had written the outline for a science fiction novel. Now he brought this out, lugged his old typewriter into the shade and began to go through it. I had never felt any interest in science fiction but wanting to show willing and be encouraging I took to looking over each section as he completed it and offering little suggestions here and there. He appreciated this and for a while it became a routine each evening for him to show me what he had produced during the day. I will admit, now, that although I was pleased to see G happier and absorbed in something, it bothered me that he was spending quite so much time "away" from our island. It seemed to push the possibility that he might one day find himself drawn deeply into the world of Tuin as I had become, further and further away. But if a woman will not share her body with a man, how can she expect him to share her infatuation with a few grains of sand and a lot of sea and sky?

Diary
The colour scheme today ranges from rich ocean turquoise stretching away to a vivid purple near the horizon where the deep currents of the Arafura and Coral Seas meet and vie with one another. The sky is bright forget-me-not blue merging into soft violet among huge snowy clouds. The air is warm and stirring borne on a rousing south-easterly wind.

On my way here, to my writing rock, I stopped to watch the touching struggles of a hermit crab attempting to drag its too-large home into the fast receding tide before it became stranded on the hot, flesh-shrivelling beach. He seemed so desperate and determined and yet his task was quite hopeless. The coral wastes are a deathbed for many small sea-creatures; birthplace and nursery for others.

There is a ridged bank of small shells in the bend of Long Beach where the golden sand ends and the coral flats begin. Treading there, my feet make a soft shirring disturbance. Sometimes sitting in a round indentation of shells, I bury my hands in the pale speckled masses all around. It is sheltered in this crook of the shore. I might just sit like that and wait for the sounds I made settling down to recede, leaving only heat and stillness. Occasionally there is a sharp crack or pop from the coral, as a mollusc snaps shut or a passing bird drops a shell. They do not scream their presence, these birds, not a rowdy lot and often solitary. I have found that utter quiet reveals the life of the island more than any foraging.

At first glance Tuin on this side seems windswept, dry, husk-like and harsh at low tide. The coral gardens are not pretty. Their grey bony acres sprawl out to low crinkled folds all the way down to where a yellowish foam marks the beginning of the submerged reefs. But there is life and death everywhere. Far away near the water's edge I can just make out the delicate, busy movements of little beige birds with long, narrow bills poking hither and thither as they run about and feed. They dash about like miniature Hovercraft, no bounce at all in their running motion. Slender white cranes come singly. What looks to be a white blob on a rock will suddenly detach itself and rise slowly into the sky on slim wings, long legs dangling, long neck outstretched. A pair of red-billed oyster-catchers momentarily cause a flurry among the little beige hunters who whizz over the ground in a flat crowd until they gradually calm down and resume their individual picking.

Perhaps they are picking out the live bodies of creatures that live in shells like those under my hands. So many tiny houses and all so perfectly wrought. There are many like hinged moth wings with rounded edges, some with a triangular squiggle of red or yellow on a pale background, others with a dark design on mauve. But the ones I like best are the miniature Grecian Urns, black or indigo with a white calligraphic pattern. Sometimes I will keep one of these in my hand all through a walk, but I rarely take them back to camp.

I can relax now because the most important part of the day's work is over; the securing of a meal for this evening. I caught two parrot fish this morning straight after breakfast and G used one of the heads for bait on his sharkline. The beast he hauled in was either a grey nurse or lemon shark.

I remember that shark. It took absolutely ages to die. G's sharkline was a colourful affair made up of a bright yellow plastic clothesline, last-minute gift of friends in Brisbane, and a blue painted metal clothes hanger. The plastic tubing around the clothesline was good because it did not burn the hands as badly as rope. G brought that particular shark in straight off the beach in front of camp. He waded a yard or so into the water and threw out the baited line. The shark was on within two minutes. I had mentioned that there was one around when I went swimming before breakfast.

When the shark did eventually deign to die, we were faced with the problem of what to do with it. The body was too heavy for us to drag all the way up to camp, so G hacked off six good steaks on the spot. It seemed sacrilegious to waste the rest of the meat so we agreed to try a little wind-drying. G chopped, twisted and tore the head off with the aid of the machete while I went back to camp with the steaks to preserve them for a couple of hours in vinegar and salt and pepper. We were fast running out of these commodities, so it was important to us that the wind-drying should prove a success. I wanted the shark's head for the teeth, thinking that if I buried it in the sand for a while insects would strip off all the flesh. But the ants on Tuin, so importunate when it came to trying to get at our own food, took no interest whatsoever in the shark's head. When I dug it up several weeks later it did not appear to have been touched. The decomposition that had set in put me off the idea of making a necklace or bracelet.

Amongst other odd useful items thrown in at the last minute, G's sons had included an old string bag. I think it was originally intended as a prawn net, but we used it, unravelled, to make ties for the pieces of shark on the line. I tore the bottom half of a dress in half to make additional ties. The work of cutting and hanging the shark was an enjoyable team effort. Pushing what remained of the shark back into the sea, to be eaten by its brothers, we carted great lumps of meat into the shade of One-Plum-a-Day tree and made ourselves comfortable with knives, ties and a ration of cold tea to hand. With shark steaks waiting to be cooked and all that flesh about to be laid up as emergency rations, we felt rich.

G did the cutting while I poked holes in the lengths of flesh, varying thicknesses for the sake of experimentation, and tied loops of rag or string around each one. I then threaded these onto the washing line and stepped back to admire the effect. One learns by trial and error. This first line was not a dramatic success. First we found that despite the precaution we had taken of soaking the posts supporting the line with salt water, ants still managed to find their way on to the strips of meat. I could not understand how they did this until I noticed the thin branch of a tree hanging close to the line. The cunning little ants had climbed all the way up the tree and were queueing on the end of the branch to drop off on to the fish-drying line. We put a stop to this by transferring the whole line on to the beach where the strips of fish hung unmolested, dried by the action of both sun and wind. The other problem we encountered was not so easy to remedy.

At roughly the same time as we began catching and eating shark in large quantities, G developed an irritating rash on his hands. Once before, on Cocos Island, he had had the same thing and he felt that it could well be caused by shark meat. Medical advice had been available there and he was ordered to keep his hands completely dry and away from all contact with raw meat or fish. This presented us with twofold difficulty. One, a great deal of the point of our shark-drying efforts was lost if G was unable to eat the results, and two, ordinary handline fishing was out for him until the rash had cleared. We were to discover, over a long period and with much trial and error, that it seemed only to be the flesh of the lemon shark that brought on the problem; black tip, the other common cruiser around our coast, did not affect him adversely at all. But meanwhile we had to find other food.

One of the stories G had told me from his childhood days involved the annual family outing to the seaside. As well as striped sticks of rock candy, a big bag of freshly picked winkles was always brought back in the car. It was Father's job to pick out the winkles with a bent pin after Mother had boiled them thoroughly on the stove. So the Shades of Margate crept to Tuin.

To the north of camp, around Armchair Rock, there were any number of tiny grey and black winkles. We began by collecting a billyful of these. I made the mistake of boiling up the first lot in the all-purpose billy. It took hours of soaking and scrubbing with handfuls of gritty sand to get rid of the smell. On future occasions I made use of the mug-shaped dipper for all shell cooking. G sat on the board and drum table which had now become part of our camp, and hooked out the minuscule bits of meat with a safety-pin. It was a long job. He dropped the winkles into a puddle of vinegar at the bottom of his stainless steel birthday goblet. We always used this if we wanted to keep the less tasty variety of oysters for a while, too, the narrow shape of the goblet ensuring no waste of precious vinegar.

While he was picking the winkles I cooked one-fifth of a mug of rice, adding a handful of sprouted mung beans when it was nearly cooked. These beans had been an instant success, good soaked and then cooked whole, or left in a drop of fresh water in a cleaned-out clam shell and allowed to sprout for a few days. I planted several rows of them as an experiment and they seemed to do remarkably well in the arid conditions.

Picking out enough winkles to make the main part of a meal took an entire afternoon. While he picked, G talked. It was rare for us to go on a mental excursion off the island when it was daylight, but the gentle occupation of winkle-picking seemed conducive to spoken reverie. The antipathy that had dogged our every move since Brisbane was by now far less pronounced. There had been rough patches, some misery for both of us, but now we had been together under the Tuin sky long enough for acceptance and a kind of understanding to have built up on both sides. G was relaxed enough with me now to speak of things that meant much to him. When someone as outwardly ''tough'' as G does this, it is like being given a present. He summed up his feelings well by saying, ''Well, Lu, I think you're a bloody bitch not to fuck, but I suppose you're all right in other ways.''

He had commented on several occasions that he had never met anyone who wanted to please him so much. He was referring to small everyday things, how I made every effort to ensure that his tea was not smoky, or cut him a pillow if he came with me on a walk and needed to rest en route, and the way I reminded him to wear his hat out fishing because

I knew too much sun made him nauseous. These things were nothing to me and yet they seemed to touch and surprise him. We had even reached a stage where we could crack the odd suggestive joke without risk of a flare-up of bitterness.

One subject very close to G's heart was that of his three sons. Sitting there over the winkles, head down so that I could not see his eyes, he spoke of the farmhouse he had had in Wales, and the happy days he had there with the boys and their mother, before things began to go wrong. His descriptions of life in Wales produced ripples of nostalgia in me for Scotland, where I had spent the years of my adolescence. From somewhere in the vaults of memory I unlocked the words of a wistful Scottish ballad about gathering wild mountain thyme. It seemed in the yearning simplicity of its tune, even though sung in a tremulous, untrained quavering, to sum up our mood very well. G asked me to sing it again, and I did, staring blindly out at the glittering miles of sea. Then we ate our winkles.

To go with this meal I had made a refreshing drink from an infusion of dried lemongrass. The day after we arrived on Tuin I had planted the sheaf of scented grass I had been given on Thursday Island, tucking its roots into the sandy soil right beside the creek, where for a while it seemed to thrive. When the water fell lower and lower in the pool the lemongrass began to droop ominously so I cut it down close to the root and spread the long blades out in the sun to dry. When they were brown and brittle I tied them into a sheaf and hung this under the shelter of a piece of flattened-out petrol drum. When we wanted a change from ordinary tea, and to make the one packet we had last longer, I would snip off two or three teaspoonfuls of lemongrass and made a kind of tea-bag out of the corner of my orange sari strip. Allowed to dangle in hot water for a time, the leaves imparted their lovely scent to the water. It was good cold as well.

To ring the changes while G's hands were recovering, I collected some of the large greenish-black winkle-shaped shells that lived in the mangroves lining Crocodile Bay. Unfortunately these turned out to be extraordinarily unpleasant. The flesh, normally a dirty yellow, oozed out in hideous bright green streams when subjected to boiling water.

"I'm not eating those horrible-looking bits of snot," said G. We stuck to the ordinary small winkles in future.

One fish which we found dried very well was the queenfish, or wahoo. On the rare occasion that we would bring one of these in on a handline, G would slice the flesh we did not use at once thinly and

I would hang it on the line. After a day or so of hot sun it was ready to eat. It made a delicious and nourishing between-meal snack and was not unacceptable reconstituted with a little fresh water and simmered with a few strands of chopped spaghetti into a stew. We had so little in our provisions in the way of bulk that to spin it out I literally used strands or grains at a time to pad out an otherwise all-fish meal.

The condition of G's hands improved greatly after a week or so of keeping them out of water and for a while he was able to resume normal fishing activities. By now we had come to know exactly where the water and the fish would be at First Fishing Rock at all states of the tide. On my walks in the interior I had worked out a way of getting to our rock even when Crocodile Bay was under water. It meant walking the length of Coconut Alley and scrambling under branches and over rocks to emerge the other end on the corner of Palm Beach. If the tide was very high, we had to make a long detour over a green ant–inhabited tract of the interior. This took such a time that if we caught nothing in the morning we would not return to camp but stay near the rock all day until a change in the tide brought the fish around again. G would take a snooze during the hottest part of the day and I would divert myself watching the sky from under the tall Palm Beach palms or wander further along where it was good to swim.

Understandably, G did not like me to swim out far. Telling me that I was a bloody idiot to float around in a vacant dream in waters where there were known to be not only shark and stingray but also sea-snakes and poisonous puffer fish, was one of his ways of letting me know that he cared. However, I found the water irresistible, and alone on the other side I was aware that sometimes I swam out perhaps further than was wise. Somehow I felt that we were taking so many risks just by being on the island that not to swim because of something that might happen seemed rather like buying a fast car and then never driving it in case one had an accident. I was actually far more perturbed by the thought that one of us could have appendicitis or a stroke and there was no way of summoning help from outside. Without an aerial the CB radio was useless and it was extremely unlikely that one of the flares we had been given, in the event that it would function at all, would attract any attention. There was nobody near enough to see it.

Speculations about things that might happen never occupied our thoughts or conversation for long. We had sufficient cause for worry in immediate realities. There came a time when the water situation threatened to wreck our life on Tuin in a matter of weeks if we were not saved by rain. Without water we had no chance whatsoever of survival. For the past month our intake of fresh water had been limited to three-quarters of a billy between us per day. This included fresh water used in cooking. We found that four mugs, two thirds full, drunk at spaced intervals throughout the day were adequate, and with the supplement of peepa juice, we were still far from the danger of dehydration. What concerned us was that we had no guarantee that the creek, already half the size it had been when we arrived, would not dry up altogether before the next rainfall. The anxiety was with us constantly, but aside from G's hopeful comments already mentioned, and the hope we shared for the sound of rain in the tent each night, we did not voice our fears.

We knew that life would not end the minute the creek ran dry. There were emergency survival methods of obtaining water, even if it were only half a mug between us. If necessary we would build "Arizona Stills" by digging out troughs in the dry soil, filling them with roots, and covering them with a piece of plastic sheeting, pressed down in the middle. A container placed underneath would slowly collect drops of condensation formed by the heat of the sun from above and the drawing power of the roots below. This operation might yield just enough water to prevent us perishing of thirst for a while, but not for the months that stood between us and the expected monsoon season. We were prepared to resort to dew gathering, with bundles of grass attached to ankles, or sucking the moisture from plants, but none of these emergency methods would be any good in view of the length of time we had to survive and green drinking coconuts on the island were not in endless supply. Our life would become a matter of existing solely for the next drop of water. All activities that created thirst would have to be minimised and then finally cut out altogether. Lack of water would finish us off long before we had time to die of starvation because we would no longer have the strength to fish.

But now, in the hot sun, dangling our lines off our fishing rock, thin but not skeletal, thirsty but not agonisingly so, at an impasse sexually but no longer fighting about it all the time, we felt we were managing all right. We played "Botticelli" until we knew all the famous people the other one knew, bar musicians and painters on my side and obscure inventors on G's. We indulged ourselves in one or two highly extravagant food fantasies, made desultory or otherwise comments on the fishing, chatted inconsequentially or simply sat in companionable silence. Less and less, as the months went on, did we find other people cropping up in our conversation, apart from when G reminisced about his boys and there came a time when he stopped mentioning even them.

References to ex-loves or bed-partners were rarely made; however close they may have been in another environment, they were not in context on Tuin. Whatever our differences, G and I were all each other had in the way of human contact on the island, and as the assumed importance of personal standards and the concept of "rights" faded, we achieved a better than acceptable emotional *modus vivendi*. On the night it rained, after weeks and weeks of drought, we actually hugged each other and exchanged a warm clumsy kiss out of sheer exuberance.

Diary
Rain! Glorious gurgling blessed and bountiful come-again-don't-go-to-Spain rain! Dear Jesus Christ and God in Heaven and all you other Gods of the world and Powers that Be—thank you. Oh lovely lovely sweetest sound lemme get out so it can trickle right in my ear!

It really was like that. A boisterous wind trumpeted over Tuin all through the night, and for once brought with it fat black clouds that did not sail over yielding none of their load. G and I woke at the same moment, lay shock-still for a second and then the magic word burst simultaneously from our lips. Then we lay in snug comfort thinking happily of the mugs and mugs of tea we could have in the morning and of the grateful ground soaking up the moisture and pushing through our vegetables. I wanted to have a look at the catchment system G had rigged up using poles supporting a bent piece of corrugated iron "borrowed" from the shed near camp and angled into a drum, so I left the protection of the tent for a few moments and allowed the rain and wind to buffet and sing against my naked body. Already there was half a twenty-litre drum of water. The dark clouds were moving fast, sweeping the precious rain over the sea. I stumbled down to the kitchen area and made sure all receptacles were upturned to catch water, including all the halved coconut husks I had ready for the fire. The rainfall was brief; back in the tent, the steady tacka-tacka on the roof that had woken us soon stopped, but this shower was to be the first of half a dozen that came over the next few days. Hope for the garden, of which we now confessed we had both privately begun to despair, was revived, and that meant hope for our life on the island. We had survived well so far, even if we had lost weight, had trouble with legs and ups and downs between ourselves. It was going to be all right.

PHASE II

Being Away

DUGONG

5

SCHISM

Diary

Soft rays of morning light stroke the treetops, falling in a fanshape under pale sun. I walk far down the beach to fetch a bucket of sea water. I am hardly awake and might still be far away in the realms of sleep fantasy so dreamlike are my surrounds. I have been up for some time moving quietly about the camp, but the feeling of being wrapped in the cocoon of sleep is still with me.

I am preoccupied with the passage of my feet over acres of sandhills. Jumping from one hill to the next becomes a game, satisfying as my stride is forced to lengthen to avoid falling in puddles. Satisfying because that stride pulls a belly chord that tells me the woman in me is not dead. There is a story about a boy who played a private game every time he walked on a pavement. He must not step on the cracks, or else the bears would get him. In my case crabs are the bogey. My eyes are lowered, concentrating on the sequence of footfalls. I can see nothing, to left or right or ahead but this lunarscape of yellow-grey mounds. On top of some of the mounds are the pursed lips of a shell-creature's hidey-hole. They go deep, deep down, these holes. I have tried to follow their paths with hands. Nearly always the white, whelk-shaped shell has gone. Where do they go?

My mind wandered with my feet. When I was very young, fifteen, and had finally escaped the well-meaning clutches of the Education Authorities, I managed to get a live-in job as a monkey keeper. The idea was that I should further my own education in a field which particularly interested me, that of animal and human behaviour. Unfortunately the laboratory and guiding light I had hoped would be there to show me the way failed to materialise. Basically my job was to clean out and feed the monkeys. I chucked fish to the seals in my lunchhour, and acted as a tree over which the reptile house man could drape his charges when he was cleaning out their cages. But seeing the monkeys every day, I could not help observing certain behaviour patterns. Most interesting were the confused little characters just flown in from their native habitat. After a few weeks, during which they showed mostly fear and aggression, as one would expect, they calmed down and adopted individual patterns of repetitive neurotic behaviour; muscular tics, endless masturbation, cell-pacing. But there was one tiny spider monkey who never gave up; he invented a system of behaviour that afforded both him and me great amusement. At weekends the zoo was opened to the public. Cooing Americans and floral-frocked Birminghamites would come in gaggles. The main monkey house was small, so I only let in one or two groups at a time. As they wandered past the pretty Diana monkeys, ooed and aahed at the cuddly Woollies, my little Spider friend would begin his game. Oiling his way shyly up the bars at the front of his cage, he would chatter softly and beckon to the nearest, biggest human male, who, if not seduced by these gestures, would invariably fall for the pouting kisses my hero would now throw to him. When the man was very close to the bars, and all the rest of the group had turned to watch, the monkey would position himself carefully, and accurately piss into his victim's eye. He would then fart, leap and splatter all over the cage, shrieking with delight.

I wondered if my preoccupation with footfalls could be compared to a neurotic tic, but I preferred to think of it as a return to childlike fascination with simple things.

Diary
The funny, half mournful cry of the "Oh Dear" bird tings out like a tuning fork from somewhere far inland. We first heard his call one night about an hour after dark. It began *pianissimo,* a clear, off-key two-tone lament. The second call followed almost immediately, much louder. The third rose in anguished crescendo, a ludicrous *cri du coeur*, the first of the two notes piercing and long: Oooh Dear! I like that bird.

Now at the edge of the far-away sea there is a gentle lapping of water as my tilted bucket fills. Whisper whisper of little waves, within, without. The growing day has nudged past a tranquil dawn. I want to swallow oceanfuls of this peace and hold it within me always.

The island had me like a lover. I was totally captivated by the very indifference of its charm, aware always that my soft body was the alien, but as it toughened and moved more naturally to the rhythm of Tuintime

I felt that I was beginning to blend. It was almost as though the less I consciously observed, the less frequently I recalled the fact that being on Tuin was something to do with a plan, a project, and the more I simply existed, obeying the few rules that made existence possible, the more "at home" I became. Feeling at home meant no longer gushing effusively about the beauties of the island or shrinking from the harshnesses. It meant fewer and fewer comparisons, voiced or in thought, between conditions on Tuin and those in "civilisation."

But the presence of certain ugly facts made a sensation of complete absorption impossible. The sores on our legs could not be ignored. I had more or less accepted that it was unlikely that my limbs would ever be free of small wounds so long as I was on Tuin; they were as much a part of daily life as water rationing and watching the sun set behind Tukupai. But the sores on my legs did not blight my life to anything like the extent that G's did. The swelling of his ankles and sometimes the whole below-knee area indicated that the poison from the deeper sores was inclined to spread, although the heat seemed to cause the swelling as well. And it was not only our legs that were affected. Every time a parrot-fish spine punctured the palm of a hand or an oyster shell grazed a finger, we knew that infection would follow; by the next morning a thick droplet of yellow pus would be pressing up the skin where the jab had been. A graze would be lined with a thin scab of pus mixed with blood. Every activity laid us open to the hazard of collecting yet more sores. G, sensibly avoiding wandering near the coral which caused the worst wounds, might venture a little way into the interior to look for suitable saplings for the shelter; invariably the just-healed tissue on one of his leg sores would be ripped off by a backlash of tough grasses or a scrape from a spiky pandanus leaf on the ground, and infection would set in anew.

Treatment of the sores was made almost impossible by the fact that the very sea was awash with coral poison. Anywhere else in the world a saltwater bath would probably have done our legs good; here, it was an invitation to deep ulceration. Heat and increasing humidity exacerbated the condition, and when on the odd occasion a sore did seem to have healed, it was not uncommon for a fresh bag of pus to be found pushing through the newly healed tissue several weeks later. The most dangerous were those that turned into tropical ulcers. These seemed impossible to cure with anything in our medical kit. Antibiotic creams and powders were useless; the problem had gone too deep and needed to be attacked from the inside. The one course of antibiotic capsules I had bought in England had long gone, melted, despite silica gel and a sealed bottle, to a sticky mess.

There came a time when G's legs were so bad for so long that we had to devise a way of transporting him to the fishing rock without any salt water touching him. I had an ulcer on my ankle bone then as well, so a bridge was necessary for both of us. The only long, strong, remotely manageable piece of wood we had was the base of the peepa pole. This we divested of its bindings and trundled laboriously all the way across Crocodile Bay to First Fishing Rock. About twelve feet of water separated us from where we needed to be. When the tide was right out this gap was dry; a rough bed of barnacled rock and jagged chunks of coral. At high tide crossed currents caused this narrow space between outcrops of rock to become a deep, swirling channel, well frequented by shark coming in to feed off parrot fish and snapper. G and I tried to time our crossings to coincide with half-tide; this way there would be plenty of water the other side of F.F.R. for good fishing, but not so much this side as to make a tumble into the channel stupidly hazardous. Before the arrangement of the Pole Bridge, we had taken one or two risky plunges to get back to shore off our rock. One of us would stand lookout as the other hurled himself across. We were never quite sure what attracted shark so often to that spot, perhaps they enjoyed the turbulence of the water.

The pole was rounded and no more than a child's handspan wide. We balanced it in several different places before we were satisfied that it was stable enough for us to attempt a crossing. The whole aim being to keep feet and legs out of the water, we did it by sitting astride the pole, legs tucked out of the way underneath, and used our hands pressed down on the pole to shuffle over in a seated position. We had to make each forward heave as smooth as possible as the pole had an alarming tendency to roll. Once I rather let the side down by getting giggly and rolling right round so that I finished the journey like a sloth, upside down. It would have been the best way had I been equipped with a long prehensile tail.

The condition of G's legs not only restricted his fishing and general mobility, it also played a large part in sapping him of all desire to do anything. The shelter, after an encouraging start, had now come to a standstill. We had found just enough rusty pieces of corrugated iron on Palm Beach to make a shade over the area where G worked on his novel. The ground where the completed shelter should stand was littered with rafters of slim mangrove and gum saplings that I had cut down with the machete and carried from Green Ant Hill and Coconut Alley.

Making the few ties necessary for a structure to support the irons was agonising for G. As he stood up on a petrol drum and stretched his arms above his head to tie a crossbeam into the fork of an upright, pain shot up his legs. I did as many as I could to save him the pain, but was unable to make the bindings as tight as they should have been. I hated the sight of the corrugated iron at first, but palm thatching would have to wait a while. At least G's mind was off his legs when he was typing.

One hot noon out of the many. The sun had just peaked at maximum sizzle and was arcing off slow motion to postmeridian grill. It was a blue, silver and palomino day. Cloudless. A slender ribbon of white foam undulated along the distant edge of the sandspit. Low tide.

I was feeding a hot little roasting fire in the scant midday shade of the utensil-hanging bush. By way of experiment I had scooped out the tender, pinkish flesh of an adolescent peepa and was trying it out grilled. The odour it gave off was not very encouraging and it looked like a slice off a sow's backside, but I was sure it must be full of goodness and was determined to make it appetising somehow. G was up at the shelter site, tap-tapping away in sporadic bursts on his science fiction novel. Events found the rites of our present norm in full swing.

Seven grand black-and-white Australian pelicans had taken to patrolling the end of the sandspit each day. Static, they lost their elegance, assuming a squat ceramic quality, beak pouches tucked fatly onto puffed chests; but when, as to a signal, they launched as one into the air, they were magnificent. I watched for this moment every day. Prodding at the smoking peepa with the chopped-off backbone of a palm leaf, I kept my eye on them now. The scene out there was as familiar to me as the pattern of veins on the back of my hand, and I was quick to notice any unusual changes in cloud formations or the white lines that denoted the pattern of currents. Two distant, unfamiliar white shapes arrested my attention. They appeared to be moving swiftly in unison, heading towards Tukupai away from behind Wia Island.

I pushed the peepa away from the fiercer heat and picked up the green bucket. It was an absurd time of the tide to be going to fetch water, but if I was going to walk out all that way to get a closer look at those white objects, I might as well bring back some water to sluice down the camp table. I walked slowly, enjoying the firm texture of the sandhills. When I stopped and raised my eyes a moment, it was to see the flight of the sentinel pelicans. Away they went, great black-and-white wings tilted to catch the upward draughts, perfect RAF formation. As they flew out of sight those two other flying shapes swooped nearer to view. In a split second of sheer wonder I recognised what they were. They were not flying, not vast white prehistoric birds, which somehow would have seemed less unexpected; they were *sailing*. They were men.

The banalities of housework forgotten, I dropped the bucket and without any thought in my head but to get close enough to wave as they went by, I sped over the sandhills in the skipping, dancing motion that by now came so easily to me. The beauty of the full white sails breasting the brilliant blue water moved me like an exquisite phrase of music. I can think of no more apposite description. The vision, as can sound, produced the sensation of a long drawn out frisson of delight. I had to stop to gaze more fully. They were changing tack, coming towards Tuin, towards Crocodile Bay.

I still had a fair way to go to reach the edge of the water. The craft were close enough now for me to see that each was manned by a single figure. It was hardly surprising that I had mistaken the boats for great white birds, they seemed to be almost all sail and no hull. In fact they were catamarans, so light and trim that their passage did indeed appear to be more of a flying than floating motion. The figures in the catamarans, one was standing up, were definitely not Islanders. Wrong shape and non-fuzzy hair. One of them was waving. Both my arms shot above my head and I returned the greeting like a cheerleader. Once again the booms swung over and they tacked away. I thought that was it, they were passing on their way, wherever that might be. But no, they had headed out again only to turn and come in through a deeper channel. They were going to land.

The leading catamaran shee-ed gently onto the sand and settled with voluptuous ruffling of sails. Its occupant jumped out, secured his craft temporarily and walked towards me. The other was quick to land and catch up. I was moving more slowly now, but still going forward to meet them. Some kind of verbal greeting was called before the gap between us closed to a yard, but I do not recall the words, I was too absorbed by the impressions of their physical presence; two young tanned white men radiating health and energy. They were talking to me. I was saying something about beautiful birds. The taller of the two was holding out a buff envelope in a slim brown hand. I noticed how white and unsullied their feet were and was suddenly conscious of the grubby bit of rag I had tied over the sore on my ankle. Other than that I was wearing only my knife-belt and flimsy strip of *crêpe-de-chine* around my hips, I had been using it to tuck my palm-leaf spoon into while feeding the fire. I was so accustomed to being naked that this much dress seemed perfectly within the bounds of decorum, my mind being adjusted to Tuin standards.

As I took the proffered envelope, thinking it must miraculously contain mail from England, I saw the blond one's eyes looking beyond me towards camp. I turned round and saw G starting the long walk across the sandhills. We set off to meet him and on the way they introduced themselves again. I had taken nothing in of what they had said in the first moment of greeting. They were on their way from Cairns, on the coast of Cape York, to Manila. It seemed a very long way to go in those small catamarans. I said as much and they laughed and explained that it was a special venture, sponsored by various bodies. I remember automatically telling them my name in exchange for theirs. Again there was laughter, they said they already knew it, the envelope I held was not mail from England; it was a census form! They had been asked if they could pass by our island, as it was not far off route for them, and deliver it to us. Now I laughed, hooted, what a wonderful way for the far-reaching ribbons of red tape to get to us!

G was limping. As the three of us strode over the hills to meet him I had a sudden sharp twinge of disquiet. For a moment I had been seeing him with the eyes of an outsider, a slow stooped figure with a hesitant look of greeting on his face under that hat. It was almost formal when we met. I left them to follow on to camp at G's pace while I scampered excitedly ahead to set a billy on to boil. I was dithering and reckless, slinging wood on the fire to hurry it up, filling the billy with our entire daily ration of water to make plenty of tea for all. It was ready soon after they arrived in camp, where they made themselves comfortable, one on a big stone, the other astride a petrol drum, and continued to tell us about their trip. G mentioned that on the way up, Peter, the taller one, had told him that he needed to make a repair on his catamaran; could they stay the afternoon to fix it, spend the night and then catch the high tide first thing in the morning? It seemed an extraordinary prospect. G and I were both tentative at first in our reactions. It had not occurred to us that anyone besides us would be spending any time on Tuin.

I poured the tea, explaining that as there were only two mugs G and I could have ours afterwards, I could fetch a couple of coconut shells later. No, no, they said, they had their own mugs in the cats. Peter took a polite sip of his black tea and then casually let slip that they also had milk and sugar. That finished any hesitation on the part of the Tuin hosts. They were more than welcome to stay the night.

The tide had begun to turn. Soon the sandhills would be under deep water where the cats were anchored now. They would have to be brought in gradually with the tide. The boys went down to pull them up a first stage, and fetch some milk and sugar. I jabbered away excitedly to G while they were gone, saying how we must get them some fish for supper, bring down a couple of peepas to celebrate. Already I was breaking wood in preparation, cleaning out the fire which had contained the frazzled and forgotten peepa.

"I think you ought to put something on, Lu."

"Something on?" I thought he meant put something on the fire.

"Cover your tits and put some knickers on."

"Oh, yes, I suppose so. Damn."

I rummaged and found my old bikini top. The bottom half was now far too big. A small pair of briefs under the sari cloth would have to suffice. I had to tie a knot in the back of the top to make it fit. I felt as though I were wearing a harness. I took a squint in G's little mirror. All I could see was part of a brown face with the furrows of a question mark in the brow. I pushed the teeth of half a comb through my hair, which was hanging in a plait over one shoulder.

The boys came back to camp well laden. Evidently the twin hulls of the catamarans were all designed as storage space. Our eyes raked through the wealth of materials and containers they set out on the table. There were water bottles, with water in them; plastic tubs with labels such as "Tea," "Rice," "Greens," "Honey," all visibly filled with these treasures. There was a big orange plastic sheet with a "V" on it, another sheet with silver reflector material on one side; fishing gear, sunscreen lotion, and a businesslike-looking medical kit which Derek, the blond one, was already opening with the intention of dressing our sores. But first, like a conjuror, Peter brought from behind his back something that set me gasping with delight, an orange. I pounced on it and began ripping off the skin immediately. The boys watched, struck that the small gift should have produced such a fever. Peter started to roll a cigarette from a tartan tobacco pouch. I saw G's top teeth bite his lower lip.

"Er, could I, er, would you mind . . . ?"

Peter handed him the pouch and papers.

"Go on, Lu," said G, savouring the ritual of rolling. "You have all that orange, I'm happy with this."

I insisted he have a couple of segments, for the vitamin content, and then drooled and guzzled my way through the rest, catching the juice that flowed down my chin with a hand cupped underneath.

"Vitamins?" one of the boys said, and produced a jar of coloured capsules. G and I swallowed two each immediately.

"Is that really honey in that tub?" I asked.

"Yes," pronounced "years": they were Australian.

Everything was real, but if someone had told me this was a daydream, I could easily have been persuaded.

Derek sat me down on the edge of the table and unwound the rag from my ankle. He cupped my calloused heel in one hand and probed gently at the most painful sore with a scalpel. He announced that it was an ulcer which had gone deep and ought to be lanced and drained. With the spare water they had brought, and recent rainfall, we felt that a little could be afforded for medical purposes. I showed the boys our creek and ladled a few inches of top pool water into our metal bowl. Derek kept reiterating that I would have to keep sand and salt water out of my sores until they were healed. I warmed to his solicitude.

Back at the table everyone watched the lancing operation with interest. When I felt a wave of nausea with the pain, Derek stroked my ankle soothingly. All the time G was explaining to Peter how difficult the sores had made our lives, and I confided to Derek that the swelling of G's legs worried me. It could be a symptom of some other disorder, unconnected with the sores. He agreed but we could both only make layman's guesses. Derek had very bright blue eyes with immaculately clear whites and a beautiful set of strong white teeth that gleamed out from his tanned face as he smiled up at me while expertly bandaging my foot. The aura of health exuded by both of them was an almost tangible thing. When I rested my hand on Derek's shoulder to keep the weight off my sore foot as I stood up to make way for G, the muscle under the smooth skin seemed to pulse with vibrant resilience.

While G's legs were being dressed, Peter carefully counted out ten antibiotic capsules from their own supply. He told me to take two now and then three per day until they were finished. G's legs were a mass of painful sores, but at that time he did not have any deep ulcers. Derek thoroughly cleansed all the sores with hydrogen peroxide and then

applied antiseptic ointment and pink splodges of an antiseptic preparation reputed to be good against coral infections. Cross-gartered with
bandages, G looked like Malvolio with scarlet fever by the time Derek
had finished.

I suggested that we all go fishing to get something for supper; Peter
could mend his cat in the morning, the tide would not be high until
well after sunrise. All were in favour of this, but G said he would
probably only watch because he did not want to wet his legs after they
had just been dressed. I knew mine were bound to go in the water
before long, it might just as well be now. But the boys had other plans
for me.

Earlier that day we had caught two small parrot fish. We took one
of these for bait and Derek brought along a handy little spear with a
rubber spring-release handle with which he might stab the odd crab or
even a fish. He had a diving mask, too. The boys went down to pull
the cats higher up the beach while G and I gathered our kinked and
knotted lines and odd assortment of hooks together. I was racking my
brains to think of something I could give in exchange for a handful of
Peter and Derek's hooks. There was always a bottle of Vidal Sassoon,
but somehow that did not seem appropriate.

"I know," I said, "I'll give them a roll or two of film."

The boys had still and film cameras with them, they were making
a film of their voyage as they went along. Their project was obviously
very well organised, and sponsored by companies who had kitted them
out with clothing and watches as well as the catamarans themselves.
All we had behind our venture was the price of a single airfare from
a magazine, plus later possible payment for an article written during
the time we were on the island, good old Vidal and a broken Puma
knife. However, I did have eighty rolls of Kodachrome and Ekta-
chrome. Aside from a little I kept in the camera case, the bulk of the
film lay buried in an old army ration tin three feet under the sand where
it was supposed to be cool. I took the spade and went to dig some up.

I was sweating freely, shovelling dry spadefuls of sand that would
keep sliding back into the hole, when Derek's quiet voice behind me
asked what I was doing. I told him and he firmly took the spade and
made short work of the job himself. I suddenly felt deliciously feminine.
Derek asked how come G did not do this sort of thing for me. I explained
that I had been the one to bury the film and therefore it was my job
to unbury it.

The boys were happy with the exchange of film for hooks and gave us a generous handful. Comparative monetary values had no relevance here; hooks meant food, film was merely a disposable luxury. The four of us trooped out in the direction of F.F.R. As we neared the water's edge Derek went ahead and walked in the shallows with spear poised. "Watch out for those blue stingrays with red spots," I called. He nodded. G, Peter and I discussed the various dangers of the sea, agreeing that although shark, ray and stonefish posed a more immediately frightening threat, it was the poisonous quality of the water itself that was perhaps most discouraging.

I collected a few cucaracias as we approached the rock. G settled himself in what little shade he could find. I pointed out to Peter the good spots for fishing and was about to wade out myself to the farthest rock when Derek called out for me to wait. Leaving his spear and mask on a rock, he came over and picked me up bodily. I let out mild squeaks of protest, but he just told me to hang on. Peter was smiling. G was watching. Derek waded all the way out to the rock I had my eye on and deposited me unscathed on the end of it. I thanked him and he went off to try his luck with the spear in a deep pool not far from where Peter was fishing with a handline. None of us had any luck for a while. The boys moved further away and, uncomfortable in the unaccustomed straps, I removed my bikini top. I noticed that Peter had also dispensed with unnecessary clothing. At last a fresh piece of "cuckoo" brought a medium-sized parrot fish splashing in on my line. I waved it at the others and gave a thumbs up. There was another long wait. Sun dancing hot silver on the water. Muted gurgles and splashes where the incoming tide filled in rock pools further along the shore. Then Peter caught another parrot. Jubilant cries.

It was a little disappointing that we did not manage to bring in a big varied catch of the better eating fish, but this was better than nothing. After some time longer, G said that he might start walking back to camp. He and I knew that it was unlikely that we would make a good strike now, but I wanted to keep on trying just in case. I said I would follow on shortly with the boys. He decided he might as well wait.

When the sun moved to the point where I knew it was time to start a cooking fire and the tide was beginning to fill Crocodile Bay, I knew we would have to be content with our small catch, and waved to the boys that I was ready to go. The water between my rock and the main island was deeper now. Derek made his way carefully towards me keeping a wary eye out for rays and sharp coral near his feet. I could see that it would be no good his carrying me back in the same way as he had brought me over. But he was not going to let me wet that ulcer. Finally I came over riding on his shoulders, which was both comfortable and fun. I had complete confidence in his strength and sure-footedness and crossed my feet behind his back to keep myself steady; I was holding bucket, fish and line in my hands. It was almost with reluctance that we separated as he set me down on the dry sand near Peter and G. Peter had his swimming trunks back on, but I had not bothered to replace my bikini top.

As we neared camp I stopped at a pool and began to scale the two parrot fish. Derek squatted down beside me to watch and lend a hand. The tide was now far enough in for the boats to be secured for the night. While I started the cooking fires and the boys saw to the boats, G dabbed more pink liquid over his legs and had a good look at the various medicaments they had given us. When they came back they encouraged me to use rice and dried peas from their stores. Both offered to help in any way they could but I declined. They had brought plates, cutlery and condiments with them, also a spare billy and an attractive straw hat, both of which Derek insisted I keep. I was in my element seeing to the fires and cooking, revelling in the luxury of not having to ration the rice to spoonfuls, boiling up a billy of tea which in our individual mugs Peter and Derek made thick with milk and honey. To us it was a marvellous, extravagant feast. By way of a small return I demanded that in the morning I should be allowed to cook the last of our porridge and send them off on their way well fed. They countered by announcing that they could not let us use all the oats without leaving an offering of muesli. My God, these boys had everything. It was a deal.

Accustomed to retiring to the tent the minute the mosquitoes came out after the sun was down, G and I made a move as soon as I had washed the dishes. Again the boys had offered to help but I had been genuinely happy to do the few things myself; after all, this was the first time I had entertained in my own home as a married woman. It was because I was a married woman that I went straight up to the tent with G instead of staying for a while with Peter and Derek, who had lights on their catamarans and ample supplies of insect repellent. Even if I was not married in the fullest sense to G, I was married to the island and I knew that in my present rather euphoric mood to stay chatting in the silky warmth of the night to those two young, fit, gentle fellows while G lay folded in on himself in the tent would be an imprudent move. They would be passing on tomorrow, G was the permanence for the year on Tuin.

We did not chat much in the tent, although G did make some mildly remonstrative comment about the fact that I had abandoned wearing my bikini top. I said I would put it on again in the morning if he liked.

I was awake well before dawn and impatient to be up and about. I combed out and re-did my hair in the tent. Crawling out for a pee, I saw the wan spreading saucer of light that preceded sunrise. The tide was coming in, gently rocking the grey shapes of the catamarans that looked sleek and mysterious lying in Camp Bay. Last night I had rinsed out my sari strip and briefs in the sea. I walked down naked to where they hung in the branches of the silvery leafed tree beside the creek. Underneath the lazy sensuality of a luxurious stretch from toes to nose I felt the strong, unequivocal demand of my blood. I hugged myself for a moment watching the grey light yield to dawn through half-closed eyes, then plucked down the bits and pieces that were nothing but an affectation of modesty and put them on, strapping the knife belt over my hips.

There was movement on one of the catamarans. One of the boys was peeing over the side. I recognised Peter's naked profile, tall and relaxed, no spare flesh. Silently I jumped the creek landing in soft sand, and then moved briskly to the kitchen camp area and set about the morning chores. I had burned a lot of wood last night, would have to make up for it by gathering in an extra load today. I used the new billy for tea and the old blackened one for porridge. Looking down towards the beach, it crossed my mind that the boys would have to be quick making their repairs if they were to go on the high tide. I wanted to dip my body in the sea as I usually did before breakfast but was inhibited by the presence of the boats. Peter was strolling up to camp. He gave a soft greeting in keeping with the barely awoken day and sat down at the table yawning and smiling. Although Derek was more obviously the warm and body-conscious one of the pair, Peter exuded a stronger male presence, which I was feeling acutely now. I busied myself making tea.

Derek joined us. He said he had lain awake a long time watching the stars. His bright eyes were restless in a still sleepy face. G was up now, making a slow tour of the vegetable garden on his way down to camp.

"Porridge up," I called.

He waved. "Been up a long time, have you, Lu?" he asked after a general greeting.

"Not really, I haven't been for a swim yet."

My purpose in saying this was to demonstrate that I had not made an exhibition of myself in front of the boys.

"Well, it would be foolish to get that foot wet, wouldn't it?"

"It's feeling much better."

The subtleties of my reassuring ploy were lost in a discussion about the progress of our sores. Immediately after breakfast Derek carefully dressed them all again. He chided me for somehow having allowed moisture in under the bandage, it must have been last night when I was doing my washing. He told me I should take more care of myself. Seeing to the many small sores on G's legs took some time. Peter went to pull his cat close in and take off the rudder, which had suffered some damage on a reef. I went to collect some wood. In Coconut Alley the sight of a fine bunch of drinking peepas sent me hurrying back to camp. The boys could not go without taking a few Tuin peepas with them to quench their thirst on the way to Merauke, their next major port of call, on the coast of Irian Jaya.

It was not far to the nearest peepa-laden tree. Derek went up like a graceful golden monkey and hacked down a whole bunch, enough to keep G and me supplied for over a week as well as some to take with them. The boys had not heard the term "peepa" before. It was a word used by the guards on Cocos Island. Now, like "cucaracia," it had become a Tuin word. When we got back to camp Peter was regarding his rudder with some dismay. He said it looked as though the job would take longer than he had originally thought, involving some messy fibre-glassing for which luckily he had all the necessary equipment. We would have to see what position the tide was in after he had finished the work. Nobody actually said it, but I think we all realised at that stage that it might mean their staying a second night. This probably meant little to them; having planned everything meticulously, they had even allowed for a generous quota of days when for some reason they would be held up. But it was different for G and me. We had enjoyed their company yesterday afternoon and evening. We had been more than grateful for the extra food and the generous help with medicines, but the shock of their arrival "out of the blue" and the excitement of talking once again with other people had already had a telling effect on both of us.

G was very calm and almost indifferent-seeming in his attitude. He even appeared to take a perverse kind of pleasure in making it clear to everyone what he would probably spend the day doing, and I quote: "Fuck all." After briefly showing Peter and Derek round the garden, he lay down on the grass daybed, rolled one of Peter's cigarettes and shortly went off into a doze.

My reactions were quite different. Already tense from a pleasurable although irrational excitement, I now began to feel very overstrung. Totally out of practice at the usual deceptions of normal social behaviour and aware of a number of questions the boys' presence had raised in my mind, I was no longer at ease with G and unable to be my relaxed Tuin self with them. Vigorous activity would keep these awkwardnesses at bay, so I launched myself at the task of collecting wood with a will. Derek joined me with the axe and chopped down a number of good burning trees I had been wanting for ages. While Peter's fibreglass was drying he helped drag in the heavier wood to camp. Between us we built up a pile in the space of a morning it would have taken me weeks of effort to achieve alone. I was very pleased with the results of the work, but uncomfortably aware each time one of us added a piece to the pile, of G's recumbent body close by. I knew he was not asleep.

After we had all refreshed ourselves at midday with peepa juice and were sitting supposedly relaxed under the shade of One-Plum-a-Day tree, my restlessness became acute. It was swelteringly hot but what I craved more than anything was a long walk. I wanted to get right back in touch with Tuin, have the sun and the sky and the sea drive the complexities of human relationships out of my head. I announced that I was going.

"Oh, Lu, in this heat? You're daft." Then, to the boys: "She's always doing this, you know, can't stay quiet for a minute. Drives me bloody nuts with her dashing around. I tell her she ought to learn to sit still and do nothing." Somebody said he was certainly expert at doing that himself. It was not quite a joke.

"You youngsters, you're all the bloody same . . ."

He had hit on the thing that had been galling him since the moment they arrived. Youth. Although, when with him, I behaved almost maternally towards them, concentrating on being housewifely and a good hostess, it was obvious to everyone that I welcomed and responded to their youth like a long-lost friend. They reminded me that I was young too.

Derek said that he would love to see some of the parts of the island I had described to him and Peter said he would like to take some photographs around the island too. It was clear now that they would not be sailing today. I muttered about fishing, but they said we were welcome to use more of their stores. It was obvious that G was not going but I had to go through the motions of asking him.

"No, you go, Lu. Enjoy yourself. I'm all right here."

We walked to Palm Beach along the shore, not talking much to begin with. Although I did not feel quite right leaving G to go walking with the boys, it seemed absurd to allow an unfounded guilt to interfere with the pleasure of the walk. Soon I was happy and confident, leading Peter and Derek over the rocks I knew so well, pointing out the places I had found turtle tracks, stopping to look at a hole where a large lizard or a goanna had been digging for eggs. Between the bays around the coast were rough areas of loose boulders under black plateau-like shelves of rock. Where I usually scrambled and clawed, Peter and Derek lent strong supportive hands. I loved the way they moved with such ease. They commented on how fit I was, how energetic.

At last we neared the small bay behind which I hoped to find some late passion fruit. There were tall palms here, their yellow-plumed heads waving blind and free far above the choking undergrowth around their lower trunks. We gathered up a few fallen nuts and I made the boys laugh over my descriptions of the difficulty I had getting the milk cleanly out of a nut by myself. They said they would have to do something about that. Derek asked to borrow my knife. He broke off a strong sapling about two feet from the ground and sharpened the rooted piece to a sturdy point. Holding a coconut in both hands, he brought it down hard on the point and peeled off sections of the tough outer husk. When the nut was cleanly bared I pierced a hole in the drinking eye and Peter stuck in a straw cut from a hollow stem. We passed it around, enjoying a rest in the shade.

Suddenly the boys began telling me how they would live if they were stranded for a year on Tuin, how they would build a good shelter, hammocks, a raft or dugout; how they would clear a large space in the greenest part of the interior for a garden, weave mats and wall-coverings for the house out of pandanus and coconut leaves, make furniture out of rocks and wood, make the camp area attractive and homely by decorating it with conch and bailer shells and any flowers or pretty ferns that could be found. "Yes!" I interjected, wholly at one with their enthusiasm: "Yes yes yes!" Why, they said, even when they stopped to camp for the night somewhere, they always made a point of making themselves as comfortable as possible. They worked as a team in everything they did. If there was some point on which they did not agree, they talked it out until some mutually satisfactory ar-

rangement had been reached. They were amazed at the apparent lack
of communication between G and me and by the way I seemed to do
all the heavy work while G lay around and did nothing. They said it
was crazy.

By now I had got up and was pacing about, ready to bang my head
against the nearest palm tree. They had touched on all the points that
most disturbed me about G's company on the island. They made our
whole approach to our project seem unenterprising in the extreme. The
fact that mentally I had to team myself with G irked me beyond words.
His slow, disorganised way of going about things was not my way. I
went along with it for the sake of harmony, and because he had not been
well. I told them that, but they swept aside the plea of his legs as though
it were an excuse, acknowledging that although they were bad they did
not excuse everything. They found his general attitude to life on the
island very hard to understand. Most of all they did not like the way
he treated me. What about, I thought to myself, the way I treated him.

Allowing the talk to go this far was a fatal mistake. Now it all burst
out of me in a staccato torrent: "Yes yes, I can't stand him, I love this
island but I loathe being stuck with him. He never shows any enthusiasm
about doing anything constructive, he sleeps half the day, he makes
me feel guilty for not sleeping with him but I just can't stand the
thought of his body on mine, he acts as an instant depressant the minute
I get back to camp after a wonderful walk, he is a lazy, ignorant, boring
old fool and why in God's name"—here my voice rose in petulant
fury—"do I have to be stuck on an island with *him* of all people in
such a potentially wonderful situation, and worse, why the hell do I
have to be married to him . . .?"

"Why *are* you married to him, Lucy?"

"Do you think I would be married to him if I could help it? It was
your bloody Government and their idiotic antediluvian ideas about
propriety. We wouldn't be here if it weren't for having a marriage
certificate. I resent it more than I can say and I've said too bloody
much. It isn't fair. G has reasons for being the way he is. Let's not
talk about it anymore. I feel terrible for speaking behind his back."

But feeling terrible was no good. The damage was done, cat out of
the bag and vicious claws striking everywhere.

"But you can't stay here like this. It's a horrible situation. We can
take you with us to Merauke, or put you on another island."

"No, no it's no good, we have to be on Tuin. I *want* to be on Tuin.
I'm all right. I give as good as I get."

"Well, sure, but it doesn't seem that way to us. I think we ought to have a little talk with G, get him to pull his weight and stop taking you for granted."

"No!"

I was horrified. I had broken all the unspoken rules of loyalty, showed myself up as a mean, weak-minded, tattle-tongued female of the sort I most despised. Going deeper, I had personally trampled ruinously over the hardwon harmony of the last month or so. I would never be able to convince myself again that I was happy with G for more than a few isolated moments. It all boded very ill.

During the rest of the walk no further reference was made to this disturbing exchange. I showed Peter and Derek the passion fruit, the plain, and took them through the interior past the tee-tree groves all the way over to Long Beach. They particularly liked the lovely shaded bower carpeted with soft thick grasses at the far end of the beach. We sat down here for a spell, but fearful of a revival of conversation I soon stood up and made to go. Some very minor pejorative comparison was made between the limitations of Tuin and some other places the boys had seen. Although my loyalty to G was unsteady, my devotion to the island was absolute. I said nothing, but sped on ahead along the hot sand of this my most beloved shore. One of them called out to me in friendly tones, but I paid no attention. In the space of being alone I tried to get my riotous feelings under control. By the time they had caught up with me I was calmer. Derek, aware that something they had said had touched an angry chord, had gathered up some long black and bronze feathers. These he affectionately wove into my plaited hair. I wore them like that until we neared camp, then I took them out and stuck them in my belt. I did not feel like G's wife but I was not Derek's Minnehaha either.

G still lay under One-Plum-a-Day, but there were signs that he had been up and made some tea. It was late, we had been away the whole afternoon. "Have a good walk then, did you?"

"Yes, fine." Guilt and confusion made my speech stilted and unnatural. It must have been glaringly obvious to G that something had happened during the walk. I could not imagine that his conjectures could be worse than the truth.

Taking refuge in action, I prepared the fires for the evening meal. Earlier on Derek had expressed a wish to take some film of me walking out on the sandspit. In order to reach the spit he carried me over a channel of water, on his shoulders again. He made every touch caressive. He said gentle things. It was getting later and later. Routine had gone haywire. I was slow and late with the meal. We all covered ourselves with insect repellent, and light was produced from a tiny hurricane lamp.

When I had eventually served out the meal, almost entirely made up of items from their stores, there was an atmosphere of falsely companionable quiet around the table that made me want to stand on my head and scream. All my movements were jerky and nervous. During the meal I kept finding reasons to jump up and fiddle about with tea or the fire. One of the boys casually asked G why he did not do the washing-up tonight. I moved away, could not bear to listen. I did not want G to do the wretched washing-up. It was my one excuse to get away down to the sea. I did not give a damn about the dark.

When I came back up, Peter and G were quietly talking over a cigarette. I heard the words "When I had money, you see . . ." from G. I hung back by the washing line. Derek came over and told me I must learn to relax. He started soothingly to massage my back. The flames from the dying fire shuddered in a night breeze. The small pool of light from the lamp barely illuminated the table at which G and Peter sat. I knew that it was foolish. I knew that it could in no way possibly improve matters, but I let him go on stroking my spine and shoulders with long, deft fingers, pushing away the tension with the palms of his hands. It felt so good.

"I'm off to bed, Lu. You coming? What are you two up to, anyway?" His tone was bantering and light but I could hear the weariness in his voice. I was sticking a knife in someone who was already down.

I said an overcheery "Good night" to Derek and Peter and went with G to the tent. Our proximity in that small rectangle felt horribly awkward. No familiar talk united us tonight. G said once before he went into a deep motionless sleep that lasted all through the night, "You know, I don't understand you, Lu. You are a most peculiar person."

It seemed impossible for me to settle in any position. My half-aroused body was ridiculously sensitive to the roughness of the old muslin I was lying on, my brain was like a bruise; every thought that pressed on it seemed to find a point of pain. How could I go on living with G now that the way I really felt about him had been expressed? And yet as I lay there and looked at his lonely sleeping figure, there was no harshness in my mind. Only confusion. I yearned to lay my head on someone's chest and be enfolded, to hear someone tell me that I was not living with the worst mistake of my life.

Morning came at last. The boys had made everything ready for an early departure the night before. The four of us gathered in camp for the last time. Derek heaped muesli on to a plate and pushed it towards me. G sat down at that moment and I stood up to pour the tea. He started eating the muesli.

"Hey, that was meant for—"

"Derek! here's some tea."

Peter asked G casually when he reckoned to get the shelter finished.

"Oh, it'll get done. It'll get done before the rains come. It doesn't need much, you know. Once the rafters are up it's just a matter of putting the roof on."

The tension beneath the superficial conviviality pressed in on me from all sides. I went down to the creek and crouched there, slowly filling the billy. After a few moments a figure dropped down quietly beside me. I did not look but I knew it was Peter.

"What are you going to do, Lucy?"

"I don't know. I don't know. I'll be all right."

He would have spoken more, but I could discuss nothing. I turned away. Derek was coming up the beach from his catamaran. He saw me and came towards the creek, but slowed when he saw Peter. I stood up and joined G by the camp table. Our legs were to be dressed one last time, but I said mine was all right, the antibiotics were working well. Peter had gone to pack the final bits and pieces onto the boats. He left the reflector tarpaulin and the orange "V" sheet for us. Derek was talking to G as he finished dabbing his legs. Unable to stay near, I wandered down to the sea, ostensibly to rinse some bandages.

"All set?" I called to Peter as he worked on his cat. Yes, he thought everything was about ready. He had the bottom half of his diving suit on. Sun and salt had bleached the top of his hair like mine, the few bright hairs on his young chest glistened. As he walked towards me I stood up. Grubby strips of bandage rolled over and over in the sandy shallows. The sun was already above the northern hill. I felt it now warm and growing on my bare flesh. Peter opened his arms wide and our lean bodies collided into a hug of long, gripping intensity. I had my eyes squeezed tight shut, chin burrowing in to the hollow of his collarbone when G's voice boomed out over the beach: "I'll thank you, sir, to unhand my wife."

He was standing at the top of the beach with Derek. They were both smiling, but G's smile was only on his mouth. It was time for the boys to go.

We said goodbye to them together. Polite, meaningless things were said. Absurdly, Derek and I shook hands. G went back into camp as soon as the sails were hoisted, but I stayed to watch until they were out of sight. When at last the white wings had vanished and only the miles and miles of blue sea and sky remained where they had been, I still stayed, choked with the chaos of my own mind.

6

DEPRIVATIONS
AND COMPENSATIONS

Diary
Although it was fun for us to have visitors, and made a tremendous
change, we did find the experience left us a trifle disorientated.

That is the understatement of the Tuin year. When I had finished gazing
out to sea I went back to camp where I found G about to dig a well
on the other side of the creek. The turmoil of emotions within me did
not allow for the fact that he was actually busy doing something towards
our future. I hurried across to him and nervously took hold of his
sleeve. "I had to defend you," I gabbled. "To defend you. It was
awful. I was ashamed. I am ashamed now."

"What the hell are you talking about, defend me? What's up with
you? I've never seen anything like the way you behaved with those
two boys. You were like a bloody bitch in heat."

I dropped his sleeve as though it had bitten me and took a step
backwards.

"Yesterday—" I began.

"Yes, what did happen between you three yesterday? I'd be interested to know. I expect you had a bloody good fuck. Well, I hope you
enjoyed yourself. Which one was it, or did you have them both? I don't
know Lu, you amaze me, you do . . ." He was prodding absent-
mindedly at the ground with his spade. His voice was almost toneless,
his stance stiff but stooped at the shoulders. He was not looking at me.

"Oh, for goodness' sake, you don't begin to understand."

"Understand? You give me one good reason why I should understand
you, Lu. You come out here to live on an island with me. For some
reason you've never told me you turn against me in Brisbane and that's
the end of our sex life as far as you're concerned. Two young bucks

come round and you flaunt yourself all over the place. God knows what you told those boys yesterday.''

''I told them to stop talking about you. I told you, I had to defend you, I hated that.''

''You're a lousy liar, Lu. I can always tell when you're lying. I bet you really let your hair down to those two. Was that before or after you had your screw?''

I sprang back across the creek without answering. Then I said I was going to make a cup of tea. I fiddled about, breaking up small twigs, trying to get a grip on myself by doing something normal. But my hands were shaking and my neck was rigid and throbbing with tension. All the half-aroused lust in me had boiled down to a solid nugget of gall. I was incapable of swallowing. When I opened my mouth, shaking all over, to hurl that gall at G across the creek, saliva ran down my chin. I could clearly hear my own voice explode out of me halfway between a snarl and a screech: ''I will never, never, *never*''—drool—''have sex with you again!''

G's mouth hung open, he was staring at me without a word. When he did finally speak it was with more curiosity than accusation: ''Lu, I think you've gone slightly off your nut.''

I spluttered. With the main bullet of my venom spent, I gradually stopped trembling. The stiffness went out of my body and I resumed the task of making tea where I had left off.

G came and sat down in the shade. He took off his hat and scratched his head. The hat Derek had given me hung from One-Plum-a-Day tree. G lifted it down and turned it in his hands. ''You know, Lu,'' he said, ''if you had behaved the way you do in the days when I had my Jaguar, I'd have kicked your arse out of the door. I sometimes wonder if what you need is a bloody good hiding.''

''I don't think it would help,'' I said, and poured the tea into our mugs. Into the new billy I measured two portions of the white rice the boys had given us and set it on the fire. While it boiled I packed my diary, a pencil, a book and a fresh strip of sari into the blotched remains of a shoulder bag. I drank my tea down in one draught and ate two spoonfuls of the rice.

''What are you doing, Lu? It isn't long after breakfast.''

''I'll be away all day. Yours is in the billy. See you later.''

And I walked straight into the interior and stayed there until nightfall. When I came back G was already in bed. In the morning I cooked rice again, left it with tea for G and went off again. I did not go to my favourite haunts but stayed deep in the interior, spending most of the day in a small clearing where there was fine, soft grass to lie on. I did not write, but read until my book was finished and then simply watched the sky and the path of the sun.

This pattern continued for four days. Sometimes I would wander as far as Derek's coconut spike and open a nut for myself if I became thirsty. I did not seem to feel particularly hungry. Neither, apparently, did G, for there was no indication that he went fishing while I was away and what was left of the stores was untouched. He ate the rice I left and some of the meat coconuts I brought in. There was no animosity in the air when we saw each other at night and briefly in the mornings. There was nothing.

Mid-morning of the fifth day I returned to camp for the pencil and paper I had not wanted before. G was asleep on his green towel, the one that had been to all the islands with him. His small beard was pointing up at the sky, his hands, the fingers untanned, the backs freckled or age-spotted, lay blankly on the dry grasses to either side of him. I settled myself not very far away under a low scrub tree. This is what I wrote:

Diary
Influences, opinions and comparisons hailing from the "outside world" can contribute nothing to our project. We are here as 20th Century castaways and our main aim is simply to survive, not to achieve. People do things in different ways. We have not come here to Tuin to write a book on expert Bush living or how to tame the jungle. We claim no great knowledge in any of the fields that could serve us most usefully here: raising crops in tropical and drought conditions; locating and securing a permanent supply of fresh water; being able to forecast weather and tidal conditions—but we are managing. We are alive, and all things considered, very much kicking!

We can look around the area of our camp and see very little evidence of work done. Our shelter is not yet erected; we are still borrowing storage space in an islander's deserted hut. But if we look at our time spent here with the eyes of two people intent merely on survival, our ostensible aim, and forget the drummed in notions of competitive civilisation, we have done well. Our efforts at fishing have yielded us a bountiful supply of protein and we have discovered an adequate source of vitamins delightfully packaged in the wild fruits of the island—coconuts and passionfruit plus wild native plum at this time of year. Our complexions are clear and healthy. The vegetable garden has occupied much time and labour. We have been working against the fact that it is totally out of season for planting, but in our situation we are forced to try for whatever small success might be possible; even if only the hardy beans, rock melon and pumpkins yield a crop, our diet will be substantially augmented.

The worst setback to all our little island plans, the house building project in particular, has been the ulcerous condition of our legs. G has suffered very badly and day after day has had to postpone plans for logging and foundation digging. This has been frustrating for him in the extreme and taken a fair toll of temper and optimism. He has been forced to lie like an invalid for days in camp, sometimes reflecting angrily on his loss of strength and vitality. However, we are tied to no schedules, and patient acceptance of our own limitations is a more sensible attitude to adopt than endless fretting that we cannot immediately do this or that. I have taken a leaf or two out of G's book of patience. My energy and enthusiasm must have exasperated him terribly at times.

It is difficult living beside a sea that is poison to sores. Since the many small wounds on our limbs began to suppurate we have had to try to avoid contact with sea water, not easy when one is obliged to fish for the main part of our diet. A careless step, a splash of coral-infested water, and progress on the legs is set back two days. Yet we have done better than just survive. We have learned to love this island, its sounds, its many different moods, the rhythm of the tides and sun. Each day the island teaches us something, we find a new plant or hear different birdsong, feel a wind stir the trees of Tuin from another direction, feel newly stirred within ourselves. . . .

We are not here to combat the island, to force from it a home fit for man, but to try to live contentedly within its confines, adapting ourselves to fit into a unique environment. Perhaps we will gain inwardly from the rare freedom it offers; if only we can allow ourselves to let go of other, irrelevant standards.

The above was written to be read to G. How much of it is truth and how much self justificatory cant for the sake of peace, I will leave to the imagination.

It was just before midday when I walked back into camp with my peace offering. A short while later G made a start on a well. "I'm going to see if I can get a fish this afternoon. You coming, Lu?"

"Yes. Are you hungry now?"

"Bloody starving."

"Right."

I quickly brewed up some tea and boiled rice with two spoonfuls of dried milk in it. G's eyes opened wide when he saw this luxury. "Hey, rice pudding!"

"Near enough. I got the extra milk off those two boys."

I deliberately threw away the dangerous mention of the boys with a dismissive and slightly contemptuous air. They had to firmly be put in the past, banished from any position of importance in the history of Tuin.

"This is bloody good, Lu. Any more?"

"That's the lot. We're back to basics now, normal starvation rations!"

"Ah, don't you worry. We'll get ourselves a beautiful great coral cod for supper, and a snapper or two. O.K.?"

"O.K.!"

We were back on our own, and together, in our own peculiar way.

The weeks that followed were unremittingly hot and dry. We seemed to have entered a new phase of weather. There were no longer grey clouds gliding by to taunt us with unreliable promises of rain. The magnesium flare dazzle of the sun hovered in the pricking blue of the sky like the vapour of a burning breath. The hours of cool, after dawn and before sunset, seemed shorter and shorter. The dry heat brought sounds of its own to the quiet interior. Brittle branches crumbled off trees with the softest brush of a shoulder and fell in powdery lumps among paper-dry grasses. Petrified streamers of heat-faded pandanus leaves detached themselves from their moistureless sockets and crackled like Christmas wrapping paper as they broke on the baked ground. Footsteps through the rustling tissues of the dying undergrowth were loud. Daily it became easier to see through to the blue distance on the other side of the island as the trees sloughed off their bleached foliage. The colours, russets, ochres, bronze, reminded me of autumn, but here death came from the sun and there was no rich, dark winter to come.

G wrestled with the lifeless soil. Deeper and deeper he went, pocking the surface of the island with waterless wells. The spindly vegetable shoots that had come through so eagerly fell like pieces of straw, there was nothing to hold their roots in the earth. Older plants, like the tomatoes and sweetcorn, stayed upright, electing to die on their feet. A recently planted bed of kohlrabi, tiny purple leaves just formed, stayed two inches high for weeks on end and then died as a body. It was a struggle without hope and yet we hoped all the time.

From Long Beach I collected all the washed-up petrol drums I could find and brought them back across the island strung by their handles on a yoke of mangroves, some falling apart with rust on the way. With these G made shades for all the vegetable beds. The drums, more convenient than stakes in the ground because they allowed for mobility, were positioned at each end of the bed with a mesh of poles laid across them and heaped over with cool palm leaves. As the sun moved in its course, G moved his shelters, protecting the parched plants from its shrivelling rays. But it was all no good without water. For a time we had hope of some seeds I had thrown in experimentally in an area on the other side of the island where the grass was still green and luxuriant. But within weeks all those plants, which had shot up very quickly, suddenly went brown and withered.

Drinking water was now rationed much more stringently. We were down to two mugs each per day and the only water used for cooking was the meagre puddle in which I boiled the breakfast rice. Once G struck sweet water when he was digging out a well not far from the creek. But our moments of jubilation were brief; the water was none other than our old creek top pool, slowly draining away to come out filtered through sand in another place. High tides now gave us greater cause for alarm. When the sea swept right into the creek we feared that our precious fresh water would stay constantly saline. But after twenty-four hours it always cleared, leaving the same small vital pool. If we knew there was going to be a high tide at night I took freshwater for the next day from the creek the evening before; this way we never had to go a day on coconut juice only. Because the water ration had been reduced over a period of time, we were not conscious of a sudden deprivation. We urinated less and even our sweat seemed to dry up, as if our bodies were conserving every drop of fluid, but we did not suffer unduly from thirst while we still had peepas.

By now an almost pure protein diet had pared us down close to the bone. I still found I had plenty of energy but strength and stamina were beginning to go. The buckets of water I brought up from the sea felt heavier; sometimes I had to stop and rest halfway up the beach. Both our sets of sores had responded well to treatment and our legs were going through an easier time. It was the failure of the garden and the horrifying and never worded thought that it might never rain again that threatened out future and burdened our minds. Day after day there was not a cloud in the sky.

Strange—we had not scrupled to tear each other apart with all the refinements of verbal cruelty when things were not so bad physically; now, faced with a threat so much larger than the sum of our two selves, we gave each other all the encouragement we could.

My lone wanders became a constant quest for food and possible leads to where there might be more water. G concentrated all his powers on trying to save the sweetcorn and tomatoes if nothing else. Sometimes he would pour a little from his own ration of water around the roots of one tomato plant that yet had hope, he called it "Elm tree." The corn had been doing well until this complete drought. Now, at a height of less than two feet its leaves began to yellow and droop. With it died our hope for a bulk food to take the place of rice as it ran out. Then God or fortune chose to lead my feet in the way of a wonderful discovery.

I had walked far around the southern point of Long Beach, so far that I was almost on the western side of Tuin again. The sun still had a space to go before it touched the top of Tukupai, but I knew how long it would take me to go back the way I had come. I decided to take the risk of plunging into the unfamiliar part of the interior at this end of the island and trying to take a straight course directly back to camp.

Diary
The grasses there are much longer than any I have encountered in the waist area of Tuin. At times I was ploughing through vegetation which rose way above my head and obscured my view of the hill towards which I was aiming. But the voice of the sea, behind and on my left, told me that the course was roughly right. As I pushed my way forwards the tall grass scraped my arms and occasionally whipped my face, but its height protected me from the still hot sun. I wondered if there might be a colony of snakes at this end of the island and hoped that the crashing noise of my approach would send them slithering away.

The high blades of grass were pale in the sunlight. Sometimes my feet encountered soft springy ferns wispy as maidenhair. The octopus-like tentacles of a young screwpine at ground level, vivid green and prickly, occasionally caused me to swerve from my straight line and take a slight detour. Sudden drops in the ground gave me one or two little alarms, but otherwise I felt just like a child let loose in a field of tall wheat on a beautiful summer afternoon.

At one point I climbed up on to a massive boulder that suddenly blocked my way. From the top of this I could clearly see the guiding contours of the hill I knew well. Between me and that hill was a valley, shallow and broad, studded with other randomly positioned rocks almost as big as the one I was standing on. There seemed to be an unusually square patch of dark soil down there near the base of the hill. Curiosity and surging hope drove me towards it. That shape had been made by man. It had been worked as ground is worked for a garden. And if there had been a garden here, then there was surely water nearby. As I scrambled blindly in the direction of the patch, I slipped into a deep crack in the ground. A creek bed! I crouched down and felt the ground. It was bone dry and ridged with raised splits. I moved on along the path made by the creek. It took me close to the abandoned garden. It was all too obvious why it had been abandoned.

Evidently the earth had once been painstakingly formed into tidy mounds. Now the crumbly grey soil cracked off the little hills in dusty clods. They looked like so many heaps of ash. But out of the tops of them some yellowed vines sprouted like skeletal fingers, wandering in knuckled lines to bury themselves under webs of a reddish fern thin as the hair on an old woman's scalp. I sat down on one of the mounds in the middle of the patch and thrust my fingers deep under two of the dead vines. At first I could feel nothing but dry, warm earth, then my hands met with something hard and rounded. It would not easily free itself. I felt the grey soil enter the gap between my short nails and questing finger ends, bending the nails backwards as I dug my hands under the round shape the better to grasp it. With a tug, the long roots broke and the treasure was released. I sat looking at it for a long moment. It was about the size of a small turnip or a large potato, pale, smooth and bulbous. I brought it up close to my face, and sniffed at it. It smelt of root and earth and vegetable. I pushed the hard flesh against my teeth and bit into it deeply, careless of the dirt. It was sweet and good and solid. Dropping the bitten fruit into the pouch of my sari strip I bent low to the earth and scrabbled among the mounds, arms covered in grey dust to the shoulder. There were many of these things. Some were wizened and soft at the ends, but I took them all.

I wished I could be magic-carpeted to G's side immediately with my find, but I had a long walk ahead. To make carrying the "yams" easier, I opened out the sari strip and piled them in the middle, then knotted up the corners to make a hobo's parcel. This I slung over my shoulder. Every time they bumped my back on the way to camp I thought with joy of the meals to come.

The discovery of the sweet-potato or yam patch—we were not sure exactly what they were—was a tremendous boon. Instead of just co-conut for lunch now we had steamed, roast or boiled "yams." They made delicious fishcakes mashed with flaked parrot fish or blue. Sometimes I made plain "yamburgers" which always went down well, but we were so low on oil that these were served only occasionally. Although we always took a pinch of salt with our evening meal to guard against cramps, we did not need much as most of the food was prepared with some salt water in the cooking. Also, we were wary of encouraging thirst. Our morale rose considerably after a few good meals. When we began to run out of "yams" I was delighted that G wanted to accompany me back to the garden.

We decided to make a day's outing of it. G emptied the geckos out of his blue rucksack, put a box of matches in one of the pockets and tied the dipper onto the back. He made a cigarette out of a tea-bag I had been drying on the line for that purpose and puffed away on it as we set off on the long trek. Instead of going back through the interior, which would have been wretched on his newly healed legs, we went right around the coast via Palm Beach, until we neared the place where I had gone into the interior before. It took me hours to relocate the garden. I could not see the boulder I had stood on before anywhere. Eventually I told G I would have to climb the nearest hill to get a good view of the whole area. He patiently sat himself down on a raised piece of ground and waited while I puffed and sweated up the hill, rather cross with myself for showing what a poor sense of direction I had. When at last I reached the top and looked down, I laughed. The path I had taken showed up clearly from this height; I had missed the garden by a matter of feet. G's piece of raised ground stood directly above it. From here I could also see a clear way out to the beach.

I went straight back to G's mound and jumped down off it right into the garden. We filled the rucksack right up with "yams." Taking the way out I had seen from the hill, we came to an attractive shady area just back from the beach. Here we made a fire and cooked up an instant picnic of yam boiled in sea water. We had found that if the flesh was not cut, the salt did not spoil the taste at all. We finished off the meal with the juice and meat of a coconut, which left us feeling pleasurably replete.

On the way back home we noticed some more old sheets of corrugated iron scattered around some broken poles. We thought it probable that whoever had tended the garden had erected a shade for themselves on this site. After we had built up our strength a little more we would come back and fetch these irons for our own roof. By now my antipathy towards using debris from the other world had softened. If there was something useful on the island, we would use it, "natural" or otherwise.

With the improvement in the condition of our legs, a new ritual was added to our day. Every morning and evening I was in the habit of taking a bath in the sea. In the mornings I was often joined by an inquisitive little black tip shark I called Sammy. If the tide was low, I would walk all the way down to the end of the sandspit and dip myself in one of the deep valleys between the sandhills. I loved to lie there for a long time with just my head sticking out of the water. It was easy to imagine I was the only land animal left in the world; an image that gave a sensation of enormous self-importance at the same time as an awareness of being no more significant than one of the myriad minute life-forms in the sea all around.

One day, when the tide was closer to home, G saw me revelling like a seal in the warm water. As the water lapped up between my breasts while I lay on my back, I would flick over onto my belly and let the small wave tumble over my shoulders, then onto my back again to wait for the next one. It was a game I could play for hours.

"Do you know what?" he said, to both our surprise. "I think I might join you."

Diary

When the tide is in and the sun is beginning to drop, we sometimes go down to the water and bathe together. The shallows, stretching out for hundreds of yards before the far side of the sandspit shelves into dark blue depths, are warm and welcoming, lapping soothingly over grimy sweat-stained skin. Keeping a wary eye out for the oval shadows of blue stingrays, we lower ourselves side by side into comfortable hip-accommodating hollows and slowly slide down until only heads remain unsubmerged. We loll luxuriously, dappled in sunlight and ripples. Our bodies undulate, long and golden as we roll and float, resting on elbows; two strange, touchingly awkward land creatures made momentarily streamlined and lovely by the sea.

The business of actual washing is less romantic. Briskly we rub sand into legs and arms in a vain attempt to clean off thoroughly ingrained dirt. I submit my grubby backside to the same savage treatment I give the inside of an encrusted billycan. We emerge glowing and refreshed, and are dry before reaching a towel.

It seemed cruel that the penance G had to pay for this small pleasure was so harsh. Whether or not the sickness in his legs would have flared up again had he stayed away from the water, we will never know. His ankles blew up like pale, pocked sausages and an ominous lump rose in his groin. I encouraged him to keep his legs up as much as possible to reduce the swelling. But at the same time I was worried that this position might make the poison spread more quickly. It was frightening to be so ignorant.

Rest always eased his legs, but this setback brought a return of all his former depression. I now made a conscious effort to spend more time in camp. G was not driving me away with his apathy and irritability these days. He was the reluctant victim of something over which he had no control and I felt that I should not add to his load by appearing to desert him when he was most in need of comfort.

I brought out my flute, which I had not played for some time, and asked if he minded if I practised nearby. Far from minding, he seemed pleased, so I propped my music in a tree and laboured breathily to produce vaguely familiar airs. To keep myself occupied close to camp I started to make a bookcase. The clean, blond bones of stripped, slender mangrove pleased me so much that I tried to use nothing else in its construction. Unfortunately the bindings were a great letdown. At first I tried knotting the sticks together with a twine of twisted vines wound tightly into grooves made in the wood, but these split when fresh and cracked when dry. All good binding material had to be saved for the shelter, so all I had left to play with were ragged strips torn off my sari cloth or pieces of soiled bandage. The look of these so spoiled the effect of the wood that I abandoned the bookcase and used the smoothed and polished sticks to play solitary games of spillikins or Pick-Up-Sticks, observed by rows of little glinting lizard eyes.

We had grown fond of our camp lizards. When G was grating a coconut to add to the morning rice a long silver-grey lizard, whom we called Oscar, after Wilde, would casually appear from nowhere, hoover up the crumbs and then retire to the safety of the woodpile from which he would observe the world with bright, disdainful eyes. My special favourite was a handsome little fellow with a shining, brazen back and a bright orange underbelly. He had a great number of progeny who were constantly in danger of being drowned or burnt to death as they hung around the places where I threw used sea water and ashes for the garden. When we sat at the table they would run boldly over our feet, sometimes freezing suddenly in mid-course, their little cool claws light on our skin. When we were very hungry I considered eating Bronzey and Oscar, but there did not look to be much meat on them.

The geckos in the shed were weird, rubbery creatures with huge round eyes like owls. They were pale and broad with thick curved limbs and flat heads. There tails came off very easily if they were alarmed, and when a new one grew in its place, it often did not match the rest of the body in colour. One, who had the unfortunate experience of being accidentally shut in my flute case for a week, grew a new tail which came out quite black.

A newcomer to camp was the Poo Poo bird. He announced his presence one morning by making a formidable rustling among the grasses just beyond the garden patch. G and I stood and watched, intrigued, as this extraordinary bird performed a series of inexplicable antics. He jumped up into the air, wings askew, and landed back on the ground on his head. At first we thought he must be unwell, but as this performance was repeated quite regularly, we came to realise that it was some kind of rite, either peculiar to the species, or to this particular member of it. We called him Poo Poo because of the sound he occasionally made, but according to our bird book he was the pheasant coucal. Certainly he had a tail like any other pheasant, but his head was very large for his body and shaped almost like an eagle's. In time, he adopted our camp as his territory and we became very fond of him. With a great deal of effort and many undignified failed attempts, he could just about jump into the implement-hanging tree. From there he could launch himself into flight with no trouble, but he simply seemed incapable of cranking himself into the air straight off the ground. Later, we were to find out what a useful weather forecaster he could be.

All the time spent in camp while G's legs were recovering meant that we got through a great many yams. It was the poorest time of the moon for fishing anyway, and to be frank, the change from unrelieved platefuls of white fish flesh was a relief. However, the yam patch was a by no means bottomless pit, so as the moon went into its quarter phase and G's legs showed signs of improvement, we fished daily again and used yams only every other day.

I had been looking forward tremendously to making the trek back to the other end of the island to fetch the irons for our roof. However, I knew better than to mention it while G's legs were bad, as it would have made him feel nagged and helpless. I brought it up tentatively when he was well on the mend, and he smiled and said he had been waiting for me to start on that. "Oh well, I suppose we had better get the bloody thing done or Madam will never be satisfied."

"That's right," I said, and winked.

We were deceived by the coolness of the morning on the day we set off to fetch the irons. We started out feeling strong and confident, forgetting that despite the bonus of starch in the yams we had still been on a diet of under a thousand calories a day for months. By the time we had reached the plateau rocks, all chatter had ceased and G was looking strained. I asked if his legs were aching and he said no it wasn't that, he just felt very tired. The sun ground and ground at our senses, sucking all the moisture from our throats, stinging our nostrils with its dry heat, seeming to squat on our shoulders like a dead weight. When at last we reached the place of the irons, we rested for a long time, I in a deep rock pool, G in the shade where we had eaten our picnic before. While he was snoozing, I went off and found a couple of good coconuts to give us some sustenance before we bound up the irons for the trek back.

The unbroken sheets were about eight feet long, two and a half across. A single sheet was not heavy, but it was awkward. We had five whole sheets and three half pieces to get back to camp. G rigged a kind of stretcher cut from strong saplings upon which we laid the irons and tied them in place with the camp rope. Poles stuck out as handles at either end of the stretcher.

"Ready, Lu?"

"Ready."

"O.K., you grab the back end. Probably be easier for you. One, two, three, lift."

And away we went. At first, like any cumbersome carrying job, it did not seem too bad. Then came the first lot of rocks to be crossed. G lifted up the front end as he wobbled on to the uneven rocks and immediately the whole of the jagged edged load slid into my belly. Fortunately my leather sheath belt bore the brunt of it but I bellowed for G to stop. As he lowered his end carefully, a loose iron from the middle of the bundle shot forward and hit him behind the knees. Extravagant curses and a halt to tie the thing more securely. It was a blessing that the worst rocks were at this end of the journey, otherwise we would never have made it. Both my arms were screaming in their sockets by the time we reached the bay on the other side. The fronts of my thighs were scraped and the backs of G's. Language, strong and basic, was jerked out of G every time an inadvertent movement of mine put an extra strain on his end. Behind his back I made frightful faces when the same thing happened to me. There was a single pine tree with long, coolly waving branches half way along this bay.

"Shall we have our first rest under that tree?" I asked.

"What, you getting tired already?"

"Well, I'm all right, but I'll go on better for a rest."

So we stopped under the tree. G flopped down and closed his eyes. I whirled my arms round and round to get the blood back to its proper place, then lay on my back and waved my legs in the air. I was so relieved to be free of the load.

"Lu, I thought you were supposed to be having a rest."

"I am, I am. A rest from the carrying. I'm not *tired* tired."

"Ready to go on then, are you?"

"Soon as you are."

We swapped ends. Now it was my skinny bottom getting bumped and the front of G's legs. There was another lot of rocks to negotiate at the end of this bay. We reckoned on taking the next rest the other side of that. I did not think I would last out, but nothing short of my arms actually falling off would have made me ask for an earlier halt. Clearly G was as relieved as I was when the next bay came into view. There had been less swearing and more sweating on this leg of the journey.

Again, as soon as the irons were safely on the ground, I danced around recharging my batteries with freedom. G sank down on the sand as if someone had pulled his plug out.

"My God, Lu," he said. "You've got a lot of strength for a woman."

"Don't tell me you're beginning to feel the strain!"

"I'm just bloody tired, that's all."

The edge of irritation in his voice made me bite back any further teasing remarks.

On the next leg G plodded onwards, in his position at the front again, without a word. I felt the same strain as before and longed to drop the load, but I knew the worst of it now and was becoming a little more adept at balancing my end satisfactorily. Every single familiar wrinkle on the back of G's neck was filled with sweat and I could feel the droplets break out from my hairline and flow down into my eye-sockets and behind my ears. I wished for a third arm to wipe my face. This was a long bay, no palm trees, loose white sand. Towards the end of it the sand covered our feet with each step, which made the going agonisingly slow and exasperating. G grunted out a single, all-encompassing obscenity. I nodded without thinking, feeling he had summed up the situation neatly.

"It is Palm Beach after this lot, isn't it, Lu?"

"No. There's that small bay with the wide gully in it first."

"Bloody hell. Let's sit down a minute."

"Can't we get to the other side of the rocks first?"

"Fuck the rocks. Sit down and shut up a minute, Lu."

There was a gravelly unevenness in his voice as though he were utterly drained. He lay on his back with eyes shut. I sat beside him and inspected the calluses on my feet. We were in a cube of shade beside the rocks.

"What's the matter with me, Lu?"

"You mean you are exhausted?"

"If you want to know the truth I feel weak as a kitten. I'm fucked. Haven't got any bloody strength left."

"Well, it is jolly heavy, that thing."

"Heavy? You don't know what you're talking about. As a young man I could have stuck that on my back and bloody run with it. My boys would carry that like a piece of paper. You don't know what it's like for a man, Lu. You should have seen the body I had on me when I went into the army, they said I was muscle-bound. Jesus Christ, look at me now."

"It isn't surprising. Your body has been deprived of all sorts of things it was used to over these past months. You can't expect to feel on top form on the amount we eat."

"Well, you seem to be all right. I know you're skinny, but you've always got energy, it seems to me."

"Don't hold that against me!"

"Oh, I don't. You know I don't, Lulu. In some ways you're bloody marvellous to have around. I've never known a woman like you. You're like one of those pioneer women."

I had never seen G so beaten down. He was shocked at the state he was in and it flattened his morale. It was at times like this that I wished we had some way of crossing the touch barrier. I so wanted to show him affection. To encourage him, I used the cajoling language that had become our code for warmth.

"Come on, you feeble old fart, we can make it."

"Bloody old cow. Nag, nag, nag."

"Get that end of yours up, Kingsland."

"Filthy little bitch."

In this manner, in ever decreasing hops, we managed to get the irons back to camp. At one point G so revived that he tried strapping the entire bundle to his back. He staggered about ten steps forward, then yelled out: "Lulu, help!" and managed to laugh at his own weakness for a moment. At the final halt before home, he said, as I emerged streaming from a reviving dip in the sea, "You know, Lu, you're almost as good as a bloke to have around."

Team efforts brought us closer together than any amount of talking could do. Two horses in separate harnesses but both striving in the same direction. Inactivity, on the other hand, eroded the harmony disastrously. Had I been content to stay in camp with G, doing nothing in between bouts of fishing, cooking and wooding, the differences in our characters might have been less pronounced. But it was never long before the other side of Tuin beckoned me and I could no longer stay away. I was a different being over there, and when I came back to camp I brought some of that stranger with me, an alien at our table.

Diary
What is it that makes the texture of the grass so different from one patch to another? Near camp it is like flattened straw these days, over near the scrubfowl haunts beyond Long Beach it is thick and when it bleaches it is not blond, but blue. Here it is dry but so fine that there is softness. I like to lie stretched out on my side and let the heat melt all inner and outer tension so that I don't even flinch when an ant crawls in my ear. He'll crawl out again. Sometimes when I lie here quite still I witness from under drowsy eyelids the coming alive of a bush. There is a whispered rustling of hundreds of tiny wings. At first I thought they were butterflies or that a freak wind had descended on a bush thick with brown and yellow leaves, but they are birds, scores of tiny, dapper, doe-eyed things all smartly tailored in chocolate waistcoats. Their wing rustling prior to take off is like a great breath stirring the bush. Then whoosh, they are blown away, high in a sky-speckling crowd. I suppose I should be dutifully crouched here behind my camera, but I don't seem to care any more, I just like to be here.

When I jump down on to Long Beach after I have missed visiting it for a day or so, I cavort up and down in a great burst of physical release, running, jumping, dancing with my shadow, doing great lolloping, floppy handstands for the sheer joy of it. When I am finally out of breath I bathe and then abandon myself to the sensual delirium of the sun.

My body has become an instrument of the sun. I am its acolyte, cup-bearer to the Gods of white fire. The giant hand of the sun plucks me from my refuge in the sea and flings me upon a flat rock spread-eagled and wanton as a flame. The heat from the baked surface of the rock flares throughout my limbs, thrusts deep into the bone at the points where it touches first, elbows, shoulder blades, coccyx, heels. Far up the beach there is a quivering heat mirage melting the sand. If I were standing there, looking this way, the mirage would be here. I am lying within the mirage.

Words. Jetsam of memory. Toasting to "Lepanto." After the third verse I will lie upside down and the sun will come right up underneath my breasts and between my toes. It has burnished the ends of my pubic hairs and bleached my fringe and the short down at the back of my neck. The top of my coiled plait is going fair. I am a golden gazelle with the head of a striped tiger. I am going to commit adultery with a sunbeam. Whoops, I am not going to read this aloud to G. You have to have a concave navel to make love to a sunbeam. I have the most beautiful navel on Tuin. They enter directly from above when the sun is perpendicular to the earth. If caught on a rock alone at this hour of the day you are almost certain to be ravished. You cannot deny the sun. His seduction is absolute: invasion, conquest, occupation.

G reckons I have sex with goannas. It is not true. The sun is my beloved.

In such a condition, radiating contentment and vibrant with after sun glow, I would return to G where he lay in camp. It was not a wonder that he suspected I had a lover hidden away on the other side of the island, but I did not know then that that was what he seriously imagined. In the absence of a stabilising order of other human beings with commonly held beliefs, it was easy for fantasy to mingle with reality so that the edges of both began to blur.

TINY SHELLS PLUS BALER

7

POWER AND POISONS

How differently, I wonder, would my diary have read had I given free rein to my thoughts. Strange how it seems such a betrayal to fold away a piece of paper with words upon it. Kept in the vaults of the mind, thought is safe because it is ultimately mutable, one has limitless control over its presentation, but that does not make it any less extant than had it been recorded. Only nobody can wave it in your face.

G was more given to contemplative thinking than I. On Tuin I found that away from the world of words and attitudes my mind seemed to dissolve into my body, becoming less of a separate, organised entity. The impressions that fed themselves in came in shapes, textures, colours, temperatures and sounds; I was a receptacle of sensation as opposed to an instrument of observation. It was only occasionally in my diary that I looked at the island with words in my head, and I wrote and mused less and less as the months went on. But G did think. Lying on the ''daybed,'' his chances of finding pleasure in the barren little world of Tuin spoilt by the pain in his legs and the anger of a thwarted heart, he thought about all sorts of things. But the subject that rolled around in his head and recurred time and time again was that of our relationship.

Weaving slowly through the labyrinth of bushes and trees across the island, pausing to touch a leaf or stroke a long curl of peeling bark, brimful of the rich, mind-mocking influence of the sun, I would return to find in G unwelcome reminders of other realities. There were times when I would get within sight of camp, see the familiar form stretched out on the old green towel, and turn tail, retreating for a little longer into the easier world of the dry interior. Finally I would come back and make tea and maybe all would be well. We would go fishing or chat inconsequentially until it was time to start making the supper fires. But sometimes G would say, "Lu, you know I've been thinking . . .", and I would know by the tone of his voice that it was not about the garden, or water, or fishing.

There is little justice when two individuals marry for a set purpose and then one has the misfortune to fall in love with the other and wants that paper union to stand for all the things we are brought up to believe a marriage should. G felt angry, used and humiliated. I felt trapped, guilty and afraid and, whenever I thought about it, which was not often, full of resentment against the notions of another world which had forced marriage into our lives. That kind of morality seemed a fantastically irrelevant, bogus import on Tuin. When G, alone under the shade of One-Plum-a-Day, feeling already sick and irritable from the pain in his legs and his diminishing strength, reviewed in his mind the cold way in which I had behaved since our wedding, he was confused and disgusted. In such a frame of mind he would attempt from time to time to confront the wandering creature he had on the island as the only human company. My reactions were usually vague and evasive but if he persisted I would eventually start to spit back. Recriminatory bickering is always ugly and often pathetic; ours was both, and of course, it got us nowhere. What made our differences dangerous was that they were undiluted. There was no one else to talk to, no moderating outlet valves for our steam, and no accepted community standard against which we could measure the viciousness of our barbs.

We had no standards to measure our physical condition by either. Being thin had become normal, along with not having much stamina and always having sores. Always wanting to drink more than we could became an accepted part of our lives, as did being unable to lie on our sides anymore in the tent because our sparsely covered bones bruised so easily. Minds and bodies were adrift in a country ruled only by the elements, and proportion entered our lives only when consciously recalled. It was possible for thoughts in that state to step easily across the accepted boundaries of the other world and feel neither wrong nor unbalanced. There was no one to judge us. We could have got away with murder.

There was a long bleak patch when from one quarter moon to the next the fishing was poor. Nothing but the eternal parrot fish and lemon shark, which made G queasy. Although I had stumbled upon a second small yam patch, well hidden under tangled undergrowth, this and the other one were virtually stripped bare by now. Even meat coconuts were becoming difficult to find and there was no wild fruit around anymore. The floor of Coconut Alley, carpeted with fallen brown meat nuts when we arrived, was now bare but for a few stunted or split specimens, most of which emitted a foul stench when opened. I harvested all the tiny, prematurely fallen baby nuts, even the ones that had already planted a root in the ground, and piled them up in camp. Inside the shooting ones there was a spongy white fibrous seed, about the size of a tennis ball. It was feathery light, very insubstantial, but delicious raw or simmered with the ever diminishing rice.

Hoping to find a few good nuts left under the Palm Beach trees, I scrambled over there one hot still morning when the tide was high. I was disappointed to find only two very small coconuts. These I knotted into the sari strip and left on a rock while I went in to bathe. But my mind refused to float with my body that morning; there was something lodged in it, like a fishbone in the throat. I drifted slowly on my back for a while, staring up at the blue heat dome of the sky. The tide kept nudging me in to shore, bumping my heels against the steep sand shelf. I allowed myself to be pushed in and rolled over so that the dry sand clung all over my wet body. Then I stretched and flexed and bent over backward into an arc, gazing at the sea and sky upside down, but still the bone in my mind stuck.

Impatiently I tossed my body back in the sea again to wash off the sand, then I climbed dripping up into the interior behind the palms. There I crouched on a rock overlooking the beach, rocking very slightly back and forth on my heels, arms clasped over knees, chin resting on them. There was a dark, brooding presence in my mind totally at odds with the scintillating brilliance of the day. It seemed to tick in rhythm with the throbbing heat on the back of my neck.

Surely it was quite impossible that I was pregnant. But not quite quite impossible.

There was no bulge, but then, I was very thin. Like a stick insect. Since my hair had begun to fall out I did not feel beautiful any more, and then there were the veins. It was G who brought my attention to them. A few days back I caught him looking at me with an unusual expression on his face.

"What is it?" I asked.

"It's you, Lu. Your veins, they're sticking out all over your body like a map. Look, they're even up on your belly and on your chest."

"Must be the heat. My legs have been aching recently, have you seen these lumps in them?"

"Yes. I didn't want to say anything, though. You're going to have to take things easier, Lu."

"Do you think they're varicose veins?"

"I know they are. Those purple lumps are what they call 'grapes.' "

"Will they go away?"

"There's an operation you can have these days."

"Oh."

Women who are pregnant sometimes get varicose veins. Oh, surely it was impossible! It must show by now. But it would be so hard to tell because I had lost so much weight. Were my breasts tight? I felt. Again I could not tell because my whole body was so changed. I did sometimes feel nauseous but I thought that was just the endless fish and perhaps the rather dirty water from the shallow creek pool. And what if I were? I had visions of a dead, squashed, stunted thing, life choked off in a shrinking belly. I must find something more to eat. Just in case. It must be all right, must be fed. I'll call it "Tuin."

"Lucy, shut up."

I said that aloud, crouched there on my rock.

"What you need is a good swift kick in the belly."

Those words, recalled and chewed over now, came from the depths of G's hurt, but I was in no mood to be understanding. I still slept with the knife by my side every night.

I looked out towards First Fishing Rock. The shark would be murmuring their blunt lengths through the swollen water now. I thought of the way their lazy shadows erupted into charging missiles after a bloody parrot-fish head, how clean the water was when they had finished the offal of one of their number we had caught. G and his good swift kick, his talk of hidings. If once he laid a violent finger on me, I knew I would explode and then he would flatten me because he would have no choice. Young wife torn apart by shark. No trace of husband's body. Pregnant wife distraught. No headlines here. Only the dawn of another rainless day, a hot bland sun far above the little dramas of our lives.

Cramming my fingers into the fast-drying scrub of my hair, I scratched long and deep at my skull and pressed my palms against my ears. Once I had a lover who used to do that, whose body fitted mine almost as perfectly as the stone fits the fruit.

"Lucy, pull yourself together."

I laughed aloud at this antique exhortation to sanity and jumped down off the rock. Not wanting to return to G yet but lacking the energy to walk far these days, I meandered to the end of the tall palms, humming an inane little tune. I threw myself down against the last trunk and sprawled apathetically. Trailing along the ground in front of me was a dark green vine, evenly punctuated with threesomes of oval leaves. There were purple flowers growing out of it in places. It was a vine I had not noticed before. Curiously, I took the nearest section in my fingers for a closer look. As I bent over I saw on the ground dozens of strangely uniform brown pebbles. Coffee beans, I thought illogically in this bushless area. Vine in one hand, "coffee bean" in the other, a conclusion began very slowly to dawn. I followed the vine on my hands and knees and within seconds came upon a pod, and then another and another.

"Not coffee beans," I yelled to the ether. *"Beans* beans! *Green* bean beans!"

The pods were fat and full. Some had burst, scattering their pale succulent-looking contents on the ground where they had dried brown in the sun, but there were hundreds of perfect ripe ones clustered along the vines, which criss-crossed each other in a net that seemed to extend right along the beach under the rocks of the interior. The dried beans looked exactly like the sort of thing you see in jars in health-food stores. "Oh perfect, protein packed pulses," I jingled as I scrabbled up handfuls. But it was the thick green pods which attracted me most. I took one and bit off the end. Inside, the beans lay cushioned in soft white viscous skeins. I popped one out and cut it in half with my teeth. The half sat on my tongue tasting like a big old pea. I scrunched it and big old cannonball-pea taste filled my mouth. I had the bitten bean still in my hand and I took an experimental nibble of pod. It was good. I tore off a mouthful of both bean and pod and munched hungrily. Clutching two more for sustenance on the way, I ran to fetch the sari cloth so that I could fill it with beans to take back to camp. G, you old wallaby, look what I've got!

By the time I had got back to camp I was full. I must have eaten at least two dozen beans raw. There was no sign of G. Then I remembered how bad things had been when I went coconutting earlier. He was probably curled up in the tent. This would cheer him up. He was a little dozy when he woke up and could not take in at first why I was so excited. Then I thrust a load of beans into his lap and he understood. "They're wonderful," I told him. "Delicious!"

"Hold on a minute, Lu, you haven't eaten any raw, have you?"

"Just a few. I'm sure they're all right."

"Did it look as though they had been planted, like the yams?"

"Not exactly, they looked wild."

"You bloody idiot, you don't know what they might be. Go and get that plant book."

I dashed off and found the book, flipping through the pages as I walked back up to the tent. There was my bean, clear and unmistakable, with a description that fit perfectly. I read it aloud to G.

" 'Leichhardt or Mackenzie bean. First mentioned by L in his notes of . . . blah blah blah . . . found it could be used as a coffee substitute when dried, roasted and ground. Edible when boiled but'—Oh my God!—'poisonous in the raw state.' "

"There now, what did I tell you. You're probably going to fall down dead any minute."

"Of course I'm not. I feel fine."

"It would serve you right if you did, Lu. Why do you have to be so impulsive? You've made yourself ill once already with those yellow plums. Just like my boys, eat bloody anything."

"I wasn't ill. I was just sick."

"All right, you were lucky. Now I want the truth, how many of those beans did you eat?"

"Just a few—well, quite a few."

"How many, Lu?"

"About twenty-five-ish."

"What? Oh well, that's it. You're going to be ill."

"I feel perfectly all right. I'm going to cook some for supper. You'll try some, won't you?"

"I'll try some, but just make sure you cook them really thoroughly."

I went down to the kitchen area of the camp and reconstituted the last of the dried shark to make a stew with the beans. When I went to collect the beans G had cut up, he casually enquired how I was feeling.

"Marvellous, better than I have for ages," I replied defiantly. The stew did not look very appetising but G was hungry enough to give it a try. An inky purple fluid seemed to be oozing from the cooked beans. The smell of very old peas was overpowering. Without any warning at all my bowels and stomach were suddenly squeezed with a grinding nausea. I felt dreadfully giddy.

"Gerald," I said falteringly, "you were right."

"Lulu? What is it?"

But I had gone.

Behind One-Plum-a-Day tree there was a broad row of low trees which cut off our eating area from the flat space of sand where we dug pits to bury rubbish. I had just managed to get as far as this space before I collapsed on to all fours. One frantic hand began to scratch out a hole and then all propriety, all conscious care, all modesty, vanished as my body became one convulsive organ of explosive evacuation. After the first double-ended eruption, which had flooded the sand fore and aft with flowing pools, I just had the strength to move sideways to a clear patch before the next storm swept my guts. Involuntary tears sprung out and mingled with the foul strings swinging from nose and mouth. Through the black and red mist that seemed to be all around my eyes and ears, I was aware of G approaching saying things I could not hear properly.

"Rag," I managed to grunt out with the next ragged stream.

G laid some oddments of cloth near my head. I swayed as I lifted one to cut off the choking chain that clung to my lips. After the next bout had gripped me I was incapable of wiping or moving or replying to G's words of concern. All I could see with my head, which seemed to weigh a ton, hanging down between my arms, were two long wrinkles of loose skin hanging from my belly. Slowly I keeled over on to my side.

I have no clear recollection of the order of what followed, but I know at one point, thinking the worst was over, I shakily stood up and somehow covered the distance between kitchen camp and tent. In the dusk G was digging a trench to one side of the tent. I had to use it before he even had time to get the spade out and start digging another for the front end. Biting insects were about. G settled himself on his side of the tent and I lay down beside him feet by his head so that exit from the tent was easier for me. Soon I lost count of the number of times I went in and out. I was too weak to stand after a while so I crawled. The pain in my belly was worse with each fresh bout. As I retched, my stomach seemed to touch my backbone. I remember that the wind was high that night. At one point I lay outside, unable to reach the trench, unable to pull myself back into the tent. I mentally cursed the wind because it took away the thin sound of my voice which sounded low even in my own ears. I knew how deeply G slept. I was trying to call his name but all that came out was a feeble moan. It was like one of those awful dreams when you shout for help but no sound comes out.

Then G's voice came to me. "Lulu, where are you? Come back in, love, come and lie down. Have you been sick again?"

I was trying my best to answer but he could not hear. Then he was at my side.

"Oh my God, poor old shithouse. Come on, let's get you inside. Don't worry, you'll be all right."

He tried to get his arms underneath to lift me up, but his own strength was so diminished that he could not stand up with my weight. I heard him muttering: "Jesus Christ and you only weigh as much as a feather."

Finally he had to drag me in by my feet and arms. He was as gentle as possible.

I was unconscious before he had me properly settled in and the next thing I knew was waking in the quiet hours before dawn and lying there warmed by the knowledge of his concern. Whatever mad, bad thoughts both of us had from time to time in our lawless world, in moments of need we did not let each other down. I felt for the knife beside me and silently unsheathed it and put it out of the tent. A small symbolic gesture to myself. I needed to get to the trench again but knew I could not get there alone. I shook G's foot and he stirred. This time he manoeuvred me in and out as if he had been coping with invalids in tents all his life. He informed me all the while in no uncertain terms that from now on I was jolly well going to have to rest and take much more care of myself, and let him take care of me sometimes. He cursed me for an impetuous fool using rough rude terms, but kindness and care were shining through.

In the morning I lay on in the tent while it was still in shade and then G helped me down to the daybed. It seemed so strange to languish there, wrapped in the huge blue maternity gown, watching G fuss round the fire and brew up tea for me. More than anything else I longed for a thorough wash, but did not yet trust my feeble body to stay upright in the sea. G brought me a damp rag and my piece of comb and I went through the motions of tidying up.

"Queen coming to tea then, is she?"

"Silly, it just makes me feel better, human if not exactly feminine."

It was then that G told me how for the past weeks he had been racked by doubts and a terrible feeling of responsibility. He had seen me changing from a golden energetic girl to a stick-like, elderly creature with deep lines and wrinkles on my face and frightening veins swelling everywhere. He knew he was in a bad state too but the change in him had been more gradual. For so long I had seemed to thrive on nervous energy and our almost-pure-protein diet. Now neither of our bodies seemed to be able to absorb the goodness of fish anymore. We ate, but it just passed through. G said that once he had looked at me when I was doing something by the fire, and he had thought: My God, that girl is going to die, and she's here in this godforsaken place because of me. But I pointed out that I had known when I came it was not going to be all roses. Risk and the unknown were part of the whole venture.

"I know all that, Lulu, but you didn't reckon on kicking the bucket, did you?"

"Now listen, Carruthers, there is going to be absolutely no bucket kicking around here. Now get me down to that sea, and stay nearby to haul me out."

"Hello, I can see Madam is well on the mend, she's giving orders again."

By the evening of that day I was able to potter around gently on my feet. By then G was beginning to flag. He had been digging out a new well that looked particularly hopeful, but he had had to stop and lie down, feeling nauseous and weak. So for a while both of us were lying in feeble heaps, waiting for strength to return. But I knew that it would do no good just to lie there, so before it became too dark I roused myself and, moving slowly and gently, made a fire and cooked up the very last spoonful of semolina, making a thin, comforting gruel, which we both managed to keep down.

In the atmosphere of warmth and consolation I told G how worried I had been about him, too, and said ruefully that I was sorry not to have been much fun as a woman to him.

"That doesn't matter now, Lulu. I couldn't do it now even if I had the urge."

So many things did not matter anymore, now that finding ways to continue supporting what life was left in our bodies had become the only value. Sex became irrelevant. Crudity of language had no meaning that could be offensive. My accent did not grate on G anymore. Physical and intellectual prowess became immaterial, and the consciousness of class which had given rise to a few gibes between us in the past disappeared. Our differences diminished as our mutual needs increased; we were companions in want.

With the last of our rice gone we were down to fish, coconuts and roots. We tended to consume very few oysters and other shell creatures now because we found that, without bulk to accompany or follow them, they disagreed with our stomachs. To ensure that all possible ways of bringing in a regular supply of fresh fish were covered, we rigged up "George," an automatic fisherman who could keep a line out while we were asleep at night. We had abandoned night fishing ourselves early on as, apart from the annoying attentions of mosquitoes and the risk of sandflies opening up a whole new batch of sores, it was pointless deliberately to court disaster by clambering around sharp coral in the dark or wading blindly in shallows where there were certainly rays and possibly the odd croc.

"George" was a petrol drum sent bobbing out on the end of a long line baited with several lightly weighted hooks. He could fish in the deep channels of dark water which were too far away for our thrown handlines to reach. On the second day of his trial period George delighted us by bringing in a good-sized coral cod. It was thanks to George too that we discovered a natural fish trap. One morning G went down to inspect George's hooks. There was no catch on this occasion, but on the way back to camp G was distracted by mysterious flapping noises coming from behind a row of rocks. He approached cautiously and peered over. There, evidently caught as the tide went down, two large plumed trevally flapped vigorously in a couple of inches of water. They were trapped by a triangle of rocks with an opening only on the side farthest from the sea as it went down. Triumphantly G marched up the beach holding lunch by the tail in one hand and supper in the other. They were not a fish that had ever come onto one of our lines, so provided not only a bonus but also the treat of a change.

Further evidence of old gardening efforts had been revealed in the few cassava roots we had dug up around camp. They were thin and stringy and under different conditions I might have hesitated to feed them to a pig, but to G and me in those days they were a wonderful find, and we only wished there had been more. Carefully we tucked in the roots once we had taken a tuber, in the hope that the plant would start to grow again once the rains came.

Diary
The water from the well G has dug is strangely white and has an unpleasant smell. It makes tea which would be undrinkable if we had any choice in the matter. The creek pool seems to get shallower every day and yet there is always just enough to give us a mug each which we divide up and take in the morning and with the evening fish. We share one peepa at midday.

I was disconsolate this morning, wandering vacantly behind Coconut Alley. My last piece of sari strip is filthy with fire grease, which will not come out in the sea. It is stiff and itchy on my coat-hanger hips so I tie it loosely diagonally across my body. And this is partially to hide my breasts, which make me sad. They are slack and wrinkled like an old woman's and so tiny they might as well not exist. What a fool I was to imagine this frame could support a second life. It is obvious my periods have stopped through weight loss, as happens to anorexics. Makes me feel like an androgynous eunuch of some sort. G is sweet to me about it in his way. We make jokes about each other's decrepitude.

It is quite a while now since either of us had any extravagant food fantasies, but occasionally we become victim of a wild craving. Before now G has woken in the night cross because he does not know where I have put a non-existent square of Cadbury's Fruit and Nut Milk chocolate. It has become a melancholy little joke between us and he pretends to berate me when we are fishing for forgetting to pack the chocolate. Today I found myself craving for an apple with a vision of the crunch and flavour and sheer appleness of it so palpable that saliva flooded into my mouth. I groaned aloud and laughed at the sound of my own voice raised in such an incongruous wail. A scrubhen bustled away clumsily from where I had disturbed her matinal snooze.

They are so gauche and funny, those scrubfowl, absurdly bold and yet at the same time easily shockable. They all manage to resemble ill-groomed, gawky blue-stockings and I can imagine them wearing lopsided pince-nez and laddered lisle stockings. Joyce Grenfell would have done a wonderful take-off of a scrubfowl. Wish I could catch one and roast it, even if they do look scrawny. Still have not found one of their eggs.

I was shaken from my ponderings by an extraordinary sight just eight or nine feet from where I was standing. What caught my eye at first was a steady flow of what seemed to be neatly thrown handfuls of earth issuing from the side of one of the scrubhen's ounds and landing with soft, gravelly thuds in two tidy piles. Aha, I thought, at last I have found where the scrubhens lay their eggs. But no scrubhen has a tail three feet long and scaly legs like those I suddenly saw working away and slinging out the earthen trajectories. Evidently the rest of the body was busy far down the hole.

Without really thinking what I was doing, I unwound the sari and spread it in front of my body like a net. Creeping forward noiselessly, I advanced upon the preoccupied creature. As I drew closer I could see that my prey was some kind of reptile. When I was almost upon him he must have sensed my presence for he started to back rapidly out of the hole. He had a thick, dark tubular body and thick claws on his handlike feet. I pounced, flinging the sari over him and covering the entrance to the hole with his head still down it, so that he could only go in and not wriggle out. I flattened my body over the struggling animal and tried to grasp him across the shoulders through the cloth, but his movements were vigorous and determined and I had to press myself down as hard as I could to prevent him getting away. His threshing front legs scattered dirt over my neck and down my back, his hind legs pumping away under my belly.

At this stage, steaks for dinner still foremost in my mind, I realised that I had not yet seen his head. I suppose I had assumed that it was a large goanna. It seemed very strong and had a tough hide like old dry leather. Did this fellow, I wondered, have large teeth? As this thought was going through my mind the reptile's movements became more frantic and with a sideways heave he managed to squirm from under me and dash away over the mound without giving me time for a proper inspection. All I saw was a flash of light markings on a matt background. The head was quite large but I did not catch a glimpse of its dentistry.

This incident succeeded in completely altering my mood. Even though I had failed to catch the animal, the activity had served to jolt me into a happier frame of mind. Back in camp, G and I shared a laugh over my antics.

Laughter, that precious commodity. A shared joke was almost as good as a snack on a desultory fishing trip or in the stupefying heat of the day.

I had one plastic bag, which I rinsed out and used over and over again, mostly as a cover to prevent geckos from shitting in the stores' box. Now that all the dried provisions had gone and all that was left was a tiny drop of oil, some salt and, as sole emergency survival kit, a tin of butter, the cover was hardly necessary. I hung out the bag on the washing line. When I went back to fetch it later I found that it had melted and stuck fast to the line. For some reason I found this hilariously funny. I began to giggle and the sound infected G. We laughed idiotically until we felt sick. Even when we wanted to, we were unable to stop. Then we were both depressed for hours.

Mood swings of this sort became more and more frequent. It was as though with the lightness of our bodies we were becoming weak in our heads. At times I felt almost euphoric, usually when alone, and then back in camp, sitting by the dead garden and G's wasted figure, utterly flat and grey. Sometimes too, G would be full of positive thoughts, sure that rain would come soon and that all would be well. In a forward-looking mood he would even speak of the future.

"When this is over, Lu . . ."

It was a subject in which I felt curiously little interest. All I really wanted was my energy and strength back again—and rain. G would talk about settling in Australia, perhaps starting up in publishing again, having a comfortable home, a cellar full of wine. None of it meant anything very much to me. I could not think of life off Tuin, and yet, if it did not rain soon, there would not be life on Tuin for much longer.

Since the episode of the Mackenzie beans, all my violent feelings towards G had dissolved. I had learned that he was a man who spoke out his feelings, sometimes viciously, without qualification or subsequent retraction. He called me ugly names, made unpleasant threats, used abominable language, but when it "came to the crunch" he was solid and reliable in the ways that matter on a barren tropical island. When he called me a "fucking old cow" it was only his way of showing affection, and when I fussed at him for picking his sores or failing to wear his hat in the sun he knew it was mine. He planned to start his book during the wet season, it was too hot to concentrate now. Meanwhile, he encouraged me to go on with the odd little diary pieces I was producing, although when we were weak and low-spirited, neither of us had the smallest inclination to keep a record of our existence in any way. During the very bad patches we could not even be bothered to take photographs, and the only word I could think of to write was "hot," repeated over and over again like a bird sound, thothotho-thot . . . thothotho, and I would turn the pencil over in my hand and wonder why it was there.

Very occasionally I would vaguely ask myself what the hell I was doing on this island, what had made me so badly want to come, temporarily abandoning the other world. It is not necessary to make a deep study of recent social history to see what happened with the decline of established values. My generation, born on the heels of the postwar mob, who still tended to adhere, at least superficially, to a reasonably clear set of values, were both the victims and the perpetrators of a chaotic pendulum swing away from all that. When I was at school respect for the older generation was still being pushed, but it was rapidly on the wane. The fabric of the stable home concept was being rent left, right and centre by the increasing incidence of divorce. God was out of fashion and there was an ever growing loophole in the argument for not "dropping out"; there was no longer any guarantee that if you did stay in the education system and go through all the proper channels, there would be a promise of a good job at the end of it. In a way, though, it was a Golden Age of opportunity. Theoretically, the possibilities for young people of any class, colour or creed, were endless. Barriers were toppling in all directions and one could either help push them down or just stand and watch.

All this may seem irrelevant to Tuin, but it has its place in that it helped to get us there. Also, inevitably, the problems that arose on the island that were not directly concerned with simple physical survival stemmed from our former existence in the other world and our assumption that somewhere beyond the miles of blue it was all still going on. In fact we would have no way of knowing about it if the Superpowers had suddenly started annihilating one another. We might have wasted years waiting for rescue instead of buckling down to the business of being Adam and Eve Crusoe.

G and I were a far cry from the tradition of Great British Adventurers. Our operation was more on the lines of Small International Escapists. Before we met, we were both on our way to a Tuin situation from opposite ends of the social dilemma. G had been through it all; worked himself up from farmboy to publisher, been married, had children, divorced, set up home number two and had more children, gone bankrupt, been on the dole, fought in a war, travelled and mixed with all kinds of people. I had participated in life very little by comparison but had taken in enough from the periphery to feel in need of a change and a break before deciding where, how and if I was going to join in, or whether to stick to Tuining for the rest of my life. The only way possible for two individuals as different as we were to get together was through having a mutual cause; because the island year was virtually a fait accompli in our separate minds before we even met, as a vital next step in our personal lives, we latched on to each other with grim determination. I did not really mind what I did for what I had come to think of as my "year out," so long as it took me into areas of mental and physical experience I had never visited before. This was in no way a reflection on any lack of interesting possibilities in any of the lives I had been leading up to that time. In fact it was quite the reverse. Tuin for me was an exercise in reduced options.

Like many of my contemporaries I was thoroughly confused. I longed for guidance but was doubtful of the solidity of my own generation's convictions and had left it rather too late to slide comfortably back into the safe arms of the old establishment, which was looking less and less safe all the time. I embraced the liberty of permissiveness but had grave doubts about whether in the long run it was going to create more hang-ups than it purported to cure. It was as though I saw a great many doors open in front of me but did not yet want actually to take the plunge of stepping through any one of them. Tuin would provide a limbo where I would not be subject to the usual influences and where there were far fewer doors to worry about. I welcomed above all the idea of knowing exactly where my boundaries lay.

In totally different ways G and I were both very self-contained, perhaps G in his knowledge of himself and me in my lack of the same thing. There are many levels of individual insularity, some of which merge comfortably in two beings isolated together, while others clash painfully. Between us, the strongest interdependence existed on one level, but there were secret parts in both of us that it never touched. A power balance exists in any relationship, sometimes heavily weighted on the least expected side. In our situation we held perhaps greater sway over each other's feelings than in a more conventional set up, but it is surprising how quickly one adapts to the limitations of a single other human contact. Just because the other person is the only emotional receptacle around, one is under no compulsion to throw all one's eggs into that basket. Also, a large tract of the personal power threat is removed when there are only two of you on an island, because so many of our fears, secret or expressed, have to do with other people. There are no facilities for public shame, judgements or back-biting. On the other hand one is deprived of the mirror of other people's reactions to use to please, reassure or impress one's partner. There is no one to attack or defend either of you except the other, and there are no witnesses or scapegoats. Our one encounter with other people on the island had proved divisive. As yet we had had no opportunity of solidifying the pair aspect of our relationship by clanning together in a united reaction for or against any other people. Our friends and enemies were all elemental.

In many ways we took the faithfulness of each other very much for granted, and this belies the petty traumas of surface hostility. However much we might criticise or castigate the other, we never had any doubts or fears of being forsaken half way through the year, and not just because it was too far to swim to civilisation. We were loyal to the venture and therefore cemented by a cause. In a way, despite all my solitary inclinations and G's justified resentment towards me, for Lucy the island was G, and for G it was Lucy. Nevertheless, we both knew that should an accident befall either one of us at that stage, the other would continue with the year on the island. So long as we had Tuin and so long as Tuin had water.

GIANT GOANNA

8

APPEARANCES

Diary

I was comfortably ensconced on Armchair Rock, dabbling a line rather idly in the slowly rising water, when an unfamiliar sound parted the sea silence. I thought at first it must be a helicopter, but it was only a very light thrum. A boat then. Occasionally G and I have both thought we heard the echo of engines coming faintly over the water. As we do not actually see any craft we have called them "ghost boats." Once G even thought he heard something land on the other side, when I was over there, but I assured him I had seen nothing, and strangely, not heard anything either.

But this was not a disembodied sound. Standing up to look, I saw a small, silver-coloured dinghy buzzing along just past our northern end. To come in as close to the reef as that the driver must either be ignorant of the danger, or else be very familiar with these waters. As the boat came more clearly into view I realised it was the latter. There were two men in the boat. Torres Strait Islanders.

The only contact we had had with the native inhabitants of the Torres Strait so far was right at the beginning of the year when we had stopped off at Badu Island on our way to Tuin. We had spoken briefly to the chief man there who had a very reasonable command of English, with only the odd slide into hard-to-understand pidgin. The crew of the *Torres Strait Islander*, the boat that brought us from Thursday Island, were all Islanders, but they were comparatively sophisticated, living on Thursday Island if not among the whites certainly heavily influenced by them. About the outer Islanders we knew little beyond the fact that as a race they had once had no rivals in the known world among head-hunters and cannibals. We also knew that there are three main island groups in the Strait: the western group, the eastern and the central islands. We were closest to the western group

(*Diary* contd.)
The thought uppermost in my mind as the boat came nearer was fish. I was having no luck and we needed something for supper. Poor G was laid up under the tree with his legs bothering him again. I wondered if perhaps they had some good bait in their boat. I waved.

They did not respond immediately and I assumed they were just going to pass by so I threw out my line once more, this time as if I meant business. When they saw that I was fishing they turned the boat in the direction of my rock. Suddenly realising that it was perhaps not a very good idea to remain naked, I hastily spread my sari cloth over the front of my body—not that there was a lot to cover—and held it up with one hand, the fishing line in the other.

"Hello!" I chirruped as the engine slowed to a quiet chug. One man raised his hand and the boat stopped. They both just looked at me. I joggled the line up and down and said:

"No fish!"

There was silence as the steady contemplation continued. Their faces were totally impassive, although the younger of the two had very thick eyebrows which gave him a slightly fierce look. He now called: " 'E gud peesh?"

Have I got a peach? No, fish. "No, no fish."

"You want peesh?"

"Yes, yes! We are hungry."

"We go peesh."

Silence again.

"Can I come?"

A long reactionless wait.

"Hokay."

"Oh goody, marvellous! I'll go and tell my husband. Don't go away."

I dragged in my line, awkward with one hand, and rushed up the beach to tell G what was happening. It was obvious that he was feeling very low because he did not feel up to coming himself, but he smiled at my excitement and told me to go along. I tied on my bikini bottoms with the knife belt and knotted on the top. With the fishing line and a couple of hooks bundled up in the sari I was ready.

"Don't worry, I'll bring some fish back for supper. They'll know where to go for the best."

And I ran off down the beach. It is incredible how energy revives with the adrenalin of adventure.

Sometimes events happen so quickly that one has no time to react to their unexpectedness. That was how it was with the fishermen finding me on the rock. There was no time to weigh up the pros and cons or consider the wisdom of getting into a boat scantily clad with total strangers who might live by a code unknown to me. It was a chance to fish where there was likely to be a good catch and that was all that mattered.

Once aboard the little craft and settled unsteadily among petrol cans, diving masks and native spears, I did momentarily experience a slight twinge of apprehension. If I were to disappear out there in the vastness of two seas, on one of the scattered islands or swallowed by the ocean itself, no one would know of my loss but G, and he would have no means of coming to find me. Seeing Tuin get smaller and smaller as we headed away was a strange sensation. It was the first time I had left the island since our arrival and the first time I had seen it from a distance.

(*Diary* contd.)
The shock-headed younger man revved the motor into high speed as soon as we were clear of the reef. No words were exchanged as the boat sped out to sea and met larger and larger waves with a fierce slap and splash, jarring my bony backside on the petrol cans. Progress seemed erratic; we would tear forward at top speed and then all of a sudden crash back almost in our own wake. Gradually I understood that the man steering was in fact doing a masterful job of avoiding high reefs visible by the different chop of the water covering them only to an experienced eye. The sweeping zig-zags grew longer and Tuin disappeared behind another small island.

I felt a great surge of sheer speed exhilaration. One forgets how fast it is possible to be carried on transport other than legs. The sun was throwing dazzling pinpoints and sheets of brilliant silver on the sea all around, and the novelty of other island coastlines held my gaze as we passed by. I could feel an involuntary beam of pleasure spreading over my face. It was answered by a cautious lip twitch from the driver. Shame on me for my white woman's prurient anxiety; was it the animal in them or in me I was afraid of?

Finally we swirled in a tight circle near a group of small islands and came to a rocking standstill. A word was spoken in the native language and the older of the two men donned a diving mask and sprang into the water, holding a short homemade spear attached loosely to his wrist by a piece of rubber. I watched the place where he had dived closely but the water was too turbulent to be clear. Seconds became long minutes and I wondered at his ability to control his breath for so long. Suddenly there was a splash and a shout as the diver surfaced on the other side of the boat brandishing a great multi-coloured creature like a gargantuan painted prawn on the end of his spear. He tossed it into the boat and dived again at once. I ventured a couple of questions. "Is that a crayfish?"

The young man kept his eyes on the water. "Cray." Affirmative.

"How do you know where to find them?"

No immediate answer. I peered into the water over the side of the boat.

"Dat bloke know."

With the conversational ice broken we progressed to personal topics. Speaking, he seemed shy and gruff but his body was arrogant and at ease. Speaking, I was at ease, but physically I felt gauche, conscious of bones and veins and an over-mobile face. He told me his name: Titom Nona. I told him mine.

"Wish way your 'usban'?"

"Gerald."

" 'Deral'. Wish way 'im?"

I was lost. I did not know which way Titom wanted to know which way G was. Perhaps he wanted to know why he had not come. "He has bad legs. Sore legs."

" 'em seek?"

"Yes, a little bit sick."

Then I began to ask about the crayfishing. He was obviously very proud of the boat but when I asked if it was his, he did not answer. However, on an enquiry as to whether he got money for the cray, he became quite eloquent.

"Plenty dollar," he said. "No worry. Tousan' dollar," and he gave a happy grin, which vanished instantly when his partner came up with another cray. I was beginning to understand that a face empty of expression was considered correct. I learned that both men came from Badu Island.

After Ubia, the older man, had been diving for some time and the already crowded floor of the dinghy was beginning to fill up with cray, Titom spoke to him and he climbed back into the boat, effortlessly pulling himself over the side with powerful arms. Titom started up the engine again and we went in search of a fresh patch. This time when we stopped, Ubia stayed in the boat with me while Titom took to the water, plunging in with a jolly flash of red gingham undershorts. Ubia was either very shy or could not speak English very well, so we sat quietly and watched Titom's efforts.

It was a fine show. In the water his face lost its rigidity and became as expressive as his joyously mobile body. Every time his bronze-streaked fuzzy head broke the surface he shook it and grinned, scattering sparkling droplets all around in a dancing spray. I wondered if it was common among the Islanders to have thick black negroid hair touched at the ends with this fiery bronze. Ubia's hair was shorter, but whether it was cut or curled naturally that close I could not tell. Both men were well muscled with deep chests. They had very little body hair and their features bore no resemblance to those of Australia's Aboriginals.

Remembering the purpose of my coming on the trip, I cast my line over the side farthest from where Titom was diving. When he bobbed up again and saw this, he dived under the boat and swam under water near the line. In a moment he surfaced, waving this time not a cray on the end of his spear but a fat black fish. Half a dozen more dives, producing two more cray and two more fish, and then Titom took his place once more in the boat.

As he started the engine I wound in the line, which had not got a bite. When I commented on this he said, "Spear more better."

I asked if they ever used lines and the answer was an expressive throwaway: "Womans."

Twice more the men swapped roles. They tried one place where there did not seem to be any cray at all, another where there was only one. It was obviously not all that easy. I noticed that the sun was no longer high; they had been diving for several hours. Now Titom appeared to be heading straight for the beach of a small round island consisting of a single hill. He cut the engine the instant before we hit the beach and the boat slid neatly on to the sand. Obviously he knew these waters very well. Ubia took a long single-pronged spear and walked away round the beach. Titom told me he was looking for turtle eggs and we followed him, carrying a large crate between us. Ubia was working his way slowly along the top of the beach, an area well meshed with turtle tracks, stopping every now and then to dig the spear experimentally into the sand. At one place he stuck the point in deeply several times and then felt the tip with a finger. Titom knelt down and began to scrape away the sand carefully, going down about one and a half feet and making a wide well. I was kneeling opposite him. He reached across and, taking hold of my wrist, firmly pulled my hand down on to the place where he had just stopped scraping. I felt cautiously with my fingertips and extracted a soft, semi-transparent egg, revealing others underneath. In parts the otherwise perfect rotundity of the egg was dented.

"Is it good?" I asked.

"Plenty good. Go," and he gestured for me to bring up the rest. When forty-three sand-dusted eggs lay beside the hole and I could feel no more down there, Titom reached in and knocked away a shelf hiding a dozen more. We piled them into the crate and went farther along the beach to where Ubia had exposed two more nests. Titom rejected the first one, pointing to footprints of goannas nearby. The cooling layers of sand had been dug away and the eggs left exposed after the reptile's feast were dry and opaque. The last nest was a bonanza find: seventy-one perfect eggs. These ones were half the size of those in the original nest, which were almost as large as tennis balls. I asked Titom if they were laid by different kinds of turtle.

He shrugged and said, "Might one woman turtle more bigger."

We had left the crate by the first nest, so we used my sari strip as a basket. The small eggs looked exactly like seamless ping-pong balls, except for one which had been punctured by the end of Ubia's spear. It was the moistness of the yolk he had been feeling for with his finger. Titom now announced that he was hungry.

"Me too," I said emphatically.

"You been try wongai?"

I said I never had and asked what it was.

"We go."

Ubia stayed by the boat, rolling a cigarette. I followed Titom as he walked round the island in the opposite direction to the turtle tracks. While we were walking I asked how to cook the turtle eggs and was told, "Boil 'ems."

"How long for?"

"Little bit time."

"Like an ordinary egg?"

"Little bit long time."

And how many eggs, I asked, would one eat for a meal? He did not look at me and there was a curious pause before he replied. Then he said airily, "Me I eats twenty, eats every eggs."

I was aghast. No wonder they needed whole nestsful to take back to their families. "Big ones or little ones?"

"Every eggs."

We crossed over some rocks onto another small beach. Here there were three or four tall palm trees covered with huge green peepas. I ran forward and picked up the few that were on the ground, telling Titom I would take them back to Tuin to drink.

" 'E gud water there Tuin?"

I explained just how poorly off for water we were and asked about the water situation on his island.

"Badu," he said grandly, "got every things."

We were approaching some trees similar to the silver-leafed one near the creek on Tuin. But these trees were bearing fruit. All the ground beneath them was a mass of oval pips and squashed purple skins. Titom was already high in the first tree and rustling the upper branches. "Wongai!" he cried happily. " 'E gud good one here."

"Give me one," I begged, standing underneath the branch where he swung languidly plucking them from a cluster three inches from his nose and stuffing them into his mouth.

"No, I go eat every ones."

"Oh no you don't!" and I scrambled up the tree to join him. The taste of the fruit intoxicated me, I could never imagine having too many. In fact the ripe ones were rather scarce, the majority being small, hard and dusky green. After this they graduated to a bright red stage with a bitter-tasting white fluid coming out of the ends. The properly ripe ones were luscious fig-purple. Between mouthfuls, I said I must take some back to G.

"Tuin got plenty—they go come nother time."

Marvellous! Tuin is going to produce another fruit for us after all. In answer to my enquiry as to why the wongai on this island should be ripe and those on Tuin not even have reached the green stage, or if they had, they were very tiny, he just said, "Small island funnykind place."

In more ways than one, I thought.

When there was not a single ripe one left, we came down from the tree and Titom headed into the shade of a vine covered bower. Here he sat on a fallen tree trunk and parted the undergrowth carefully with his hands, evidently searching for something. When I asked what it was he said "Gooseberry."

After a few moments he extricated a delicate vine with pea-sized fruits strewn along it. Each "gooseberry" was nestling in a green papery casing. Inside, the fruit was mild and pleasant-tasting, not unlike a miniature lychee.

"In England," I ventured rashly, "we have gooseberries as big as this." I held up a thumb and forefinger to show him.

"You lie," he said with smiling conviction. "I been lie you too."

"Turtle eggs?" I asked, seeing now his mischievous boast.

"Wa. We eats maybe two, three."

After nibbling a few more gooseberries, Titom stood up and stretched. "We go for coconut now."

Under the palm trees he took my knife and held it in his teeth. I was glad he did not want the sheath belt as well, as it was all that was holding up my pants. It took him no time at all to shin up and cut loose a dozen fat peepas. I ran out of the way as they bounded all over the beach. We made our way back to the boat loaded down with peepas and found Ubia tying up a large bag filled with red wongai. Obviously he had found a good tree somewhere unknown to Titom, who poured out a flood of light-hearted abuse, the only words I recognised being "fuckan bastard" which occurred several times and gave no offence. Apparently Ubia was going to wash the viscous white stuff off the fruit and leave it to ripen in the sun. I bore this in mind for future use on Tuin.

It was getting late. The pre-sunset flare was already spreading a uniform sheen over the waves where sharp rays had played before. I imagined G battening down the mosquito netting across the front of the tent and wondering if I would ever return. The dinghy was well loaded down with cray, turtle eggs and peepas, but Titom still went at top speed wherever there were no shallow reefs to negotiate. As the flare turned to orange and the light left the water I realised how totally lost I was. I could not recognise the shapes of any of the islands we were passing. As we crossed the rougher patches I was surprised how chilly the sprays that washed over us had become. It was a long time since I had been out after sunset.

At last three unmistakable palm trees appeared out of a long dark ridge ahead of us. I pointed and exclaimed joyfully, "Tuin!"

It was going to be impossible for the boat to get anywhere near to camp because the tide was right down. I was in for a long dark stingray-haunted walk through the sandhill shallows, with twelve coconuts full of precious liquid. Titom took the boat in as far as he could without grinding the propeller in the sand. As I climbed out, full of thanks, he selected two cray and handed them to me, also a number of turtle eggs. They threw the peepas out vaguely in the direction of the dry sand and then with a cry of "Yahvoh!" were gone. Bleary in the grey dark, I pursued the floating footballs and gathered as many as I could into a heap on a high sandhill. I could only carry three at a time with the cray and eggs wrapped up in the sari. Then I came to my senses and stripped off my bikini to use as ties. With the top I secured the sari bundle and slung it around my neck. Now I could manage three peepas in each free hand knotted together with their stems and the bikini bottoms. I hurried the first pile half way up the beach and ran back for the next lot before they floated out to sea. By the time I arrived in camp I was worn out but immensely happy.

G was in the tent but there was still a glow in the fire. Quickly I boiled up a billy of sea water and threw in the tails of the two cray. While it was cooking I arranged the turtle eggs in the straw hat I never wore and hung it in a tree. I was looking forward tremendously to serving G eggs for breakfast.

For once I broke my own rule of no food in the tent and took the luxurious fat white tails in to G.

"So you're back, are you. Hey! I smell food."

"Crayfish."

"You clever old shithouse."

"Well, I didn't actually catch it myself."

"Don't care how you got it. Shit, it is good! Now tell me all about your trip, I know you're dying to."

And I did. Burbling on happily for hours until G's encouraging grunts suddenly changed to peaceful snores—but not until every last morsel had gone from the plates and they shone in the dark where we had licked them clean.

In the above diary extract there are one or two diplomatic omissions. With the exception of odd times when I found myself carried away, I did always read my diary aloud to G, and I saw in this case no reason to exacerbate the worry he already had concerning the deterioration of his body which gave him an elderly mien. Titom had shown considerable surprise at the obvious difference in our ages. " 'Em old bloke," he had exclaimed. "Wish way sex thing?"

I had answered non-committally, "He is my husband. Are you married?"

"No."

"Have you a girlfriend?"

"Plenty!"

Although Titom's question about sex had in no way been a proposition, I was aware, for the first time, of using the fact of being married as a screen, which I suppose if necessary I would have tried, hypocritically, to hide behind. I was not aware at the time that a thin woman is regarded by the Island men as a poor catch. If I was all G was able to get, he could not be up to much.

The visit of the crayfishermen coincided with a notable change in the weather. The days were, as ever, hot, but now the nights were even hotter. It was not only an increase in temperature; the humidity level shot up as well. What I once mistook in the night for a silent fall of rain drenching the tent turned out on closer inspection to be condensation.

Instead of seeing it as a refuge and a place of comfortable oblivion, we began to dread crawling into the tent at night. Even G, who claimed to be able to sleep anywhere at any time, and in just about any position, found himself contending with sweaty insomnia. Our pillows, the original piles of clothes now replaced with foam packing from the CB radio covered with rag, were soaked through every night with the sweat off our heads and had to be dried out during the day. The sheet was hung out each morning as a matter of course. We would have regarded it as extremely slovenly to leave it on the bed, in the same way as the thought of using paper instead of having a proper wash in the sea seemed primitive and rather disgusting. We were civilised in our own selective manner.

This new damp heat sapped our energy far more than the dry blasting grill of the months before. We urinated less and less, losing all our moisture through the pores of our skin. It was not, however, in any way a dirty feeling because each layer of sweat was immediately sluiced away by another, and there was none of the clinging odour of armpits one suffers where clothes are worn. But this heat wrung us out from morning until night and then all through the night. There was no escape from it anywhere. The sea was warm and sluggish, and shade was no protection from humidity.

Since the veins in my legs had thrombosed and ached if I stood for any length of time, I had been forced to follow G's advice and take things easier. In practice this meant bringing in two or three branches at a time instead of whole trees. Limbs moved more slowly, automatically, in the heavy, stifling air. To and fro I would drag myself, from the interior back to camp, to Coconut Alley, back to camp, making a game of the floppy motion of my heat-drugged limbs. G would either be flat out on his back on the table under One-Plum-a-Day, legs and arms spread wide to catch any tiny passing breeze, or standing limp and dripping having manfully attacked yet another patch of intractable ground in the hope of striking water. Time and again the same hopeless, perplexed, exhausted protest would drop from his lips: "Jesus Christ, Lu, it's so *fucking* hot!"

We reached a stage where even laughter was too much.

"Lu, don't make me laugh. It makes me sweat worse."

I knew what he meant.

In case this change in the weather should prove to be an early symptom of the wet season, we decided to move the tent down nearer to the rest of the camp area and cover it as best we could with the pieces of iron we had lugged from the southern end of the island. G dug a sturdy pole into the ground at each end of the tent, far enough out at the front to allow for a sheltered porch area, and bound the main pole from the now dismantled fish-drying line across the top. We had had to abandon drying fish recently as in this weather it began to smell before it had a chance to dry out properly. We propped the uneven lengths of iron against the cross-pole, and G clouted them into a curved shape at the top with the back of the axe so that they hugged the supporting pole closely and could be tied on through holes for extra security. The ends of the irons were thrust as deep into the dry ground as we could get them, but I still had visions of a high wind catching the two sides of the iron over-tent and the whole structure flapping like a giant pair of wings, with us being stabbed by the flailing ends of rusty iron in the Terylene tent beneath. To further secure the outer carapace we heaped up sand and stones along the buried edges.

To waterproof the east-facing back end of the tent we employed the so far despised reflector tarpaulin donated to us by the catamaran boys. We hoped the porch irons would protect us sufficiently at the front. We kept a flap open at the rear to encourage a through draught but the effect of the trapped hot air between the irons and the roof of the tent made it like sleeping in a solar heated thermos flask. Condensation would collect along the aluminium piping holding up the tent and drip down on to us during the night. Every crease and crack in our bodies was soggy with sweat. There was just a blessed half-hour or so around dawn when the air seemed briefly to lighten and skin wiped with a rag would stay dry for more than a few seconds.

Inevitably these humid conditions had an effect on our already diminished health. Poor G got the most vile, oozing fungal infection on his feet. It started between his toes, like a particularly virulent form of athlete's foot, and then spread upwards in vicious little red tramlines under the skin. We tried every single ointment in the medical box, starting off with fairly sensible things like anti-fungal cream but working our way through finally to a cocktail of burn and eye ointment with an overcoating of zinc. Because of the irritation G could not leave his feet alone and was to be seen at all hours of the night and day scraping and probing and pasting, all to no avail. One day the infection cleared up almost as suddenly as it had come, but that did not happen until the weather changed again.

*   *   *

Ever since the trip with Titom and Ubia I had found myself with a new mission in life. Every day, without fail, I would cross the island to the area in the south where the biggest wongai trees grew. It did not take me long to realise that I was not the only one waiting for the moment when the fruit became ripe. Pairs of lovely white Torres Strait pigeons scudded about the tops of the trees. They became so accustomed to my daily appearance that after a while they no longer took off at my approach. Worn out from the heat of the walk, I would sit down panting, back against the trunk of the largest tree, eyes searching through the leaves to the higher branches where the wongai were already turning from green to scarlet. The peaceful sounds of the preening birds floated down calm and cooling. The sea close by licked its salt lips against the coral sand. Day after day I went there, as if overnight the fruit would suddenly ripen and be ready to fall into waiting hands.

Diary

This is a side of Tuinlife of which I never want to lose sight or sensation; to crouch animal-childlike under a wongai tree and forage among the earth and leaves for ripe fallen fruit. The high branches dance a dappling shade over the area of search, tossing their brilliant load in the sun and sea breeze. The fruit does not fall until it is mauve-black and soft, when it plummets, heavy with juice, to nestle like a softly glowing secret in the dry leaves beneath the tree. The white pigeons of Tuin are quick to swoop down and feast here. Their sharp beaks drive into the skin of the wongai and stud the smoothness with pockmarks, leaving handy holes for the ants to ravage in their turn. The sun shrivels and dries the mauve fruit within hours, making glistening, delectable prunes of the wongai after two or three days. Naked there beneath the tree I feel totally in my element. Eyes roving in a sweeping motion, hands gently turning the leaves, I work my way gradually around the entire windfall area, taking care not to miss the fruit directly beneath feet and knees.

Sometimes the tree affords no more than a handful of ripe wongai. As my eye alights upon one shining out richly from the leaf debris, a small delicious surge of satisfaction rises up in me and I move forward to take the fruit between my fingers, careless of the peckmarks of birds or a skin damaged in falling. The action of hand to mouth is unconscious. Suddenly the fruit is there, pressed to my lips, the flesh breaks between my teeth and the taste is on my tongue. I roll the pear-shaped pit around in my mouth until the next wongai is about

Peter, one of the catamaran boys, shows me the route planned for their expedition to Manila.

Hosia – also known as Timao – fascinated by the pictures in one of our fish identification books.

Above: Ronnie 'No More' hacks down palm leaves for our roof, and
below, with 'Sarls' Torres, receives rudimentary instruction in
mechanics from G.

Enid 'No More' throws a net for mullet near Armchair Rock.

Kingtucker! The great ray Ronnie speared and cooked for us.

Robinson Crusoe himself.

The engines begin to take over.

to go in, then spit it on to the ground where it joins the many others stripped before me by the birds. On and on I go, from tree to tree, like a great appreciative human hoover.

If there are plenty of fruit I work on a vague and very flexible system of eat one, keep one, slowly filling my sari pouch with those I do not instantly devour. I pick the unripe red ones to ripen in camp for G, spread out on an old piece of fishing net I found caught on a tree overhanging the northern rocks. Within three days they are soft and ready to eat.

Under a ripe wongai tree I have about as much self-control as a child let loose in a sweet shop. I know that my shrunken belly will swell, that my bowels will weaken and cry out for a reprieve, but I do not care. I go on stuffing the fruit into my mouth, both hands working, until I collapse, bulging and roll-eyed, against the trunk of the tree and laugh happily to myself, greedy animal-child that I have become.

Consumption of wongai fruit on a massive scale seemed to give me a new lease of life. My flagging energy revived and I made a concentrated effort to build up the wood store against the wet days ahead. As I could only manage one or two branches at a time now, it was a slow job, but I enjoyed it and was rewarded by the sight of the pile growing a little higher every day. G was amused by my adoration of the wongai and called me a fruit bat. He liked wongai too, but was not so keen on what they did to his bowels. They had a disturbing habit of coming out faster than they had gone in.

One afternoon, while I was away collecting paperbark, G had a visitor. He described the incident to me in detail. G had been digging out the creek when an Islander's dinghy appeared in Camp Bay. A large man and a small boy climbed out and walked up the beach towards him. The man was carrying a spear and gave no great impression of friendliness. The child had huge cowlike eyes and a nose running with green slugs of snot. Both were wearing gingham shorts and the man had a piece of rag twisted round his head char-lady fashion. His eyes, G noticed, were an angry red, his skin dark and lavishly sprinkled with black moles. He announced without preamble that he had come to look at the white man who was using his garden shed. He had heard about us from the Chairman of Badu. He poked his head round the door of the shed and seemed satisfied that all was in order, the sand, geckos and odd planks as he had presumably left them. Then he sat at the table and rolled a tremendously fat cigarette. He seemed surprised that G was not smoking too. ''You no smoke?''

G said he did but had no tobacco, whereupon the visitor gave him all that was left in his tin bar enough for a smoke in the boat on the way back to his own island. He introduced himself as Ronald Lui from Badu. G asked, as the man obviously knew Tuin quite well, where he thought the best place was to dig a well. Ronald walked straight into the middle of a clump of pandanus and pointed downwards. He then said that he would have to go but would come back again another day. Before he departed he told G that he did not mind him using his shed, he had just wanted to have a look at him. Apparently a friend of Ronald's on Badu was anxious to know if the white man on Tuin had his missus with him. When G replied that he did, Ronald said, ''Well, that all right then. No good without Missus.''

When I came back I found G digging away enthusiastically in the middle of the group of pandanus. Already a trickle of murky water was dampening the edge of the spade.

''We'll be all right now, Lu, these boys know what they're talking about. You make sure you're around next time he comes.''

I made a point of it.

When Ronald came the second time it was evident that he had made a decision in our favour. We were to be adopted. I saw exactly what G meant by the formidable eyes. There was also a somewhat startling absence of teeth every time his dark mauve lips parted, and I found the initial immobility of his expression rather awe-inspiring. However, it was clear that underneath his impassive exterior, Ronald hid a warm and generous heart. A troupe of five silent children followed him up the beach, each, with the exception of a plump toddler who trailed in the rear, carrying an item of food or a water container on his or her head. The leading child, the same plump and speechless boy who had accompanied his father before, was carrying a large bag of rice which he dumped down on the table. The second child, a thin, very dark boy, held a swilling bottle full of a bright pink liquid. These two were called, respectively, Alfie and Mypele. Alice came next, a frowning, moody, beautiful child with a wild shock of hair standing straight up all round her head like a devilish halo. She slapped down a small knotted cloth containing some kind of buns and stood glaring into the middle distance, arms akimbo and straight little hips thrust forwards. The last two members of the crew were still down on the beach.

"*Ayey*, Patti-Pat, Victor. *Ayey wal!*" Ronald beckoned them onwards fiercely, but Patti-Pat had been distracted. She was squatting down, one arm around her fat baby brother, poking among the debris of one of our shell meals. At last she came trotting up on incredibly thin and ulcer-pocked legs and with a huge, shining smile of love presented me with a minute green crab. She had abandoned her rags of clothing down on the shore and now proceeded to divest Victor of his smart trousers. These she wisely replaced on his head as he went to play in the sun. His contribution to the gifts on the table had been a plastic bottle of water.

G and I were stunned by what was happening to us so suddenly. There on the table was a bag of rice which at our old rate of rationing would have kept us going for about three years. But even more wonderful than this was what Ronald was saying about water. He was telling us that it was his intention to paint a large petrol drum and bring it over to Tuin for us to catch water in. Everybody on Badu, he informed us, had water drums. He had spoken to the Chairman about us and he too was thinking of sending over a water drum.

I was so pleased and excited, I could not stop gasping and exclaiming while flapping around making a fire for tea and desperately trying to think if there was anything among our possessions these people might like. I foraged in my suitcase and came up with some slides and hairpins for the little girls and pencils for Alfie and Victor. Victor stuck his decoratively in his hair not to be outdone by the girls, and Patti-Pat drew pictures in the sand with a hairpin.

Without thinking, I kept introducing the words "my husband" into almost every sentence I uttered. G gave me some very odd looks. It was the first occasion on which I felt proud to be married. We were Mr. and Mrs. Tuin, and Ronald was being good to us as a couple. By now I was so skinny that there was no question of wearing a bikini top, and G only put on some trunks as an afterthought. There were no feelings of self-consciousness. Nevertheless, appearances still counted for something. My repeated use of the title "my husband" was an unpremeditated presentation of a united front. G's stance by the table, smoking a cigarette with Ronald, was one of "man of the world," amused by the antics of women and children, but aloof and dignified on a masculine plane.

When the tea was poured and Ronald raised the mug to his lips, holding it off a little way and sucking noisily, I experienced a moment of social anguish. As the hot liquid went into his mouth his already much folded features creased into a rictus of disgust like a clenched fist. With one easy movement he swung the cup behind him and tipped the contents out on to the sand. Then he set the mug down decorously in front of his crossed legs and emptied his face of expression. I felt ghastly; the tea was all we had to offer by way of civilised refreshment and he clearly found it undrinkable.

"I'm sorry we have no milk and sugar, Ronald."

His eldest son was sitting close by on the table. In a very low, husky voice he said, "My fada like five soogar."

Ronald reprimanded him in his own language and then gestured toward G's mug of tea. " 'E gud salt there."

Of course! That was it. G and I had become so accustomed to the semi-saline water skimmed from the tiny creek pool that it no longer tasted bad to us.

"I go bring water from Badu if no rain."

In this casual offer lay our lifeline. We thanked Ronald profusely and he accepted the gushing with a dignified raising of eyebrows. I reiterated the fact that we wished we had something to give him in return.

"Yorrigh," he said. "You learn my kid talk proper good."

The three youngest children had wandered down the beach. Alice had surreptitiously appropriated the pink cordial and buns the moment her father was not looking and stashed them in a hole behind the shed. Nobody commented. She was now posturing on the sand with a child-sized spear and threatening Patti-Pat, who shielded herself with a small plastic bucket. From time to time Ronald yelled crossly at them to come to him, but they paid little attention, moving a few token steps in his direction and then trotting away again. Alfie whispered something to his father.

"They go to look for crab," said Ronald.

"We know a good place for crab," I said. "I'll go with them." We needed some bait for fishing later anyway.

I took our big spear and moved off. Ronald called after me, "Where you been get that spear?"

"My husband," I said proudly, "made it."

With the five children I went down into Crocodile Bay. The tide was not in an ideal position for crab-spearing, but if one looked hard enough it was usually possible to find one or two.

The children were shy of me at first, although Patti held my hand all the time. Alfie and Alice kept up a running battle of words in which the familiar "fuckan bastard" occurred frequently. Victor was really too little to walk this far but he shrank from me when I tried to pick him up. Alfie explained, " 'Em fright from white man," and sat Victor firmly on a rock out of harm's way.

Alice and Patti seemed to know exactly where to find the crabs. One caught Alice by the little finger and she dashed around shrieking with pain and delight. When she had had enough she tore off the offending claw and ate it, sucking the meat out neatly and tossing the shell at Alfie. Soon all the children were happily chewing claw meat like gum. Patti ate half hers and then gently pressed the rest into my mouth, reserving the shell to decorate my hair. Victor bellowed and his mouth gaped like a cuckoo's every time it was empty.

Suddenly Alice's eyes goggled and she slapped the other children into silence, pointing excitedly into the shallows. A small needle fish was moving there. She skipped forward in complete silence and jabbed the tiny spear straight into it.

"Gar peesh," said Alfie with satisfaction. There followed two small mullet, and then Patti, unable to wrestle the spear from Alice, caught a little round striped fish in her bare hands. She bit it solemnly in the eye to stop it wriggling. As we passed the red mangroves on the way back to Camp Bay, Alice broke off a slender twig with a few leaves at one end and carefully threaded the fish onto it through the gills; a neat and sensible way to carry them.

I felt like a swim and proposed the idea to the children. "*Wa wa sweem mika!*" It was clear that "*wa*" meant yes. I took off my sari strip and, with the exception of Alfie, the children all went in naked too. None of them had the slightest fear of the water, and Victor, who was hardly more than a baby, had to keep having his head pulled up from under the waves; he seemed more comfortable in the sea than on land. When the children had spent their energy diving and tumbling around the bay, we all went and sat on the sand. Most of the shyness had worn off by now, but the little girls and Mypele were still reluctant to respond to my questions in English. I noticed that every time I made a movement, sitting there on the sand, the children copied what I did exactly. This developed into a wonderful game. Skinny as I was, I found I could perform all sorts of knotty contortions and there were yells of laughter as the little ones tried to mimic my manoeuvres. G and Ronald appeared at the top of the beach to see what all the fun was about, and G called that Ronald had to go because the tide was dropping.

Just before he went I placed a scribbled note in Ronald's hand addressed to the Chairman of Badu. In it I asked if there was any chance of some antibiotics being sent across with Ronald. I had no idea what the medical situation was on Badu, but presumed that as the Islanders came under the jurisdiction of the Australian Government, provision would be made for their health care. We had of course been warned that the Government could take no responsibility in the matter of our health, but I felt that in view of the serious condition of G's legs anything was worth a try.

The visit left us happy, incredulous and dazed with exhaustion. We had forgotten how tiring and demanding conversation and company can be. As G hooked up one of the water bottles with a finger and swung it, watching the liquid swilling inside, we smiled at one another in the quiet complicity of understanding. "You know, Lulu," he said, "I reckon we're bloody lucky. Maybe there is some old God up there keeping an eye on us after all." He did not have to say anything else. We both knew that without just such a miracle as this, our days of hanging on with the pathetic amount of water left in the creek were coming to an end. It was one of those things that, beyond noting the necessity for increasingly severe rationing, we did not discuss because there was no point. But now this lifeline from another world had been thrown to us and we knew for certain that we would survive. As with other major changes in life, it was surprising how quickly we adjusted to the new situation and took the absence of the threat of death for granted. If ever we brooded privately on the extraordinarily opportune timing of our rescue, we never spoke of it to each other.

Over the next few days G and I stuffed ourselves with white rice cooked in sea water. It was a great luxury to have both fish and rice on one plate. We had rice for breakfast, rice at midday and rice with fish for the evening meal. G worked hard on the well he was digging at the spot Ronald had shown him. Unfortunately, although non-saline water was coming through, it was thick and cloudy and smelled unpleasant as in the other wells he had tried to make. It was too late to save any of the little green soldiers in the garden but G was now determined that by hook or by crook he was going to get a tomato to grow. He took the earth-filled drum containing the last Grosse Lisse tomato he had planted after a dribble of rain months ago. Using his own shit and a rich dressing of fish-head ashes from the fire, he lovingly nourished this single plant, tipping half a mug of the cloudy water over it night and morning. He did not pee on it because he had tried that on the kohlrabi with lethal results. Within a week, the tomato plant was showing signs of life. When it was no more than five inches high G tied it to a long thin stick and gave it pride of place in the centre of camp. One tomato would give us enough seeds to start a row of plants after the rains came.

It was not long before Ronald returned with the promised water drum and some filled plastic bottles to keep us going until the next rainfall, which he predicted might be fairly soon. He stopped just long enough for a chat and a smoke before catching the high tide back to Badu. He was talkative and quite at ease this time; G had told me that conversation had been rather uphill work before. He announced, self-importantly, that the Chairman, a relation of his, had thought it a good idea that Ronald should come over from time to time and see that we were all right. This was evidently very agreeable to Ronald, as it gave him a feeling of favoured status. He sat at the table grandly rolling one of his vast cigarettes, his round belly spilling over his shorts, fore and aft, and generous pinches of tobacco spilling over his knees. I watched with amusement as G's eyes followed the fallen tobacco. Last time, after Ronald had gone, G had gone down on his hands and knees and picked up every minute wisp that Ronald had dropped. There were no tea-bags left now, and leaf tea was unsuitable for smoking.

Conversationally, I asked Ronald some questions about his family. He told us that one of his older daughters, Daysy, was looking after his house at the moment, as his wife was away visiting another daughter. I said I would like to meet Daysy one day, and Ronald replied that she wanted to come over to Tuin for the fishing but had to stay at home making clothes for her baby. She was having trouble with the sewing because the machine was broken.

Here G jumped in quickly: "I might be able to fix that for her. Could you bring it over next time you come?"

Ronald thought that was a splendid idea.

We stood side by side on the shore to see him off. Before leaving, he looked out to sea, pointing to the sky beyond Tukupai Island: "In time of nor'west season you can't see nothing there. Black everyway." We pressed him as to when he thought the nor'west season might start, but he was vague, advising us only, "Better yous make shelter one-time." On enquiry about the note I had given him, he said that he had given it to the Chairman but there were no white sisters on Badu now: "Been trouble onetime. Might sister come I speak her for yous."

*   *   *

It was some time now before we saw Ronald again. The weather turned rough, although the humidity stayed high and the wind did not veer from the south east. G was in much better spirits. Although his legs continued to hurt him, he gave up lying for days on the green towel and set about improving our living arrangements. He was happy with his one smoke a day and looked forward to the time when Ronald would call in again and bring the sewing machine.

"I didn't know you knew anything about sewing machines."

"Lulu, I tell you, there are a lot of things you don't know about me."

Time was to prove him right.

When he had perfected the guttering system on Ronald's shed and all we were waiting for was a fall of rain to fill the drum, G decided that the moment had come to build a permanent shelter.

"We're bloody daft, Lu; up there where the shelter is now, first thing that's going to happen when the wind starts coming from the north west is the roof's going to take off."

This was true. The basic structure of that unfinished shelter was designed with the south easterlies in mind. The high front was open like a gaping tunnel to wind coming from out at sea on this side of the island. It could not have been in a more exposed position.

"Here you are," said G one morning, dropping pencil and paper into my lap. "You design a house and I'll build it for you."

"Golly," I said. How many women get an offer like that from their husbands?

"Now don't get too ambitious, remember we've only got so many pieces of iron and one bit of canvas, which can cover the wall furthest away from the wind."

"What about a palm-leaf roof?"

"You'll get your palm-leaf roof, that goes on last, but these irons are as good as anything. These islanders know what they're doing."

G lay down for a little doze, conserving his energy to withstand the shock of my design. I stalked up and down the area on which the shelter would stand. It was on our side of the creek, sheltered from the direct blast of a sea wind by the block of bushes behind One-Plum-a-Day. The ground was sandy but there was just enough earth in it to make a well dug in upright stand firm. I decided that there was ample space for three rooms plus a sheltered cooking area. We knew that it would be impossible to build anything insect-proof, so the tent would have to come in whole as the bedroom area. We hardly needed a lot of wardrobe space. The design I drew up was T-shaped, but the crossbar section of this was summarily dismissed as being too wasteful of irons. Inevitably G ended up building to the dictates of materials available rather than to my design, but I was very pleased that he had asked for my ideas. I always liked it when we did something as a team, and although it had long ago ceased to be a bone of contention between us, the shelter-building was still important to me, especially now that we had been warned about the nor'westerlies.

I wonder, though, if there had been no nor'westerlies coming, if a shelter would ever have been built. Once the feeling that somehow we just *ought* to have a shelter had been abandoned along with a few other imported precepts, there was no particular reason to build a home. It was not as if we needed to mark out our territory; on a small island inhabited by only two people, the sea provides an ample margin. Certainly, as feeling for the island grew within me, I treated Tuin as though the whole, not just a part of it, was my domain. However, it would take more than a natural arrangement of leaves to protect us from a monsoon.

Within a couple of days the plans for the shelter were complete. G had worked out exactly how many beams and uprights would be required, some of which could be pulled out of the site of the old half-built shelter. But we found that the big gum uprights we had dug in so painstakingly could not be budged, and those that could be lifted had been attacked by termites which were gradually reducing the centres of the trunks to sawdust, so we decided to use just stripped mangrove trunks for the permanent shelter.

If we thought we were feeble the first time we went searching for uprights, it was nothing compared to now. The months of subsistence diet had taken their toll. Perhaps it was the leaden heat as well. G would start out with every intention of doing a full day's work. By midday, having chopped down and carried in no more than half a dozen mangroves, we were both stupid with exhaustion and fit for nothing but to collapse under a tree and gasp speechlessly. Now that G really wanted to work, this infuriated him.

"I wasn't always like this, you know: look at me, pathetic doddering old fart."

"You're a dear old fart really."

"Poor Lulu! I used to think you'd look good in the centrefold of *Playboy*; if they put you in there now, you'd be hidden by the staples."

"You button your lip. There's a dance in the old dame yet."

Secretly, although things were going much better on the whole, I was very concerned about a particularly deep ulcer on one of G's legs. The sticky weather seemed to stop the process of healing altogether. The mouth of the ulcer had spread and small secondary craters formed underneath it, each with a deep eye of pus. If G inadvertently knocked the shin while climbing in or out of the tent, he went sick and silent with pain. It was way beyond the stage where medicines on the outside could help. The problem needed to be tackled from within; he needed antibiotics. I was beginning to fear that there might be something seriously wrong with me, too. Not only were my veins bulging out grotesquely all over my body, now several inches of rectum had started to fall out whenever I squatted down. This disturbed me because I did not understand it. G did not like the sound of it at all.

This was the condition we were in when Ronald came over again, bringing with him a wonderful surprise in the form of two white nurses who were temporarily stationed at the Medical Aid Post on Badu. Ronald must have told them how thin and poorly-looking we were because not only had they brought antibiotics, they had a whole carton full of lint, bandages, antiseptic creams and vitamin tablets; and in addition to this they had thought to bring a large motley assortment of containers all filled with clear fresh water, plus a huge tin of flour.

It is easy to relate this sudden series of visits just as they happened. It is not so easy to describe the intensity of our reactions to them. G had considerably more self-control over his externalised feelings than I, but I knew him well enough by now to see that under a *"que sera sera"* front he too was deeply moved. When the nurses came with their gifts and friendliness, their concern and warmth and curiosity, I was unashamedly and wholeheartedly overwhelmed. I was moved to hug them as they waded through the shallows of Camp Bay carrying their boxes and bottles, a pretty, slim blond woman with a sweet, delicately boned face and her younger companion, a smiling dark-haired girl. Both were wearing elegant embroidered culottes and light blouses. When I touched them I was amazed at how clean and soft and fresh they felt, in striking contrast to ourselves and our surrounds.

Ronald acknowledged our thanks for bringing them over with his customary dignity. He sat quietly in camp smoking while the girls tut-tutted and admonished us for the condition we were in. "You both look terrible," they stated bluntly. While the dark-haired girl dressed G's ulcer and measured out a seven-day course of antibiotics for both of us, Janine, the older one, pinched the slack skin over the bones in my arms to see if there was any muscle tone left. I was so excited that I felt full of energy and *joie de vivre*, but when I went to dig up some film to photograph the girls I could not hide the fact that I was not strong enough to wield the spade properly. Janine made me lie down and checked me over, saying that she thought both G and I ought to go to hospital. Would we at least go over to Badu where she could inject us with large doses of vitamins and antibiotics? I explained the nature of the project to her, saying that had it not been for the unexpected scarcity of water on Tuin we should not have lacked any vitamins, as our garden would have provided us with all that was necessary. Now that we had an emergency lifeline for water to tide us over until the Wet, all should be well. I asked her quietly if she thought G's ulcer would heal without hospital treatment. She said it was very hard to tell; it looked as though it had gone right down into the bone, and G was badly run-down, which would hinder efficient healing of the tissue, leaving the wound continually exposed to further infection. If it did not heal with this course of antibiotics and careful dressing, he would have no choice but to be evacuated from Badu to Thursday Island hospital. Amputations and death among the Islanders through neglected tropical ulcers were not uncommon, she warned. I promised that I would watch G carefully for signs of deterioration, but inwardly I was determined that he should be cured on Tuin. I knew, within the civilised remnants of myself, that now that succour had come this far, if G's life were in danger he would have to go—I would make him go—but I prayed it would not come to that. We had come so far on Tuin, surviving together through the heat and the drought and the barren days, when we entertained no hope of outside help, when all the barriers between us were broken down and we were bonded together in mutual need. We could not weaken now.

But I could not explain all that to this kind and practical stranger. Instead I told her about my not having had a period for so long. She smiled and asked if I thought I was pregnant.

"Could I be, like this?"

She gently palpated my concave belly and shook her head, saying that the periods had stopped owing to loss of weight, as I had concluded. This, and nutritional deficiency, helped to explain the falling hair. The thrombosed veins and collapsing rectum would very probably, she felt, be exacerbated by heat and strain. If I lost any more weight, I risked losing more than my looks.

These sombre warnings failed to depress me. We had water, a bag of rice and a tin of flour, the basic commodities with which to begin to build ourselves up. The sea was still full of fish and new coconuts were beginning to form on the trees. Now that we had water to drink we could allow the few clusters of peepas left on the highest palms in Coconut Alley to turn into good meat coconuts and fall of their own accord. With wongai fruit and vitamin tablets to help we had everything we needed to survive healthily on Tuin.

The nurses could not stay long, as their visit was unofficial and they could not risk being stranded on Tuin until the next high tide. But they did accompany me briefly to Prize Parrot Rock, an excellent new fishing spot pointed out to us by Ronald. Here they dabbled momentarily in the Tuin lifestyle that had become so ordinary to us; eating oysters straight off the rocks, baring their pale bodies to be branded by the sun. I chattered and laughed at my own inability to form straight, coherent sentences in reply to all the questions they asked. They told me a little about the problems facing nurses stationed for short spells on remote islands. I learned that the "trouble" Ronald had mentioned in connection with white sisters had been a double rape of two women stationed on Badu a couple of years before. Since that time no white woman had been permitted to stay on any of the Torres Strait Islands alone. Janine felt this regulation to be destructive as well as protective as it offended the island chiefs and underlined the differences between rules for whites and rules for blacks. One member of an Island Council had been heard to say:

"If man do this things to womans Down South [mainland Australia], that man he punish—'em no punish every other peoples too."

On Tuin the problems of politics and race seemed distant and out of context, but hearing about other people's lives fascinated me. It is easy to forget the existence of millions of other cogs turning in millions of wheels in another world when one has been isolated for some time.

While the nurses and I had been on the rock, G had been sitting enjoying a smoke with Ronald, glad, as he put it, of a bit of male company. Unwittingly, he had been discussing something with Ronald which was to add a whole new dimension to our already altered lives. On the table between them sat Daysy Lui's Singer sewing machine.

For all the excitement and change brought about by the visits, I was still very deeply in touch with the "other side" of Tuin. It had become an intimate, private world and to visit it often felt vital to my existence, as if the depths of the island gave me something I could no more live without than my own blood and marrow.

Diary

There is a secret place in the heart of Tuin to which I find myself returning again and again. I don't know why I say secret: it is no more or less unknown than any other not immediately visible copse in the interior. But mystery and discovery make it more mine. Perhaps every island has a heart, made or unmade by the presence of one who presumes to recognise it. But then every island is only a prominent excrescence on a great mass of land covered by water. The whole world is one big island floating in the sky, with great pools of water on it called oceans. The concept of heart and power invested in inanimate objects is one of man's specialities. Such thoughts did not rob me of the fascination of my Phallic Ring. Nature itself has done that.

It did not look like this the first time I came here. How long ago? Seven ants' nests ago. Who would have thought this great irregular lump of grey and yellow deposits began life as seven tiny mushrooms positioned neatly in a perfect ring? I am glad I have witnessed this thing. I came here originally to plait whippy ferns, lying on my back with the ends of the three stems held in my teeth, face divided from the full glare of the sun by a spidery pattern of branches. I paid little attention to the ring at first. New crops of ants' nests are always popping up all over the island. But on the third or fourth occasion I became intrigued by the regularity and direction of the growth. The "mushrooms," still with their caps on, had developed thick stalks that pushed up under the elongated caps exactly like the shafts of seven circumcised penises. The ochre and elephant-dung colour gave the group a stone-like appearance. When my footsteps led me back a few days later, the dimensions of the phalluses had greatly increased. One had outstripped the rest. It stood majestically above the others, inclined very slightly towards the centre of the ring. Of course, it was an accident of nature, but why did it follow such a perfect design?

It was over a week before I returned. That was the week Ronald came and there was lots of rice to cook and damper (flat buns) to be made, and G and I nearly made ourselves sick from eating too much wongai scone. A wonderful week when I was too busy building us up with food and rest and vitamins, all in a sensible routine, to miss the out-of-camp Tuin much. But of course I had to come back before too long.

Three of the phalluses, bending in as the first tall one had done, had formed a one-yard-high monstrosity with, fantastically, a single, huge, lop-sided cap. The other four, maintaining their shape, had risen to about two feet, growing thick in proportion to their height. I only made one other visit before today. Then how glad I was that I came. The seven phalluses had become one. I saw it even before parting the trees to enter the copse, its great head pushed up above the bushes and ferns that made the background to its totem majesty. A group of dark spoke-leaved screwpines, below and behind, emphasised its solid, risen splendour.

Today, tremulous with secret anticipation, I revisited the site of my virile idol, all ready to pledge esoteric allegiance. Alas, what a disappointment! All that remains is a splodged, pocked, shapeless lump, as if, having well exceeded his Priapic destiny, he finally succumbed to the paunchy fate reserved for all over-ambitious satyrs.

PHASE III

Turning Away

GECKO AND SMALL LIZARD

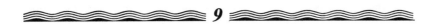

9

ROLLER BEARINGS
IN THE SAND

What G had touched on quite by chance in his chat with Ronald was the subject of engines. They had been talking about crayfishing and how it had changed and developed since Ronald was a boy. Apart from a small pearl-culture station on Moa Island, crayfishing was the sole industry on the islands of the Western Strait. It was only within the last few decades that the Islanders had started using outboard motors on a wide scale. They earned good money for the cray they speared, up to ten dollars per kilo, and with this they bought bigger and better motors for their dinghies so that they could get out quickly to the best spots for fishing. From the moment the first Islander started using an engine, it had become necessary for every freelance fisherman to acquire one or be left far behind in the race for cray. The drawback to this modernisation was that although it was successful to begin with, and greatly increased the speed with which an Islander could turn his catch into dollars, as soon as the slightest thing went wrong with the engine the whole system fell apart. The Islanders had no knowledge of mechanics and in the unlikely event that they were able to afford a repair on Thursday Island, it would take so long that the cray season would be over by the time they got the engine back.

During the War a few hundred natives of the Torres Strait had been recruited into the army on Thursday Island. Their participation as volunteers, originally courted because they knew the dangerous waters of the Strait better than anyone else, earned them greater access to the white world than they had had before. Native families were permitted to live on Thursday Island for the first time since its European development. Ronald had been among the first to benefit from this. It was in the army that he had learned to speak the quite fluent English he used when talking to us, and there also that he first started to take an interest in things mechanical. He was not, he assured G, like some Islanders who thought their engines had broken down forever the first time they ran out of gas. A few years before, he had suffered some damage to his back which prevented him from crayfishing anymore. He had had to look around for something to occupy his time and, if possible, earn a few dollars. Fiddling about with engines, which had always fascinated him, now became a passion.

By studying odd parts and abandoned engines and always taking every opportunity to watch a white man on Thursday Island fixing an engine, Ronald had picked up just enough knowledge to enable him to do the odd minor repair for friends and relatives on Badu. They paid him in tobacco and promises of money which very occasionally actually appeared. An engine would be brought to him, the cause of its sudden failure to function a complete mystery to its owner, and Ronald would take it apart with great care and concentration so as to remember how to put it together again. He would then look at it from all angles and inspect each nut and bolt in the hope of finding some indication as to what the trouble might be. A number of engines had apparently started to work again after just this treatment. In the course of his graphic and lengthy descriptions of the dismantling and reassembling process, he told G proudly that he always wiped the parts before putting them back together again and finished the job with a good squirt of something that sounded suspiciously like "Pantene." G, who knows about these things, concluded that it must be a brand of lubricant. Therein lay the secret of the "miracle" repairs. So it came to Ronald's attention that G knew something about engines and it was agreed that, perhaps, if they succeeded in mending the sewing machine, Ronald would bring over an engine of his own that was giving trouble. At least they could look at it together.

It took G nearly a whole day to mend the sewing machine, with Ronald observing closely all the time except when he felt it necessary to stop for a smoke and a "spell," which was every ten minutes or so. I was called in now and again to thread the needle. As the sun began to set and Ronald's glances at the sinking tide became more anxious, G suddenly raised a triumphant shout: "Hey, Lulu, I can make you a pair of cami-knickers now!"

It was working. There on a rickety table balanced on four rusty petrol drums on a tiny island in the middle of the Torres Strait, G was making a neat machine hem up the side of my ragged sari cloth. Ronald was evidently impressed. He said he would be coming back again very soon.

He came again within a week, bringing with him a boatload of children and a small, ancient Honda generator, plus a rusty assortment of wrenches and a hammer wrapped up in his all-purpose head cloth.

"Oh," he said, as if he had just remembered something, "this for you, Lucy," and he reached down into the bottom of the boat and produced a jar of honey. He showed pleasure that this gift was received with such rapture.

"I don't know what thing for bring you. Might yous not like Island tucker [food]. Anyway, I been listen white womans say honey proper good." He reached down again and handed me a tin of baking powder thoughtfully sent by his daughter Daysy. With the flour the nurses had brought, we had the makings of a perfect picnic tea.

"What day is it today, Ronald?"

"Today Sunday. Kids been go sursh."

I tried to imagine wild little Alice in church. Life on Ronald's island was beginning to sound positively formal.

"Well, today," I announced, "we are going to have Sunday tea."

Ronald looked doubtful at the mention of tea. "I forget bring soogar. Next time." At least he would not have to suffer salt in the water today.

G, whose ulcerated leg was already beginning to show signs of improvement, was waiting for us in camp. His blue eyes lit up when he saw the old red generator Ronald had balanced on his shoulder. They made a place for it between the children on the table. Ronald's standard contingent of five children had been joined by four newcomers and I was relieved that they had been thoughtful enough to bring extra water. Soon I was happily immersed in making fires and tea and scone dough, while G and Ronald settled down to examine the generator.

Alice was in her element, gabbling away in her own language to the others as she took them on a guided tour of the camp. She marched boldly across the dry creek bed and stood arrogantly by the entrance to our iron-clad tent while she waited for her followers to catch up. There was a great deal of peering and pointing and the names "Deral" and Lucy were repeated often. Then the entire troupe, minus Alfie, who evidently considered himself above Alice's games, disappeared inside the tent. Excited shouts and soft exclamations as they examined our sleeping arrangements. Ronald suddenly became aware of what they were up to and shouted fiercely. He must have said something impressive, for there was instantly complete silence within the tent. After a moment the children emerged in a subdued row and filed quietly back into the kitchen camp area. Alice started collecting twigs for the fire. I was curious to know what Ronald had said; usually the children paid little heed to his commands.

"I tell them Markai of Tuin go catch them."

"What is that?"

"Oh, little bit like devil."

He omitted to tell us at this time that in fact he meant us. In the old days, the "Beforetime," all white people were believed to be no more than spirits. They were pale because they were dead. It was believed that they were malevolent because only discontented spirits or those plotting mischief would wander around. The properly dead would lead a quiet afterlife on an island called Boigu. As all the white men the Islanders saw in the early days would have come by ship, apparently lost or looking for something and more often than not getting wrecked on the reefs, these conclusions would seem logical. In the beginning the whites would always have appeared either armed and aggressive or feeble and half drowned, resembling in both cases an eerie devil or spirit. It was believed that by killing them again they would return to their proper place and trouble the living no more. We were to learn more of such things later on.

The children did not remain intimidated for long. They were intrigued by my method of cooking scones in our metal washing-up bowl. I used the frying-pan, which was by now worn thin as a leaf, as a lid, a reversal of the earlier arrangement. Until Ronald had brought the baking-powder, G and I had made unleavened bread by simply mixing flour and water—salt water was fine—and beating the dough with our hands to make flat shapes that could be cooked like chappatis. G made the first batch and the luxury of chewing on a mouthful of starch was so glorious that we ate the lot and I immediately rushed to make some more. It must have been quite a shock to our digestive systems, but it was the leavened bread that had the most marked result: we both had a prolonged and impressive attack of farts, which made life in the tent more stifling than ever.

G and Ronald by now had the Honda in pieces all over the table. It was so rusty that the hammer had to be used on all the nuts and bolts to jolt them into mobility. Ronald seemed to be unclear as to when it had last been in a usable condition, but he assured G that it definitely had worked when he brought it across from Thursday Island to Badu about ten years ago. It had been one of the first generators on Badu. G was so deeply absorbed with the innards of the Honda that he did not notice when I placed one of our metal plates, piled high with perfectly risen scones, on the table. The children dived on them without ceremony and I hastily grabbed one and wafted it under G's nose.

"Wow, Lu!" he exclaimed, opening his mouth wide to accommodate the honey-dripping scone. "That's fu . . ."—chew—". . . bloody good." I rescued one more for him before Victor spread his hair with it as he had with two others. I did not care how many the children ate, but could not bear to see one mouthful go to waste. Already I was planning in my mind luscious cakes made with coconut and wongai fruit, fish pâté on toast, turtle egg and oyster rolls . . .

After tea I took the children down to the beach and we played the miming game again. I asked Alfie if he knew any songs, as he often seemed to be humming to himself. Immediately he broke into a lively rendition of a hymn, partly in English, partly in his own tongue. The theme was "Jesus Loves You," and all the children joined in the chorus, which ended with a shouted "And *You!*" for every member of the group. Alice made the point so violently that two of the littlest ones burst into tears, whereupon she pushed them on to their backs in the sand and glared directly into their eyes with a frozen grimace until they were silent. She then lay down with her eyes shut and stroked her belly, her bushy hair glinting grittily with coral fragments. She joined in loudly from her position of repose when Alfie started on another song: "Oh Jesus, Oh Jesus, What a Wonder You Are." I thought that if I concentrated hard I might just about be able to pick that one up on the flute.

Eight small amazed faces gaped in rapt fascination as I pieced the shining sections of the flute together and set the mouthpiece before my lips. Alice had gone to sleep, wearing Victor's trousers over her face, but when the first surprisingly loud note wobbled out, even she sat up. I could not bear to let them down with mistakes in a tune I did not know, so I went straight into "Frère Jacques." Patti-Pat, her mouth wide open and eyes huge, edged closer and closer on her bottom until her face was no more than a couple of inches from the end of the flute. Victor threw sand at her until she retreated, giving the others a clearer view. When I had gone through the melody once, a pretty, quiet child called Relsie began shyly to sing. Alfie added his even voice and gradually they all joined in. Those who were unsure of the words contributed by thumping the sand and yelling. The words had obviously been taught to the children in English, but the lapse into Island language on the second line indicated that they had been taken in merely as meaningless sounds to be sung to a tune:

> Ome to deena, ome to deena,
> Ayey debbel! Ayey debbel!   [Here the bell]
> Bakin an potatoes, Bakin an potatoes,
> Oll done weel, oll done weel.

That "weel" made me wonder vaguely if they had been taught by a Scot. The concert dissolved into squeals of fun as Victor took the floor in the centre of the group and executed an extremely solemn rhythmic dance, during the course of which he fell down hard on his fat little bottom three times. Each time he was assisted to his feet by hands from all sides. Although there was very little movement in the dance— one foot being raised a short way off the ground and then lowered firmly to allow the other to come up, the body bent well forward, arms stiff and fists clenched—ritual patterns of ordered motion were clearly discernible. Dancing must be an important part of the Islanders' life if such a tiny child already had the general idea.

A loud spluttering sound made us all look up. Something interesting was happening by the camp table. Everybody stood round in a circle as G, using my sheath belt as a starter rope, coaxed evidence of life from the engine.

"Try a drop of oil in her," he muttered. Alfie was despatched to look for a bottle of oil in Ronald's dinghy. While we were waiting, G beamed across at me, all sweat and grease: "She's all right Lu, she's going to go."

When he pulled her again, drop of oil in place, the engine burped and grumbled.

"Here she comes . . ."

Two more pulls and come she did. The children leapt back as a body as the little red engine gyrated hectically all over the table. G was chasing it with a knife, trying to make an adjustment on a screw. After a moment the engine came to a standstill.

"That's your trouble," said G, pointing to a trail of oil and petrol over the surface of the table. "Your oil-seal's gone, and it wouldn't hurt to put a bit of solder on that crack in the petrol tank."

Ronald sighed in admiration and sat down to roll a smoke. "You know engines *proper* good," he said, shaking his head in wonder.

G had another pull at the engine but this time it danced so violently that it fell off the table into the sand.

"Bugger! Could do with some nails to hold it steady."

"Towi belong my wife brother got nail for yous. I go send him onetime."

Ronald left the Honda generator with G, who wanted to go over it again. He also left the tools. For the next week G spent every moment when we were not fishing or sleeping lovingly cleaning up the bent and broken old wrenches. There was a file, too, so rusted that the teeth could not be felt. G patiently rubbed away at it with a piece of greasy rag until it was fit for use. He took the generator apart again and cleaned it thoroughly inside and out. Working on it seemed to give him real and private pleasure. Until this time, I had had no idea that G had any interest in or knowledge of engines. This quiet occupation, which he could do sitting comfortably in the shade with his bad leg up, fitted in ideally with the regimen I had started of building up our bodies with the extra food and medicines now at our disposal.

Morning and evening we attended religiously to our sores, carefully following the instructions of the nurses. At first I dressed G's deep ulcer for him, but because I was hesitant to probe far enough when cleaning out the root, G soon performed this task for himself. G would be the first to admit that he has a low threshold of pain, but in the case of his leg, when he said it was "agony" I knew there was no exaggeration. Cold sweat oiled his face, which despite a strong tan could clearly be seen to pale every time the wound was touched. First he fizzed out all the impurities with neat hydrogen peroxide. Then, with plastic tweezers Janine had left for the purpose, he removed all the hardened gobbets of poison he could from the core of the ulcer. The worst part was when he sloshed a solution of Milton into the crater left by this operation. Even G, with his very considerable command of extravagant obscenities, could find no terms with which to express adequately the rapier sting of this. It was a great relief when the pus eventually stopped gathering so that he did not have to dig it out anymore and a thin film of tissue formed inside the raw wound. While it was still deep, the hole had to be plugged with Milton-soaked balls of gauze, over which was laid a lint pad tied in place with a bandage.

All smaller ulcers had to be dealt with in similar fashion. When he had finished with his legs, dusted his feet with anti-fungal powder, sprinkled Milton on his itchy scalp and smeared Savlon on his piles, he felt, as he put it with a rude allusion, "all dressed up and nowhere to go."

It amazed me to see how quickly we began to gain weight and strength on our bolstered diet. For breakfast now we were having rice cooked to a porridge in fresh water and flavoured with soft seed or grated meat of coconut. At midday we shared between us a round loaf of damper or scones touched with honey, which I wanted to make last as long as possible. G wanted to open the tin of butter to have with the bread and honey, but I pointed out that once opened, the butter would have to be eaten very quickly before it spoiled in the heat, and therefore it would make sense to save it until the fishless time of the moon when we could live on bread, rice and butter. G accepted this but made a few mumbled comments about parsimonious Scots. At supper-time now I revelled in the luxury of having three main ingredients to play with. We had fish stuffed in bread envelopes, baked rice and fish rissoles ("Call them balls, woman, call them balls"); rice and oyster stew, roast fish and rice, poached fish and rice, hot, cold, mashed, flaked, served-in-a-pattern, pounded-into-a-paste fish piled on to toasted damper, toasted damper crumbled onto piled fish . . . I must have tried every combination and G was happily appreciative of them all. He was a rewarding man to cook for, and it took some discipline on my part to prevent myself from opening the butter and devastating his palate with buttered coral trout and oysters. We would save enough for that after the poor fishing time. I thought of all the good things Defoe gave his Crusoe: goat flesh, vegetables, corn, rice, cheeses, milk, flour, rum and biscuit from the wreck, sweet fruit . . . with imaginative use of that lot he could have lived like a king. I would have opened a restaurant for castaways, advertising by messages in bottles, payment in the currency of company . . .

I was to discover that an improvement in physical health was for me a two-sided blessing. As my hip bones retreated under a subtly growing layer of flesh and my breasts made a shy second debut, I caught G looking at me broodingly from time to time. But we were so generally contented, merely by virtue of the unaccustomed luxury of having enough to eat, and the memory of the close times when things were very bad being still in our minds as well as in the gentler way we treated each other, that it took the catalyst of another young male from outside the world of Tuin to make the rebirth of desire a problem.

The young male came in the form of Titom Nona, who returned to Tuin to take me crayfishing again and to see if the wongai on our island were ripe. Because wetting the ulcer in the coral-poisoned sea would undo all the good done to it so far, G again stayed under One-Plum-a-Day while Titom, Ubia and I went off in the dinghy. I made a point of asking G if he minded my going off in the boat and he assured me that he did not. There was no sexual tension on this occasion, or at least none that was expressed.

I was still very much hoping, as we sped away in the dinghy, that there would be a chance for me to learn to dive Islander fashion. As it happened, the crayfishing that day was very poor, and Titom and Ubia were expending so much energy diving with so little reward that it would have been thoughtless of me to request that they waste yet more time by taking on a beginner who would undoubtedly miss the only precious crayfish around. However, when I mentioned casually to Titom later that I would love to have a go at diving, he said at once, "I teesh you." I had no idea G would consider my wanting to take up such an offer "unwise." In the event, because of the disharmony it would cause, I did not pursue the matter; but the knowledge that something I would have done had to be scotched because of his attitude was an unwelcome reminder that I was not an independent agent. I was, however, aware that not all his reasoning was grounded in a kind of jealousy because he could not teach me himself, and that it would mean my spending a lot of time in the company of attractive young men. He also sensibly pointed out the fact that the Islanders were not accustomed to scantily clad white young females messing about under the water with them. It would be foolish to ask for trouble.

After a couple of hours Titom became fed up with the fruitless day's diving. He zoomed around moodily in the dinghy and then slowed down and sat in contemplative silence for a minute. He said, "Might I show you something."

A statement.

Off we went again at speed.

Diary
Yesterday Titom did me the honour of taking me to see something probably never looked upon by a non-native Islander before. I felt

that the privilege was bestowed largely owing to the fact that G and I are now recognised by the Islanders as being "Tuingal"—inhabitants of Tuin.

"This Islander thing, from Beforetime," Titom told me as the dinghy weaved briskly among the reefs, heading towards a small island indistinguishable to my eyes from any of the other scattered, hummocky mounds beyond the island where we had picked the wongai. Apart from two words, "Sobai" and "Wahei," Titom gave no further explanation of what he was taking me to see. When I asked him the name of the island he replied flatly, "That secret thing."

My curiosity increased as, leaving the boat tied to a rock, we walked up a short stretch of beach under a jutting outcrop of huge boulders. Titom began to climb steadily upwards. I followed carefully, planting my feet where he had trodden. I was determined not to slide ignominiously into one of the deep crevices in the rock and have to be helped, or waited for, by this proud son of a tiny island race who was about to let me into the secret of something important to him and his people. Looking up, I saw him standing silently on a prominent ledge about ten feet above me. Reaching his side without mishap, I caught my breath at the scene that came into view. A vast slab of rock overhung the ledge on which we stood. Underneath this mammoth black canopy lay a deep hollow stretching far back to form a natural cave. Towards the far end of the cave I could see white objects, pale against the dark stone. They were ranged upon what appeared to be a great shelf of rock at least ten feet wide and going back I don't know how far into the side of the hill. Titom took my arm and drew me into the cave. "Sobai and Wahei," he said. "Warrior from Beforetime." And there they were: two obviously honoured warriors laid to rest in a magnificent natural tomb. The skeletons seemed to be whole, although some bones were in odd positions and one of the skulls faced outwards. I was tempted to ask if I might handle the bones, hoping to get some clue as to their age, but felt that such a suggestion would be out of order. As if reading my thoughts, Titom said, "My fada hold them onetime, head belong Sobai and Wahei."

"Who were they?" I asked. "Did they live here?"

" 'Em chief belong fighting men there Badu. Kill plenty bloke from nother place. 'Em been die peenish along this place," he gestured out behind him towards the sea. "Pass away," he added to make the point clear. "Last time fight with canoe."

For a long time the two of us stood in silence before the bones. Finally, Titom turned towards the sea and we gazed out on to the glittering silver spread by the dying sun as it swept over the dark waves.

"Marvellous place to be buried," I muttered inadequately.

On the way back to Tuin I questioned Titom as to how many people knew of the warriors' tomb. From what he said I understood that, although the existence of the skeletons was known to be more than legend in the minds of a number of Islanders, not many of them actually knew where they were. Titom suddenly seemed rather nervous and concerned. "You no tell no one I been bring you that place. Might nother white man come from Down South take them bones go back onetime."

I promised him that I would not let the secret out to anyone who might disturb the resting place of Sobai and Wahei.

" 'E gud wongai there Tuin?" he asked, changing the subject.

"Plenty, good ones too."

"Might I go come there morning time," and he dropped me back on Tuin, without cray this time but with a good story to tell G in the tent. I feel quite safe from the temptation of ever jeopardising the sanctity of the tomb, as I know I would never be able to find my way back to that small island. Not that I would abuse my privilege by trying.

Titom did return to Tuin the next morning and it was this that stirred up the old trouble between G and myself. There was cloud about, a possibility of rain. G was devising a shelf for Ronald's Honda out of a strip of corrugated iron and two petrol drums. He was going to make a safe place for it in the little shed. We made freer use of the shed now that we had met the owner and been approved. Thoughtlessly, I went off with Titom to show him the wongai on the other side of the island. G must have been painfully reminded of the other occasion when I had gone off round the island with company.

Titom and I enjoyed ourselves like happy children, climbing trees and guzzling wongai fruit. We were so busy that I hardly noticed the drop in temperature and darkening of the sky, but Titom seemed to sense exactly the moment when the rain was about to begin, for he dropped suddenly out of the tree we had been raiding and crawled in under the shelter of some bushy mangroves. As the first volley of raindrops made a timpani of the leaves I crept in to join him. It was suddenly cold. Crouched there together in the dark of the mangroves we sat in silence for a while waiting for the shower to pass. My thoughts were with G, imagining him checking to see that the big drum was in the best position to catch the maximum amount of water.

"I tink your Poo Poo bird been call."

This statement of Titom's was something of a mystery to me at first. It was clear that detailed accounts of life on Tuin had been relayed to Badu by Ronald's brood. In the weeks to come I was to learn what Titom had meant: the Poo Poo bird called whenever rain was imminent. He proved to be very reliable.

An aura of body warmth emanated from Titom, although we were not touching. He was looking down at his hands, which were making little men in boats out of the stiff pink-tasselled cups that held the mangrove pods, with twigs and wongai pits to represent the figures.

"Kids make like this on island," he said. Then with one impatient movement he swept them all aside, saying, "You tink this kind play stupid."

"No," I said. "No."

I was dying for a pee and, unaccustomed to having to wait, wriggled away several yards and let it go, just remembering to lower my pants, which still felt strange to wear. When the rain stopped and we headed back to camp via Long Beach and the interior, Titom said, "You been make me want give you one."

Stupidly I said, "Give me one what?"

He made an unequivocal gesture with an upward thrust bent arm. This time there was an element of proposition. He seemed to be waiting for an answer of some kind. I would love to be able to say that I deflected a potentially awkward situation with a poised and sensible response, but all I said, rather feebly, was, "No, I don't think we had better do that."

As an afterthought I added, "You told me you have plenty of girl-friends."

"Yes, plenty," he said with relish. "We do them things everytime. If woman got 'usband we don't say nothing, that way no got trouble. She like all right."

He seemed to accept without offence that I was not game, and as we passed through Coconut Alley he climbed a tree and cut down a few peepas for me. But he did not come all the way into camp, turning off instead as soon as we came to the beach and swimming out to his dinghy without greeting or saying goodbye to G.

The anger and bitter recriminations that followed stirred up all the ugly resentment in both of us which had first let fly after the exit of the catamaran boys. G accused me of having "fucked" Titom and I accused him of being obsessed and sordid. When he carried on talking as though it were an undisputed fact that I had spent the entire morning in premeditated lascivious activities, I became so incensed that I could no longer reply. Instead I grabbed the axe and vented my fury on a solid branch of tee tree which was lying beside the woodpile awaiting just such a burst of activity. Between blows I heard G say, "It's not just sour grapes on my part, Lu. I just think you're being stupid, throwing yourself at young bucks. You'll get yourself into trouble one day."

As there was no response other than the crashing thumps of the axe as it bit into the branch in half a dozen different places, he started on a new tack: "How would you like it if a pretty girl came to the island and I went off for all-morning walks with her?"

Pausing in my onslaught with the axe, I stabbed cruelly at him with words: "I would not mind at all. I wish one would come, and I wouldn't mind what you did with her. Release your tension and get it off me!"

"And what place do you think you'd have with me if I got something to fuck?"

I don't need a place with you, I get along fine with Tuin."

This was not strictly true, and was perhaps the worst way of expressing what on other occasions I had already failed to put into words. I never did manage to explain adequately to G the peculiar and, to me, beautiful relationship I had with Tuin. Since the visitors had started coming and it was obvious that G was sick and tired of the rock-bottom survival business, I had given up all hope of his ever really giving himself to the island as I had done. But to be honest, I must admit that I had reached a stage where I so cherished my times alone in the depths of Tuin that had G suddenly wanted to accompany me, his presence would have felt like an intrusion. I was more possessive of Tuin than I had ever been of any man.

We wrangled and snarled on and off for a couple of days and then abandoned the subject and reverted to treating each other as the companions we had by now become, despite the unsolved problem of our nonexistent sex life.

It was not long before events began to move so fast for us again that there was no time or energy to indulge in domestic disharmony. One evening, just as we were settling down for the night, we heard, coming from the opposite direction from which Ronald's and Titom's boats had come, the now not so unfamiliar thrum of an outboard motor. It seemed to be moving at first towards and then away from the island in sporadic bursts of high revs punctuated by a sound that was definitely not familiar: a low, long, single note like air being blown through a fuzz-filled metal pipe. G and I peered at each other's faces in silent perplexity through the grey dark inside the tent. Now the boat was going slower and clearly heading into Camp Bay. The strange sound suddenly revealed itself to be a powerful *basso profundo* hum. Somebody was happy. There was an abrupt break in the engine sound and the hum changed to a broken growl culminating in the loudest belch G or I had ever heard.

"Whoever that is," said G in the voice of one who knows, "he's drunk. Now for once in your life stay quiet and let me handle this, Lu."

"I will, let me wrap myself in that gown. Have you got any trousers on?"

"Yes, I'm going down to see what's going on. You get out of the tent but stay back until I tell you it's O.K."

"Right."

We made our way to the top of the beach where G stood out in the open and I lurked close by behind a bush. There was enough light from the moon to give us a good view of the scene in the bay. A huge figure was very slowly and deliberately trying to detach itself from the boat. Balancing the centre of the dinghy, like a solid sculpture of round black rocks, was an even huger figure. Number one was now standing waist-deep in the water, not that he had a waist; I have never seen a man built so exactly like a barrel, and his legs, glimpsed as he climbed out of the boat, were like tapered standing-stones. He let go of the side of the boat, and stretched out his arms to the figure in the boat, who leaned over to hand him something. But number one had lost his balance. In slow motion, arms still held out ready to receive the bundle, he leaned further and further backwards until he suddenly gave in the middle and crashed down under the water. His head, with a broad mop of hair flat on top, emerged seconds later and floated as though disembodied on the surface. Even from this distance the moonlight picked out the shining whites of his eyes and a magnificent set of teeth displayed in a gleeful grin. He sank down again out of sight. When he surfaced, his companion, expostulating gently in a voice that identified her as female, leaned over and hit him on the head with a dark roll of cloth. His hand shot out of the water and grabbed it. He stood up, and leading the boat, waded closer to shore. Out of the bow he lifted a large anchor, which he threw, as though it weighed no more than a pebble, a good way out into the bay.

G's voice reached across to me quietly: "Are you there, Lu?"

"Yes, yes."

"Don't move."

"That man looks too happy to be unfriendly."

"Even so, just stay still and keep quiet until we see what they want."

The man had once again let go of the boat and now appeared to be trying to get into a pair of shorts. At the moment he was clad in the standard uniform of gingham undershorts riding half way down vast buttocks. It was like a moonlit scene from a custard pie comedy. Every time he managed to get one leg in the shorts and lifted the other foot to put that in, he fell over. This happened several times. Finally he dragged them on in a sitting position. Plunging back to the straying boat like a monstrous seal, he once again reached out his arms and this time the woman succeeded in passing him the bundle. He lifted it with one hand onto his shoulder and proceeded to walk out of the water and up the beach. At one point he turned around to call something to the woman, but the movement proved too much for his equilibrium and he sat down hard in the sand, jolting the bundle on his shoulder which let out a squawk.

"Good God," I whispered to G. "It's a baby."

On his feet again the huge man staggered on and halted, swaying, a few yards from G. "Meester Deral?"

G stepped forward and said hello. He held out his right hand. This caused some confusion. The visitor shifted the baby onto his other shoulder and politely patted G's palm with his left hand.

"My name no more," he announced, puzzlingly, "an' this one my son, Sarls Torres. That my wife Enid." He pointed vaguely behind him, and the sentence finished with a very long and evidently quite uncontrollable repetition of the belch we had heard earlier.

"Oh," he said in distress, " 'scuse."

G tentatively asked where he had come from.

"Bamaga," was the answer. "Me an' Enid an' Sarls Torres been come prom Bamaga."

"That is a long way." Bamaga is a small Islander and Aboriginal settlement on the tip of Cape York peninsula.

"Yes, long way. I been bring stubbies plenty for you but all peenish on long way." (A stubby is a bottle of beer.)

Weight was added to this pronouncement by the way his legs gave way unexpectedly and he sat down heavily on the sand again. Sarls Torres hung on calmly, tiny fists buried deeply in his father's corkscrew-curled mop of hair. Mr. No More twisted his face round to look up at G.

"Uncle Ronal been say me come Tuin. Morning time I go bring engine. Today I come prom Bamaga, stop by for make party but stubbies no got." For a moment his eyes shone with sorrow at the tragedy. "Peenish."

At this point I stepped out from behind the bush. No More scrambled to his feet, supporting Sarls with one huge hand. "Oh hello, Tuinlady, 'scuse, Meesus Deral."

"You can call me Lucy."

"Yes. You call me Ronnie. My name Ronnie No More." He looked at my thin face, grinning, then turned to G. "I go bring yous plenty tucker. Lucy go come fat like Island womans."

After a moment or two Ronnie looked out to sea and flapped his hand roughly in the direction of his own island, announcing that he had better go. G asked if they would be all right crossing the reefs in such poor light. Ronnie laughed delightedly. "Every water my priend. Know every rocks. No worry."

We walked down to see them off, and I waded into the water to say hello to Enid, who very shyly spread her plump hand in a tiny wave, fluttering the fingers. She did not say anything but dimpled all over her face when Ronnie handed her back the baby and I stroked its bald head.

"See you," said Ronnie, and climbing onto the bow, pulled the dinghy out to the deeper water with the anchor rope. His engine started up on the third pull and they zigzagged away over the indigo waves.

"That," I said to G as we once more settled down for the night, "was the sweetest drunk I have ever seen."

Ronnie did not appear the next day, but he did turn up, with Enid and Sarls Torres, about the third morning after his nocturnal visit. He apologised for not coming before, explaining that he had had a long sleep ("Not surprised," muttered G in an aside to me). In the dinghy lay a 28 h.p. Mariner outboard in a very sorry state. Ronnie plucked it up lightly and balanced it on a massive shoulder. Enid sat in the boat with a large plastic dustbin and Sarls Torres on her knees. There was ample room for both. She made no move to follow Ronnie, so I went and made encouraging gestures; as she had not yet spoken I had no idea how well she understood English.

"Please come up and sit with us in camp" brought no response other than an uncertain smile; "Cup of tea?" with actions was more successful. Leaving the bin in the boat and tucking Sarls' small body under one thigh-sized arm, she followed me slowly, on surprisingly dainty feet. Ronnie's footprints, next to G's in a trail up the beach, were almost as broad as they were long, and the absence of a convex shape where the instep should have been suggested that his feet were totally flat.

Ronnie left the engine leaning against One-Plum-a-Day and returned to the dinghy for a rough wooden stand and the dustbin. G had the cover off the engine even before Ronnie had set it on the stand.

"Christ," he was muttering, "wish I had a decent set of tools."

Ronnie, who was immensely shy when sober, lifted the lid of the dustbin and took out a sack, which he proffered deferentially to G, whose sandy eyebrows shot up as he peered, delighted, at the contents. I was laying out our mugs on the table and some flat buns I had made that morning.

"Could you move those things a minute, Lu?"

I did, and onto the table G tipped several screwdrivers, some large wrenches, half a dozen used sparkplugs, a handsome new starter rope and—here he paused and handled the box lovingly—an almost complete socket-wrench set. Last came a milk tin full of old but certainly usable nails.

"Uncle Ronal' been say me yous no got nail."

I poured tea from the billy into our two mugs and handed them to Ronnie and Enid. Sarls was sucking enthusiastically at a bottle containing bright green liquid. Ronnie said something to Enid and she fished out from the dustbin two big red mugs, which she held out to me.

"This for Lucy an' Deral," Ronnie said. There was also another large bag of rice for us.

"I been mean buy plenty nother things but dollar peenish gone. When cray coming good me an' Enid go store onetime."

When we tried to impress upon Ronnie that he need not bring us anything, and thanked him profusely, he merely smiled and looked down shyly into his cup. He followed G in taking a bun and pleased me by offering one to Sarls, saying, "Take 'im, little baldy 'ead, Tuin damper proper nice."

I could see that G was itching to start on the 28 Mariner. When he stood up from the table he was actually rubbing his hands in anticipation.

"Well, Ronnie," he said in a businesslike manner. "What do you find is the main trouble with her?"

"She no go."

"Ah."

He set to with the wrenches. Ronnie stood by with one wrench chosen at random, obviously dying to help but with no idea where to begin. As G took off the various parts Ronnie carefully arranged them in a row on the table. G had trouble removing the flywheel nut. He gritted his teeth and broke out in an extra layer of sweat, straining to turn it with a large wrench. Ronnie shyly stepped in and twirled the wrench round as though it gave no more resistance than cream against a spoon.

"Handy, our Ronnie, isn't he, Lu?" G crossed his eyes at me in mock horror behind Ronnie's gleaming expanse of back.

While they were taking the engine apart, I sat with Enid, attempting, with no success at all, to make small talk. Her large round head, set on a neck like a bollard, inclined forward gently from time to time but she never said a word. Sarls, seated comfortably on one mammoth breast, which in turn sat comfortably on Enid's lap, reached up and poked his fingers up her nose occasionally. This would cause a tiny little giggle to tinkle out from her huge bulk. One thing she did confirm was Sarls' name.

"Is it Charles?"

Affirmative inclination of head. At the mention of his son's name Ronnie looked up a moment from the engine. "Sarls," he said tenderly, and then made a special effort at pronunciation: "Shearles Torres No More."

The sun rose to its midday zenith and the stripping down of the engine continued. Enid lay on her back in the shade, dozing peacefully, a continent unto herself. Sarls sat on one of his father's feet, hands clasped around the great calf. This arrangement gave Ronnie a slight limp, but apart from that it seemed to suit them both. Time for another cup of tea but the water in the drum was almost used up, so that it would mean subjecting Ronnie and Enid to unappetising creek water. The single shower we had had when Titom came had given us about four days strictly rationed supply in the drum, and I had deliberately saved a billyful with which to make tea for Ronald when he came. This had now gone to Ronnie and Enid, so that we were, until the next rainfall, back to square one. By way of compromise I suggested we all have some peepa juice. Ronnie, clearly relieved at the opportunity of sitting down in the shade for a minute, neatly knocked the tops off two peepas I had stored in the cool of a bush and poured the juice into mugs. He scooped a little of the gelatinous unformed meat from the inside of the nut and fed it to Sarls, who knitted small eyebrows angrily when Ronnie stopped.

"No good small one eat many. Make belly runs," he grinned, and infinitely gently tweaked Sarls' tiny button nose between huge fingers. Then he stood up and went to our drum, evidently still thirsty. "E gud nother drums?" he asked innocently.

When we explained the water situation to him he frowned in deep concern, and then suddenly looked up with a beaming face and said, "We go Yaza!"

We gathered that this was a place where there was a permanent spring. It meant a ride in the boat for us all.

"Bugger the leg," said G to me quietly; "in this weather the best place to be is out on the sea." It certainly looked inviting.

Diary

The water was like a lake. No clear delineation between blue of sea and blue of sky on the horizon. All the distances around us were smudged with heat haze. The boat seemed a tiny, busy thing moving in a welter of still, silent heat.

G and I sat on the forward seat, our light combined weight having no effect on the bow, which rode high out of the water with the ballast of the No Mores in the stern. But as we left the reefs and sandspits behind, Ronnie increased the speed and the boat began to plane. G and I squeezed hands in the shared thrill of speed. A symmetrically rounded hump of an island wavered in the heat haze.

"That Death Adder Island," Ronnie called to us. "We go pass Soldier Point," and he waved towards the mass of a larger island coming up on our right.

Time was a foreign thing. The boat told its passage by a great white streamer of wake and the changing outlines of the land. Great slow islands of cloud hung in the pace of another dimension.

Soldier Point stood out without the need for further identification. On top of a mass of rough boulders on a jutting apex of island coastline, a solitary "figure," slim and straight, stood stiff and erect. It was hard to imagine the violent convulsion of land and sea that must have thrown up that slender rock to be cast forever as a sightless sentry, becoming a marker for the few navigators of the Strait. Without consulting each other, G and I both saluted. Ronnie laughed with pleasure. More coastline, rocks, long beaches, palm trees, then: "Yaza!" called Ronnie and we landed in the crook of a sandy bay.

The spring at Yaza was accounted for by the Islanders in the legend of a Baduleega, who, finding himself far from home without water, had struck his spear deeply into the dry ground causing a spring to gush forth. There was evidently more to this tale than Ronnie was prepared to reveal: "Little bit rude thing," he said coyly, and Enid giggled. The first thing I noticed as we followed Ronnie in single file through a tunnel-like opening into the dense interior was that the vegetation here was wonderfully lush compared to that of Tuin. The leaves on the trees and bushes were a rich, shiny green and palms of a kind I had not seen before, with delicate bouffant heads of fern-slender leaves, grew sturdily together in flourishing groups. Ronnie turned around and spread his arms to indicate that we had arrived at the spring. He stepped aside and I found myself gazing into the clear water of a jungle pool. A long black eel glided languidly away into the tall rushes on the far side.

Ronnie walked into the pool gently so as not to stir up the bottom. He scooped up a double handful of water and sucked it in joyfully, extracting every drop of sensual pleasure from the taste and feel of it. When he had finished he sighed deeply, mouth wide and glistening. "Yaza water," he said with deep satisfaction, and gestured for G and me to come and drink our fill. It was the sweetest water I have ever tasted and, leaning over, I dipped my chin and drank directly from the pool the better to enjoy it. As my face bent to the water my reflection rose to meet me, but the urge to drink was stronger than the urge to look. After thirst was satisfied I briefly regarded the brown stranger rippling in the broken surface of the water. Surely nobody I knew.

Slaves as ever to the tide, we could not stay long at Yaza, although had G and I been alone I think we would happily have stayed the night just to be close to all that fresh water and revel in the security of its presence. But Ronnie was already moving the boat out. We climbed in with our filled containers, G hopping through the shallows to keep the bad leg dry.

All at once Enid cried out excitedly and grabbed Ronnie's arm, pointing at the water and speaking guickly. All I could see was a cloud of sand spread over a broad area in the shallows. Ronnie took a long spear with three thick prongs from the bottom of the boat and, stepping cat-like despite his bulk, stalked without a sound after his prey. But Enid cried out again and now Ronnie jumped into the boat and briskly started the engine, tipping it up so that the propeller stayed clear of the sand. Enid was leaning over the side, tension suddenly making the mass of her body mobile and compact. She kept one arm outstretched, showing Ronnie where to steer. There it was, the thing they were after, a dark oval shape flying along under the water like a great flat kite. Ronnie gave the boat a spurt of speed and slewed it round in a long arc. Then he was over the side, his huge body parting the water in waves as he strode forward, spear raised high in his right hand. Down it plunged in one heavy, lethal stroke. With both hands he ground the points of the spear firmly in, and grinned at me and G in the boat.

"Tupmul," he said. "Kingtucker!"

He gestured for me to pass him a big hook on the end of a piece of rope; it was, we learned, his turtle hook. With this he pierced the creature through its pig-like nostrils and hauled it up so that it dangled over the side of the boat. It was a great brown ray. G handed him a knife and Ronnie slit its belly, to check, as he explained to us later, that it had plenty of fat. His face fell as he reluctantly decided that this one was no good. But Enid was up on her feet and pointing again. Quick as a flash Ronnie seized his spear and hurled himself in pursuit. He seemed to know precisely the path the ray would take, for this time I had a clear view of the action and saw him aim the spear just ahead of his swiftly moving quarry. He flung the spear with such force that it transfixed the ray and the bound end of the bamboo was buried in the thick skin. Again the turtle hook and the knife, but now triumph instead of disappointment. "We go make picnic Tuin onetime, this Kingtucker."

He slung the ray, belly up because its back was covered with sharp spikes, on the floor in the middle of the boat, and G and I sat with our feet in a puddle of thick blood all the way back to Tuin.

As soon as we reached our home shores, the long and careful business of preparing the ray for the table began. First Ronnie soaked the gutted body in the sea, then he cut out the fat liver from a hollow in the ray's belly. He sliced off the wings and chopped the flesh into large pieces, placing as many of these as would fit in a catering-sized saucepan which Enid had produced from the apparently bottomless pit of the plastic dustbin. The flesh was simmered in saltwater until tender. We had to have three boilings before all the edible parts of the ray were cooked, it was so big. Now the skin and bone were removed from each piece and the meat was spooned into a bucket of sea water. Ronnie changed the water three times and swished the meat around with his hands. Dripping handfuls were lifted out and squeezed like wet washing until every drop of water was removed and the meat was so dry that it could be formed into woolly balls which we piled high in a natural basin of rock. Ronnie checked all the balls made by Enid and me and with his powerful hands always managed to wring out one last drop of moisture. The next stage was shredding. Sitting round the washing-up bowl, we slowly built up a snowy mountain of flesh threads pinched off the balls. At last it was ready for the final cooking process.

While Ronnie was melting the liver fat in the saucepan I started a second fire and boiled up a billy of rice. Into six inches of bubbling fat Ronnie stirred the shredded meat, pressing and turning it until all the fat was absorbed. "She ready now," he said proudly.

The tupmul proved to be delicious, very rich and filling. We each had two helpings but when Sarls reached out his little hand to help himself to some directly from the pan, Ronnie intercepted him and, usually so indulgent with his child, would not allow him to touch it, although apparently it was all right for him to eat what was on his plate with his fingers. Ronnie now glanced up anxiously at the sky, checking to see if the moon had yet risen. "Moon see tucker, she make no good. Same thing if hand touch. I go take tupmul for Uncle Ronal. Better cover 'em now."

He encouraged me to take plenty for tomorrow, making sure I put it under the table well out of sight of the moon. He covered what was left very carefully to take back to Badu.

I went down to wave goodbye, happy and sleepy and full. When I headed back up to camp I knew what I would find: stooped over like a heron in the dusk, cursing because of the poor light, G was once again addressing himself to the challenge of the totally seized Mariner.

G worked on that engine as though his life depended on it, and in a way, it did. Not the go-fishing-or-starve kind of existence we now knew so intimately, but the new manner of living brought about by the coming of the Islanders. Contact founded on curiosity and encouraged by friendship could be cemented by the discovery of some commodity on our island of sufficient value to the Baduleegas for them to continue to maintain our present heightened standard of living with goods such as rice and flour otherwise unobtainable.

We had both seen the admiration in old Ronald's eyes, the awe in young Ronnie's, as G's experienced hands moved confidently over their engines and he gave names to each different part and knew where all the complicated little pieces fitted in. If we were to establish a system of barter, G's skill was to be our commodity for exchange. But no such advanced notion was in either of our minds the day following the Yaza trip when G sweated from the moment the sun rose to well after it had gone down, determined that by the time Ronnie came back the 28 would be ready to test. I was intrigued and impressed. This was a side of G I had never seen before.

The worst part was getting the pistons out. They were so solidly rusted in that the only way he could free them was with violent application of the back of the axe. I remember returning from wooding in the morning to find him apparently practising golf. He was strolling stark naked in a slow circle, occasionally taking a swing with the axe at the engine block on the ground. I knelt down in the sand and held the block as still as I could while G, using a piece of wood to absorb the shock, gradually succeeded in knocking one piston out undamaged. Of all the things I had envisaged doing on an uninhabited tropical island this was perhaps the least expected.

Ronald the elder was the next visitor to return to our shores. This time he was just dropping by en route to a place where he told us he was going trolling for queenfish. When he saw that G had Ronnie No More's engine all ready to put back together again but for one still unmovable piston, he decided to help with his tomahawk. Unfortunately he was a little overenthusiastic; the piston fell out in several pieces. Ronald looked crestfallen. "No much good now," he said sadly.

" 'Em broke," said Alfie, quite unnecessarily.

G, who of course had been dreading this very thing, said without a great deal of hope, "I don't suppose there might be an old 28 lying around on your island?"

Ronald seemed to consider for a minute, then told us that he thought he knew where there might be an old Mariner.

"Oh, I nearly forget," he added, just as he was about to leave, "my friend been send nother small engine." He collected a Johnson 6 h.p. from his dinghy and propped it up against One-Plum-a-Day. Then he went to get on with his trolling. Later, when the tide was low, he stopped at the end of our sandspit and sent Alfie running up with a big queenfish for us.

Although there were days in between, it seemed to us that one visit followed immediately on the heels of another. We would begin to settle back into a pattern resembling our old routine and then the sound of an outboard would remind us that our world was no longer exclusive to us. In fact, the return to Tuin ways really only applied to me. From the moment a tool was first placed in G's hand and an engine set in front of him, life on the island for him focused entirely on the camp area and, more precisely, on the part of a motor he happened to be handling at the time. His new preoccupation made him absent-minded about all things other than the task in hand, and when I mentioned the shelter, which at present consisted of four dug-in uprights—I reminded him that we even had nails now—he told me not to fuss, it would get done.

As things turned out, I need not have worried. The Islanders were not about to let us face the monsoon season with no proper shelter.

It was young Ronnie himself who brought across the old Mariner his uncle had been talking about. There were a number of parts missing but the pistons were intact. Again it was clear that the No More family was with us for the day, and this time they had very definite plans for the afternoon. Before lunch, which consisted of parrot fish as the Tuin contribution and a magnificent damper from the recesses of Enid's dustbin, Ronnie and G concentrated on the engine. While Ronnie, happy to have been set one clear task, cleaned the "new" block with G's toothbrush, G cut a couple of gaskets out of the cover of Anthony Burgess' *Language Made Plain*, a book unfortunately damaged by geckos in the early days. (Infuriating, as I had only managed to pick up the basics of half the International Phonetic Alphabet before it became unreadable. Desert islands are excellent places for practising your labial fricatives.)

It was while we were all relaxing in the shade, as G took enough time off from the engine to roll himself a cigarette, that Ronnie announced his intention to help build our shelter. He said that he knew the best places to find good straight mangroves and long bamboos to hold down a palm-leaf roof; the places where in the Beforetime his ancestors had gone for their building materials.

"Wood on Tuin," he said, "no mush good. No mush good Badu, neither. We go Carbai."

Carbai was located on the far side of Moa Island. It was not an especially prepossessing area, mostly high sandbanks and grey mud in the bays, but the red mangrove trunks were superb; straight, tall and clean. Ronnie marched confidently into the forest, casually uprooting small trees that got in his way. G tried to do the same and nearly got knocked out as the trees he pushed firmly down sprang back and hit him on the head. I always felt tremendously warm towards him when he made a joke of this sort of thing; it showed a side far more lovable than the blasé When-I-had-my Jaguar tendencies.

Back on Tuin, Enid and I sat in the shallows of Camp Bay knocking the thick red bark off the dozen trunks the men had cut down. Using the tomahawk and a length of hard wood, we tapped the bark sharply to loosen it so that it fell away in long shards. A deep magenta stain spread in the blue water as these floated away. The lovely blond limbs of the stripped trunks bobbed gently on the twinkling surface as we left them to clean themselves and soak up a layer of ant-discouraging salt. Ronnie and G had leapt a century or so and were doing another stint on the engine. I was called up once from the wood-stripping to help fit the piston rings, for G did not quite trust Ronnie to knock the pistons in gently enough with the hammer.

The day drew to a close too soon, as they nearly all did on Tuin. Over a meal of two large mud crabs that G and Enid had caught at Carbai, Ronnie stated firmly that tomorrow we would work on the shelter. "Big rain coming soon," he said, reiterating his uncle's warning. I could have hugged him.

That night in the tent G talked about the engine. He had never worked on an outboard before, but, as he put it, "an engine is an engine." And in one way or another, G had been dabbling in engines all his life. As a small boy he had played around the garage as his father worked on one of the first cars to come to the small village of his childhood. Later he had driven and looked after farm machinery. Even when he was a successful publisher he had done all the maintenance and repairs on his own and friends' cars. He simply loved engines. But why, I wondered, had he not told me about this passion of his before? Perhaps because it had not been relevant to our venture, but then, neither was publishing an "educational" girlie magazine. No, it was the old-fashioned stigma attached to labour that got your hands dirty which had inhibited G from talking about what he was really good at. Once he realised that I was proud of his skill, one more barrier between us was down.

The No Mores' arrival at noon next day was an impressive sight. They had been over to a beach called "Old Camp" on their own island and cut down ten magnificent green bamboos for us. Each one was over twenty feet long and they stuck out on either side of the dinghy like broad green wings. Underneath the bamboos were nine or ten sheets of corrugated iron, full of rust and holes but all more or less the same length. These were the contribution of the friend of Ronald who had sent over the Johnson 6 h.p. Underneath the layer of irons was a large container filled with water, and young Sarls Torres, who blinked when suddenly exposed to sunlight again. As final proof that he had thought of everything, Ronnie presented G with a saw and the news that Uncle

Ronald said it would be all right to use any old planks we found in his shed. There was a brief debate as to whether to test the engine first or get straight on with the shelter. I knew that G had put so much effort into the Mariner that he could hardly wait for the moment of truth. It was Ronnie who made the decision for us: "Little bit selter, little bit test engine. 'E gud plenty time por fix engine when selter he peenish."

One side of the shelter flew up while the sun still stood high. It took the shape of the original long stroke of my T. There were just enough irons to cover the west-facing wall once a sufficient number had been set aside for the roof, where they would be used as a supporting structure for a thatch of palm leaves. Ronnie told us that he would bring over some wire later on when the time came for tying on the roof. "Nor'west season plenty wild," he explained. When the shelter neared completion, G and I could remove the irons now covering the tent and use them to fill in the back and part of the eastern wall. The yellow canvas still up at the site of the old shelter would cover the remaining open patch on that side.

With the bones of the shelter complete—it looked, with its skeleton structure of mangroves and the one ragged wall, like a cross between a climbing frame and a seaside windbreak—attention was transferred to the engine. While Ronnie removed the present outboard on his dinghy, G tightened all the nuts on the Mariner one last time. He had told me earlier that what this engine really needed was a new diaphragm for the pump, new float and needle for the carburetor, new piston rings, new impeller and a complete set of new gaskets. He also mentioned that the block and pistons he had taken from the old engine Ronald had found seemed slightly larger than the original. The sparkplugs were old and doubtful but in the semidark last evening when he called me to help, I had clearly seen a spark off both. A temporary diaphragm had been made from a piece of rice bag, and one of my hairbands secured the tube to the pump in place of a wire clip. The engine had to be tied onto the boat with rope since there were no screws on the clamps. In lieu of a tilt-adjusting rod G used the prong of a spear.

As Ronnie poled the boat out from the shallows, G called, "Hey wait! Can't go without old Lu. Come on, shithouse, and bring down that big screwdriver."

Because Enid and Sarls could not be left alone on the island—" 'em fright from Markai"—they came too.

"My God, Lu," G said quietly, looking anxiously at the engine, "I hope the old bitch goes."

The attachment to the petrol tank was made and the hand pump squeezed. Since there was no such refinement as a proper starter mechanism, a rope had to be wound round the flywheel. G tried a couple of pulls but he could not get enough power into it. I was sent up to the bow with the spear to keep us from drifting onto rocks, and Ronnie went back to give G a hand. He stood with his massive legs apart and very carefully wound the rope into the grooves as he had seen G do. Hunched and tense, G sat by holding the steering arm in one hand and a screwdriver in the other.

One pull from Ronnie and the engine coughed, two and she cleared her throat hard, three—and we were off. The engine was stuck in forward gear and the boat weaved madly as G, his back to a group of rocks towards which we were shooting at speed, desperately tried to bring down the revs.

"Left," I shrieked, "left!" and the boat veered off just in time and whizzed round in a circle. G was blissfully oblivious of the terrifying clarity of the rocks not far beneath the surface of the water. As he succeeded in quietening the scream of the engine to a gentle roar, he looked up with an excited smile. "She goes, the old bitch goes!" and he gave an inarticulate gurgle of pure glee.

We did not go far, since now that G had seen that the engine would actually go, there were a number of adjustments he wanted to make while she was standing still. Also, the water cooling system was not working efficiently. G told Ronnie that he must try to get a new impeller if nothing else. This was not outside the bounds of possibility, as an opportunity had come up for Ronnie to work on a lugger skippered by his brother-in-law, Bul-bul. They would be calling in at Thursday Island to sell their cray at the end of the trip. If G wrote it down, Ronnie might be able to ask a mechanic on Thursday Island to send Down South for the necessary part.

Ronnie's large face shone with pride and respect. He kept patting the engine and patting G. "You my proper brudder, Deral. When come back prom craypeesh we go peenish selter good an' me an' Enid go store por yous."

When they had left, G shook his head and said there was still a great deal wrong with the engine that he could not fix without new parts. But I said never mind, he had made it go, and I was "proper proud Meesus Deral, too."

News of G's success with the 28 spread swiftly among the Baduleegas so far aware of our existence on Tuin. The man who had sent the

Johnson 6 and the corrugated iron turned out to be Titom's father, Philamon. He now sent over a Dunlite generator complete with an advance payment of flour, dried milk, tea, sugar and, obscurely, a very old packet of Brillo pads. Ronald turned up with a Mercury 9 h.p. and the news that the Chairman of Badu would be sending over a Kawasaki generator as soon as his sons were back with their dinghies from a long crayfishing trip. Ronald's own 20 h.p. Mariner needed attention, and in order to establish himself as first in the pecking order he kept the secret of G's tobacco to himself. As Ronald smoked a whole tin every one and a half days, he overestimated G's capacity, and soon G had enough stored away to keep him going for months.

There was so much rice and flour in store that I lost all thought of rationing and made quantities of bread, which I picked at all day long. With the dried milk and sugar I was able to make puddings as well, which G, with his craving for sweet things, wolfed down like a school-boy. Within three weeks of the day of the nurse's visit he was able to leave the bandage off his leg, merely protecting the vulnerable new tissue formed where the crater had been with a light dressing of gauze. My veins began to protrude less and my guts stopped falling out at awkward moments.

After G had managed, with Ronald's attentive assistance, to repair the Johnson 6 and it was taken away, we had a temporary reprieve from the attentions of the outside world. G had explained that in order to do any effective work on the generators he must have a battery for testing. This was something of a poser for the Islanders, but was eventually made possible when G said he could manage with six ordinary flashlight batteries taped together end to end. In the meantime, because he knew he only had it on loan until Ronnie No More came back, G made good use of the saw.

The first thing he made was a sturdy workbench. The only square-edged wood in the camp was like iron to saw through, and just cutting enough lengths for the surface took hours of sweaty labour. The end result was a very neat job and I looked at it enviously, commenting that it would be ideal as an alternative to kneading damper in the washing-up bowl. But G already had plans for me. In the as yet unwalled space near the front of the shelter, he constructed a proper kitchen work area. It was designed in two layers; a flat work surface with a storage shelf underneath. He even made little grooves where there was a short-age of planks so that I could make good use of the gap as a space for draining plates, of which, thanks to Ronnie and Enid, we now had five.

To the left of this he built a low shelf, using a sheet of broken iron for the surface, as he had come to the end of Ronald's planks. Another sheet of iron, nailed onto the supporting posts of the work surface, made this a fireproof corner with indoor cooking in mind. A floor-to-ceiling range of shelves was planned, but before G had a chance to complete this, engines started coming in again. I finished it off myself, using pretty, stripped mangrove saplings as slats. These built-in units looked rather attractive without a wall behind them; truly open plan. When Ronald gave us his old camp frying-pan I immediately hung it up on a nail beside my fish-slice and colander. Suddenly things were beginning to look amazingly civilised.

When in my clumsy way I tried to tell G how lovely I thought it was of him to have built these things to make life easier for me, he swept aside my gratitude.

"Listen, shithouse, I've built kitchens for a woman with all pine panelling, fitted cupboards, tiled floors, deep freezes and a Westing-house cooker, and there was still no pleasing her. I've built a banquet table with a solid oak top, mahogany panels on the walls of the dining-room, and all I got was a critical 'Hmm.' I put up this piece of crap for you and you're over the moon."

"Yes but—"

"Oh, I know there's all that. You don't fuck, and what's the good of a cunt that doesn't fuck? But you are bloody good company, I'll say that for you, Lu. There's still no other woman I'd rather have on this island."

Why did I not "fuck" G after all this time, after all we had been through as a couple? The simple, honest, cruel and indefensible answer: I was not in love with him.

But was that, I was beginning to ask myself, a good enough reason anymore?

10

COMPROMISES

Diary

Tuin is changing. There are different sounds in the night and creatures we have not seen before are making their presence known. The other day, when I was dancing in the formal ballroom of the Paperbark grove—all those stiff, gallant, grey consorts—I found a new kind of hanging nest no larger than my fist. It was tidily woven from tiny twigs and thin grey strips of bark, with a hole in the middle for the bird to get in. When I screwed up my eyes in my dreamy dance mood it looked like a pale teardrop suspended in the hot air. There were others, dangling gracefully from the bony arms of the Melaleucas.

There are new things to watch around camp, too. Ever since the flying foxes have made their home in the mangroves behind Croc Bay I have stayed out of the tent a little while each night to watch them take off on their nocturnal sorties. They make a gibbering racket during the day sometimes, when they are not hanging fast asleep in their colony, but at night they are quiet and graceful, only occasionally uttering a squeak. Wandering around camp waiting for them to fly over one evening, I stepped over a long, thin form on the sand near the washing line. I did not recall seeing anything there earlier, so went back to have a look. It moved a little as I came towards it. A snake. G's machete was leaning up against One-Plum-a-Day. I was not sure what to do for the best but I knew that it was no good dithering, so I chopped its head off. I hung the head and body on the line so that we could inspect it in the morning. When Ronald came over next he told us that it was a baby carpet python. There was a whole nest of them in the bushes.

These small ones were quite harmless, and the larger ones rarely caused trouble either, but he did warn us about some very big fellows that lurked up in the trees on Northern Hill. On his island they had been known to drop their full coiled weight around a man's neck and strangle him. That is the way they killed wild pigs before ingesting them whole. I was not sure if he was talking about the same type of snake. Anyway, something to be avoided. There are also bulbous-bodied spiders in the interior of Tuin now, but these are apparently harmless, which is a relief because I value my walks more than ever these days.

Our friend Ronald is full of surprises. The other day he arrived with his boat bursting at the seams with people. He had brought his neighbours, Olandi and Kales Aragu, an elderly couple, to show us how to weave mats and wall coverings from palm leaves. Of course they had brought with them a large contingent of grand-children and their friends. Ronald's daughter and her small baby also came, the pram taking up a great deal of space in the dinghy. Apparently it is the only pram on Badu, and they are very proud of it. Not much weaving was done—it was desperately hot for fetching palm leaves—but everyone had a jolly good time. The younger members of the party went fishing and Kales and I roasted the fish as soon as they were caught. She had almost no pidgin but was extremely friendly and did a splendid foot-shuffling and hip-wagging dance around the fire. She shrieked with delight every time I said a word to her. Olandi, old, bandy-legged, narrow at the top of his head and widening out evenly as a turnip to an enormous wobbly bum, purposely made himself the clown of the group and waggled the single tooth in his mouth with his tongue to stop the baby crying. He spoke non-stop in breathless, incomprehensible pidgin.

Another time, after swapping army stories with G, Ronald brought over a rusty twelve-bore shotgun with a sad case history. He said that if G could mend it, he could keep it on Tuin. Ronald thought we ought to have a firearm in case of crocodiles, although we still had no firm evidence of their existence on the island. "They swim pretty good," he cautioned, "better watch out." I no longer had to watch out for Sammy the shark when I went swimming; he had deserted me since the Baduleegas' boats had started coming.

G could not work out at first what was blocking the shotgun. The barrel was full of a peculiar, sticky substance. He asked Ronald what it was. Ronald composed his face into a prim expression. "In my house," he said, " 'e gud one python. I think he been use gun for toilet."

"You mean this thing's full of snakeshit?" said G, his face a study.

"Gun been there maybe five, ten year. Python sit same place every year."

"Holy shit!" said G, not quite appositely.

With the shotgun, once he had cleaned it out thoroughly, G was again on familiar ground. His upbringing had familiarised him with shotguns and rifles at an early age and then in the army he had received proper training. Now he set his heart on bringing down a scrubfowl for dinner. The thought of a piece of flesh other than fish made the idea irresistible to both of us. But we only had three cartridges and one of them had to be used to test the gun. G was not going to risk any blocked breech explosions.

There was a conveniently forked tree just the other side of the creek. Into this we tied the shotgun, attaching a long piece of unravelled rope to the trigger. G and I crouched in the dry creek bed and he pushed my head down as he yanked the rope. There was an embarrassing silence and then the gun fell out of the tree.

"Come on, Lu, we'll tie the bloody thing in properly this time."

G aimed the barrel at a large anthill and we jumped down into the creek again.

"Ready?"

"Yes."

Bang!

"She works!"

The next morning, very early, I took G to a place right across the other side of the island where I knew there would be white pigeons and scrubfowl. It was beautiful walking through the heavy dew together on our hunters' mission. We talked softly, saying how it must rain soon, the air was so heavy and now there were these dews . . . G mentioned that he would not have to water his prize tomato plant and we both giggled; it was bearing one minuscule fruit that was dull-green, shrivelled, and hard as a bullet.

For G, who so rarely left the camp area, the walk through the interior held one or two surprises. He had not realised that the flat expanse of plain in the centre of the island was so large. He said that if he decided to stay forever on Tuin he might build his house there. Of course things would be very different then because he would "have money again." There would be a proper garden and a large catchment system for water. He would have a library and an office, a proper bathroom and a big double bed with satin sheets. There would be a fridge full of cold stubbies and wine.

"How would you like that, Lu?"

"It sounds lovely, but I'll be happy when we've got the roof on our present shelter."

"Yes, but I'm talking about when this is all over, when we're not in a survival situation anymore, when I've written my book. Or are you going to fuck off as soon as the year is over?"

"I haven't thought about it."

The conversation was left open-ended, and as we neared the haunt of the scrubfowl, near the wongai copse, it was soon forgotten.

We had both put on our rags of clothes for this dawn trek. As I crouched in the leaves I could smell the bleached mustiness of cloth mingled with the ineffable scent of early-morning Tuin. G was wearing his fantastically disreputable once yellow corduroy jeans. I suddenly had a startlingly clear recollection of the first time I had seen him wearing them. It was at a party, the only social occasion we attended together apart from our wedding. I remember thinking how the corduroys were a definite improvement on the cavalry twillish things he had worn to previous meetings. When he took them off that night it was before the first time we got into bed together. When I got out again at five-thirty the next morning and took a taxi back to my bachelor room at Kew, it provoked the comment "She's a total enigma" from G's friends. Of course to them I was just another girl who had answered G's advertisement. But after that night he did not see any more girls and on the following day, which happened to be my twenty-fifth birthday, I severed my only other lovership, for I had now given myself heart, mind and body to the Island Year.

"There's one," I hissed, a hand on G's shoulder. It was just a dark movement in the scrub. G stood up quietly, moved forward a pace, and shot the bird neatly. I galloped into the bushes to retrieve it, and before I had emerged there was a second blast and a small pigeon fell from the high branch of a wongai tree. I was thrilled and kept repeating, "That's wonderful; two cartridges, two birds!"

On the way back, via Long Beach, I plucked the little pigeon as we walked along because G told me it was easier while the bird was still warm. Once stripped of its plumage it looked no bigger than a quail, and G said had he known it was that small he would not have shot it.

Back in camp I sat down to pluck the dark feathers of the scrubfowl. I had never done any plucking before but found handling the dead bird a pleasant change from fish, and the feathers came away easily. I wished there had been banana leaves on the island, they would have made an ideal substitute for tin foil. Ronald had equipped us with an ancient heavy iron pot which made a fine camp oven when suspended over a steady fire with burning logs piled on the lid. It was encrusted inside and out with rust, so I could not cook directly in it but had to place the food on a plate. It still tended to catch on the bottom, so I used a trick suggested by G of balancing the plate on three or four flat pebbles on the floor of the ''oven.'' This worked very well and I baked the scrubfowl in this way, turning it over from time to time and covering it with the largest leaves I could find when it began to crisp. Although I suspected from the stringiness of the meat that this was a grandmother hen, it made a damn good meal crunched straight off the bone, and alternated with mouthfuls of fresh hot damper. The little pigeon made an interesting couple of bites for hors d'oeuvres.

When Ronald came again I boasted to him about G's prowess with the shotgun and it was not long before we found ourselves with an air-rifle and a .22. Unfortunately the air-rifle lacked a vital screw for the sights and with the .22 came only half a dozen bullets, but as we had no intention of depleting the island's small stock of wild fowl noticeably, these handicaps did not unduly disappoint us. However, when Ronald brought word that his daughter had asked if the ''Markai of Tuin'' could shoot a white heron for her, as she needed the feathers for a dance costume, we did wish there had been a few more bullets. A white heron sat on the sandhills right at the edge of the sea every day at low tide, but at that distance, when he turned sideways, which he invariably did when we were aiming at him, he became thinner than a piece of string. Later on, G and I admitted to each other that we were rather glad we never got him. The day would not have been the same without his small elegant presence out there at the edge of the bright sea.

Once, before the time when the rice and bread had made a noticeable difference to our appearance, Titom paid a last visit to the island. This time there were three other men with him. They came chugging around from the north while G and I were making our way back to camp, climbing naked along the uneven shoreline from Prize Parrot Rock.

G's face went cold when he saw Titom but he said jovially, "Well, here's your boyfriend back again, Lu."

We had fish wrapped up in a piece of shirt. I emptied it into our bucket and tied the rag over my loins as the boat came in close to the rocks. G held the bucket vaguely in front of him. The four in the boat were regarding us in a silence which gradually became unnerving. Three pairs of eyes were riveted to my breasts, the fourth man was gazing at G. For one interminable moment it seemed impossible that there could be any common code of communication between the stolid, black, heavy-set men in the boat and the two white scarecrows on the shore. There was not a flicker of expression on any of their faces, only the staring eyes. I took a nervous step forward, an arm shielding my breasts, and bleated hello.

It was as if someone had snapped their fingers. Titom uttered a greeting and the other men shuffled up on their seats to make room for G and me. The tide was coming up fast and they would save us a wade by taking us round to our bay by sea. They looked anywhere but at us while we were sitting in the boat.

In Camp Bay, G and I were surprised to see a little dinghy, smaller than any we had seen so far, pulled up on the shore. No footprints led away from it up towards camp. I looked questioningly at Titom.

"My fada been borrow yous that dinghy," he said.

G and I could hardly take in this piece of news. As soon as their boat hit the sand, the men jumped out and strolled up to camp. G and I hurried to find things to wear.

The men were sitting at the table on petrol drums. One, a huge man with a badly deformed leg like a charred oak, produced a large bottle from a sack. He waved it at G. "You like Moselle?" he asked.

"Bloody right I do! Hey, Lulu, get some cups."

The big man poured out. I was not included in the round. G took a deep swig. "Thanks," he said, "this is great. Aren't you having any, Lu? Here, have a drop of mine." He passed the mug over.

"She drink Moselle?" They seemed surprised.

"Oh, she loves a little drop—don't you, Lu? Go on, have a drink."

I drank and passed the cup back. The small grey-haired man who had gazed at G drank his mug down all in one go and his face immediately split into a grin which stayed there all afternoon. Titom drank no wine and asked for tea.

Ubia was the fourth member of the party. He was quiet as ever, but after two mugs of Moselle he said to me so softly that no one else could hear, "We feel sorry when we look yous. Yous thin like seek." The expression of concern and perplexity stayed on his face a long time as he stared blindly in the direction of the woodpile.

"What are you two whispering about?" said G, jolly by now. He passed the mug again, and as we exchanged a smile he turned to the others and said, "She's not a bad old girl, you know. You see all that wood there? Old Lulu did that all by herself. You should see her with an axe. She's all right. And you want to see her out fishing, a wonderful little old girl . . ." and he started to sing a song we both knew straight into my eyes.

Endearing though this was, I could not help feeling that this was perhaps not the ideal moment for personal eulogies. I busied myself making Titom's tea. When I came back to the table, G and Titom were kneeling down in the sand over one corner and about to start an arm wrestle.

It was then that I recognised how savagely ironic that device of nature called romance can be. In that moment, witnessing the shuddering determination straining every sinew in G's wasted body, and the rigid smile on his face, every ounce of tender will flew from my heart like a prayer, and though I hovered and smiled with the Islanders, that will stayed fixed on his arm like a vise. Titom was young, my age; he was fit and smoothly muscled with the body of a diver. G was twice his age and only just beginning to recover from months of semi-starvation. Behind him were years of too much drinking and too much smoking, but back beyond those years lay the rigorous training of the Parachute Regiment, and transcending all the warring physical elements was the desperate pride of a man. It was this, long after all the smiles had faded and concentration became a spell, that finally—finally—brought Titom's arm crashing onto the table and made a puppy of him.

All tension was dissipated within seconds. Titom got rid of any chagrin he might have had by lolling with exaggerated exhaustion all over the table and scratching his belly button possessively exactly as young Alice would have done. The big man grinned and patted G so hard on the back that he choked on his wine. Ubia smiled gently and the little old grinning Hosia stood up and beat his palms together soundlessly above his head, like a Spanish dancer in a silent movie.

Later that night when the boys had gone and the wine had worn off and G's voice was becoming hoarse from the one-man concert he had

been giving me for about four hours, I told him how proud I was that
he had won the wrestle.

" 'Course I won. Young puppy like that hasn't got an ounce of
proper muscle on him.''

There was silence for a minute. Then he said, "But I'm glad that
bloody big bloke didn't want to have a go.''

And he chuckled.

In the morning there was the thrill of trying out the little dinghy for
the first time. In my bachelor days I had acquired the habit of giving
names to possessions that meant a lot to me, travelling at an early age
through Europe in the company of Beverly, Amelia and Harold—
rucksack, sleeping-bag and water bottle. Now I automatically christened
this valuable new aid to Tuinlife, Isobel. She was eleven feet long with
shallow sides, and her aluminium bottom was spotted with black stuff
filling in the holes. She did not have a plug of a conventional sort, but
the Islanders had thoughtfully pushed a soft stick through the hole in
the stern where it should have been. We decided to fulfil the long-held
ambition of going fishing off the tiny rock islet in front of Tuin. With
a large outcrop of rocks to one side of it, and a deep channel running
in between, it looked an excellent spot for interesting fishing.

The weather had been showing signs of change again. Now, capri-
ciously interspersed between days of broiling heat, there would suddenly be a whole morning or afternoon when it was quite cloudy and
cool as the wind swerved round to fluster the palms on this side of the
island. We noticed that when the sand was stirred up by the turbulence
of the water, fishing off the rocks around the shallow coasts was poor.
It ought to be better out there in the deeper water. Excitedly G and I
made our preparations for the trip. While he devised a solid anchor,
using the discarded block from Ronnie's 28, I hunted around for suitable
paddles. Two spades would have been ideal, but as we did not have
two spades, one of us had to use an unwieldy piece of wood. We took
the spear along as a barge-pole. We did not think it would be too
difficult getting over to the rock, as the tide was high and slack and
the weather calm. What we had not reckoned upon were the devious
currents of the Strait.

The first one hit us when we were half way between the end of our
sandspit and the rock islet that was our destination. We had been
paddling gently, charmed and lulled by the sweet sensation of floating
on sparkling sea under a sunny sky. One moment we were calmly

progressing, hardly putting any effort into our spade and wood strokes; the next, without any warning, Isobel began wheeling and scudding in a hysterical manner.

"What the bloody hell are you doing, Lu?"

Like every man I have ever known in a boat, G had fallen victim to the skipper syndrome. Anything untoward that happened must be the fault of the incompetent crew, who had to be bawled at at regular intervals to keep them on their toes. But this sudden change of character in Isobel was nothing to do with anything either of us was doing.

Had I known then what I know now I don't think we would ever have attempted to leave the relative shelter of Camp Bay in a boat with neither sail nor engine power. The currents in the Torres Strait are notorious. Coupled with the fateful coral reefs, they have been the cause of innumerable wrecks. The waters running through Prince of Wales Channel, less than fifty miles away, are reputed to have the strongest currents of any charted route in the world. If it had not been for the fact that we were still in shallow enough water for the long bamboo spear to reach the bottom and steady us, G and I would have drifted away helplessly into the wilderness of the Arafura Sea. Later we were to learn that the lives of Islanders whose engines break down are not infrequently lost in this way.

Fighting hard against the dragging pull of the undercurrent with spade and spear, we managed to push ourselves out of the way of the strongest flow. In doing this we found that we were nearer to the rock islet than home, so, rather than facing that bad patch again, we decided to risk going on. We knew from seeing the land at low tide that there were no more channels between here and the islet. If necessary we could wait to go home until the water was low enough to pole all the way.

Although we had been caught completely by surprise, G and I were more exhilarated than shaken by our experience. We had a bottle of fresh water in the boat, and we had fishing lines. We knew that had the worst come to the worst, we could have survived well for days. However, we were relieved not to have to prove it, and there was no telling where we might have ended up.

Fishing from the islet was every bit as good as we had hoped. While G, who was a great deal better at casting than I, fished from the tiny beach on the far side facing Tukupai Island, I clambered onto a high promontory overlooking the channel and dangled a tempting bait of fresh winkles in the deep water. Simultaneously we let out triumphant yells. He caught two parrot fish and a coral cod one after the other and

I pulled in the biggest snapper we had so far seen. Thereafter the islet was called Snapper Rock. But as we fished, the whole complexion of the day altered. The sun was masked over by rags of loose grey cloud and the heat vanished as swiftly as it does when day turns to night in the desert. Within minutes G and I began to feel terribly cold. I climbed down from my rock and joined G on his handkerchief of beach. The only bits of cloth we had with us were half a shirt and a flimsy strip of sari. G tied the ends of his half shirt over his chest like Brigitte Bardot. I wrapped the orange sari into a turban on my head, because that seemed to be the chilliest part of me.

When it began to rain I yowled like a Siamese cat. G became frightfully businesslike: "Right, men. In line. Chests out. One two three four . . ." And he put us through a vigorous series of physical jerks he had learned in the cold of Korea in 1952. We felt more cheerful after this, but there was nowhere for us to shelter from the rain. My eyes kept returning to our bait tin, which had been one of the containers used by the nurses to bring us water. Once upon a time it had contained ground coffee. Coffee of any description was, along with russet apples, the only comestible I actually craved occasionally from civilisation. How I wished I had my hands around a cup of steaming coffee at that moment. Tea back on Tuin would do very nicely, but however were we going to get across there now?

With the rain came squalling gusts of wind. The sea between Snapper Rock and Camp Bay now had waves on it that would wash over the sides of little Isobel and we had not a hope of negotiating that dangerous channel safely. We could do nothing but wait, passing the time with bouts of exercise followed by a rest until our limbs began to feel cold again. The rain did not last long, but the wind kept up and there was no break in the clouds. The sensation of cold was so alien that I almost felt frightened by it.

The day wore on and the wretched tide showed no sign of dropping appreciably. We were cold, hungry and dispirited. When I suggested playing "Botticelli" during the rests between exercises, G said, "Oh, Lu, can't you just sit still and be miserable like me?"

From time to time one of us would go and look at Isobel to see how far the tide had fallen away from her. But it was never enough to make it safe for an attempt to leave. The next problem would be the dark. Another immeasurable length of time passed. We could not even see where the sun was, it was obscured by so much cloud, but we knew it was getting late and the thought of spending the night on the rock was thoroughly depressing. We caught each other's eye and did not have to say a word. Apart from anything else I was damned if we were going to eat raw the finest fish I had caught yet.

Launching Isobel was in itself a tricky business. There were clusters of tall rocks all around the entrance to Snapper Rock's miniature bay and the waves tried their best to throw the dinghy onto them. I was knocked down twice while trying to steady the boat from the water while G manoeuvred the bow round to face the clearest channel between the rocks.

"O.K., Lu, give her a bloody good shove and jump in as she moves off."

I managed the first part of this operation successfully but failed the second part dismally. G had to leave the bow unattended for a moment while he dragged me over the stern, me cursing the fact that I had any breasts at all.

Once away from Snapper Rock we were swiftly caught in a current against which spade, wood and spear were as matchsticks. We drifted fast in the direction of Wia Island.

"Well, at least we'll have a croc each to cuddle there," I said. There was a swamp on the top of Wia reputedly teeming with crocodiles.

"Lu," admonished G sternly, "this is no time to be funny."

Then it started to rain again. Cold grey unglamorous rain on a cold grey unglamorous sea.

"Shit," said G, "I've got to piss."

It was far too rough for him to stand up, so I handed him the bait tin. Typically, instead of thinking brave adventurers' thoughts as the waves tossed us and the current took us farther and farther away from Tuin, with the sound of the rain on the boat and G tinkling into the tin, both of us began to laugh.

"This," said G, encompassing the whole absurdity of the situation with a broad gesture, "is the story of my life."

We were quiet for a while, helpless. When the drift seemed at one stage to be taking us towards Prize Parrot Rock, we tried again with the spade and wood to guide ourselves in a homeward direction, but our puny efforts did nothing. Then, almost lost in the sound of the rain, I thought I heard an engine.

I was not mistaken. Yet again the Islanders came to our rescue. Months had gone by without a soul passing and now, when we were so badly in need of help, a boatload of mountainous figures came buzzing towards us through the rain. We thought to begin with it was three gigantic men, but the figure in the middle was actually three children wrapped up in a cloth. In silence the fishermen passed a rope over the bow of Isobel, and G tied it on. Slowly, so as not to swamp the dinghy, which was already swilling with water, the unknown Islanders took us back to Tuin. They knew where we belonged. As the driver, having deposited us safely on shore, headed his boat away again, he threw us a couple of fat mullet. In exchange and as a small gesture of thanks, I threw him my snapper.

Before the day when Isobel became very grand and acquired a pair of almost matching oars, we used her with great circumspection and only on flat calm hot days. Occasionally we would bob cautiously out in her to fish in the deep places now no longer reached by George, our automatic fisherman, who had been swiped by a shark. Or we might gently pole round into the peaceful green water of Crocodile Bay, hunting for crabs and rays. G longed for the day when she might have an engine.

We wondered if the squall which blew up while we were on Snapper Rock had been an indication of the beginning of the nor'westerly season, but were assured by Ronald, who came over within a week of that day, that it had been nothing compared to the storms we would see when the season truly began. We were at the end of "Naigai," the calm time, when one of the Islanders' fifteen- or sixteen-foot dinghies might venture as far as Daru, an island off the coast of Papua New Guinea, or even to New Guinea itself if they had relatives there. However, the latter case was rare. We only heard of one instance of intermarriage between a Papuan and a Torres Strait Islander. To the Islanders, the Kiwais, or New Guinea men, were only one step above the Australian Aboriginals, to whom they referred scathingly as "Em bruddy brack savages." One of the main complaints about the Aboriginals was that "Em eat bruddy everythings; funnykind peesh, goanna, snake, everythings, they got no manners." There was a horrified silence once when I casually mentioned that some white men ate frogs. "You lie," was the general verdict, and I was patted indulgently like a mischievous child.

Ronald had brought with him Philamon, who had lent us the boat and sent over the Dunlite generator and food. He was powerfully built and had obviously once been very strong, but his broad legs were now bent with what looked to be a form of rheumatism or arthritis. He was very shy and at first only giggled whenever G or I addressed him.

Ronald translated the questions G asked about the generator into "lingo" but Philamon was unable to tell G much about it in any language. After a while G concluded that it was useless to ask even the simplest questions of people who had no basic knowledge of what makes an engine work, and every engine that came to him from then on was automatically stripped down so as to waste no time rectifying the one fault the owner recognised, only to discover there were half a dozen other more serious things wrong. Ronald was the worst culprit for this. He would say, with the air of one who knows, "Oh, I been look this one myself. Only little thing matter. Must be carbie, I think." And he would whip the lid off an engine missing most of its vital parts and caked with salt and rust to boot. "Carbie," a pet name for carburetor, was a word he had picked up on Thursday Island, and he used it in every sentence when holding forth on the subject of engines. To my enormous amusement it was perhaps the only word in the English language that made G shudder; the foulest obscenity was quite acceptable, but a corruption of the sacred name of an engine part—never.

While G and Ronald inspected the Dunlite generator, I made Philamon a cup of tea. When I pressed him to help himself to milk and sugar he looked up at me from under his lashes: "Yous gud plenty?"

I teased him by saying he knew we had plenty because he had been the one to send it over, and his greying eyebrows shot up and down with pleasure. When I asked tentatively if he had seen a doctor about his legs he looked embarrassed and shuffled his great gnarled toes in the sand. Finally he said, "No need go doctor. Fat from dugong make him come O.K."

He told me that for two whole crayfishing seasons—over a year—he had not been able to move from the floor of his house. Then his wife had taken quantities of dugong fat and rubbed it over him from head to foot, leaving it on him for several days. After this he had been able to get up and walk without pain. He pointed at G's not perfectly healed ulcer and explained exactly what I should do if it went bad again. To "bring 'im up bad one" (draw out the poison) the leaves of the convolvulus had to be boiled until soft, and then, when cold, three or four laid with their backs on the boil or ulcer. To complete the cure—and useful for all wounds—the centre stem was taken from a pandanus and the end shaved down until a sticky juice came out. The shavings were mashed up with the juice and placed on the wound, which was then covered with a leaf or bandage. This should effect a cure within three days. If it took longer, the implication was that forces beyond man's ken were at work. He mentioned one other natural remedy, that of the pure meat of the flying fox for "shortwind."

"I gud shortwind sometime," he added, and a plan formed in my mind.

G faced insurmountable practical problems with Philamon's generator. There were several specific tools and testing instruments he needed to make a proper job of it. He felt weighed down under the implicit faith the Islanders had in his ability, and he particularly wanted success with this engine because Philamon was simply such a trusting and gentle person. But, as he vainly tried to explain, he could not perform miracles. When we were on our own again on the island G fretted endlessly over the yeliow Dunlite. He would lie awake at night and muse about it, going over all its inner workings in his mind. When we got out of the tent for our nightly pee together he would muse outside in the moonlight; could it be that the magnet was weary? Was there something amiss in the great coil of copper wire?

One morning, when he had the engine in pieces and was scratching his head unhappily, I suggested that we go and take a pot at the flying foxes. It was an appallingly hot day but it would not be too bad if we took Isobel round and waded in through the back of Crocodile Bay. We took the .22 and pushed ourselves along through the still, clear water, taking turns using the spear like gondoliers. The foxes were quiet at this time of the day, no doubt tired out by their nocturnal expeditions. They hung singly, like macabre Christmas decorations in the highest branches of the dark-green-leaved mangroves. Leaving Isobel hooked to a mangrove hoop, we waded warily among the tangled roots until we had a clear sighting through the trees. G brought one down at once with a clean shot through the head. There was only a slight flurry among its companions and then they settled down and went back to sleep again. He shot another but it stayed hanging by one foot to the branch. I brought it down with a second shot and we decided to leave it at that, as shooting these innocently sleeping bats seemed such poor sport. When I went to pick up the dead I noticed a pathetic movement from one of the bodies. I was about to pick up a stone to put it out of its misery when I realised that it was an uninjured tiny baby flying fox clinging to its dead mother's breast. G was if anything more put out than I was over this mistake. He quickly killed the baby, which would otherwise have only died slowly. It was strange how both of us, unmoved by the death throes of fish or fowl, were affected by the flying foxes.

We took them back to camp, where, unintentionally, I hung them in a sad parody of life in One-Plum-a-Day. Ronald and his gang of little ones came later that day and I asked him to deliver the "Sapours" to Philamon, to help with his shortwind. I thought the children might like to see the baby. They loved it. Alice opened out its tiny wings and whizzed it round and round making aeroplane noises. Victor tried to eat it raw, head first, and not finding it to his liking that way, gave it back to Alice, who threw it unceremoniously on the fire. Ronald remonstrated with her and explained to us that he was telling her that that was not the way to cook it. It had to be boiled first and then skinned and baked. G and I would happily have tried this in our starving days, but as things were now, there was no necessity, and the faces of the foxes were disturbingly human.

Whenever it was cool for a few hours G would carry on with the next stage of shelter building, which consisted of laying a thin skin of rusty irons over the structure of beams and rafters and nailing them down quickly before the wind took them. I was constantly on hand to help, but he made it clear that he preferred to do the actual shifting of irons and banging down of nails himself. He was convinced that I was going to be cut by the rough edge of an iron caught in the wind, and of course, on the one occasion when he was up on the beams and an iron did flap out of control, I just happened to be standing in the wrong place and it cut deeply into my ankle as it fell. It was while I was dressing this that I saw another use for all the sticking plaster the nurses had left us. Every one of the irons had a dozen or more holes in it, and some of them were so worn with age that they were open nearly all the way along the furrows where presumably water had sat during previous wet seasons. I spent a whole day carefully patching them up with Band-Aid.

By the time the No Mores returned, the shelter was ready for the palm thatch to go on, but before this a bonus damp-proof layer appeared from an unexpected direction. The Chairman of Badu had been so pleased with the repair G had done on the little Kawasaki generator his sons had brought over that he sent them straight back with a six-foot-wide roll of polythene which fitted perfectly over the roof irons, making my patching somewhat redundant. I concluded that the progress of "Deral" and "Tuinlady" must be a frequent topic of conversation on Badu.

Ronnie had done well on his crayfishing trip, and true to his promise had been to the Badu store for us. He had brought flour, dried milk, a bottle of raspberry cordial and a tin of jam. Also, to G's delight, he had managed to get hold of a brand-new set of sparkplugs and a less chewed-up impeller than the old one on his 28. Enid had not brought the dustbin this time. Instead she was carrying a rice bag full of spare knickers for Sarls, whose maximum time for keeping a pair on was five minutes. On her head was one of her delicious, dustbin-lid-sized dampers, which we tucked into straight away while we caught up on news.

"I been miss yous," said Ronnie, with engaging honesty. "I been told Enid might next time we make new 'ouse along Tuin, make neighbour with Lucy an' Deral."

I observed that one side of Ronnie's lower lip was swollen and asked if he had had an accident. The story he told us was disturbing and sad. Apparently, while he had been on Thursday Island he had "been little bit fight." Because liquor was prohibited by the Government on the outer Islands, whenever the chance came for a fisherman to go to Thursday Island, the general tendency was to hit the bottle in a big way. No wonder Titom's friends had been glad to consume their illegal wine on Tuin. Ronnie had been with an ex-Baduleega in a bar. They had put away nearly a carton of stubbies between them. For some reason Ronnie had begun to talk about his friends on Tuin. His companion had been sneering and contemptuous, along the lines that if we were white we were no good. Angry and befuddled, Ronnie had knocked him to the floor—"I been smack him little bit an' he lie down"— whereupon friends of the fallen one had punched Ronnie. He told us this with his broad brow furrowed and a mixture of confusion and righteousness in his tone. Suddenly he looked up. "Yous gud black bloke in Englan'?"

"My doctor," said G, "was a black man."

The seriousness went out of the conversation as Ronnie grinned happily at what he considered to be a polite lie. "You Numberone bloke," he said, "an' you Meesus. Yous been eat Island tucker, fix up engine. We go peenish fix up roof onetime."

The trip to fetch the palm leaves for the roof was one of those magical occasions that will stay in my mind forever; the swill and lap of limpid water as Ronnie led the two dinghies to an opening in the mangroves that went through to Coconut Alley; the quiet vision of Enid sitting patiently in the boat nursing Sarls under a huge black umbrella against the sun, a monument to maternal majesty; Ronnie's glistening back and earnest expression as he cut down the finest leaves for us with his tomahawk; G and myself dragging them into great green piles that trailed along the sandy floor of the Alley like spectacular plumage when, following Ronnie's example, we carried them on our heads until we reached the dark tunnel of the mangrove path. Here we separated into a three-man chain. I stood in the Alley passing the leaves in heavy bunches of four or five along to G, who in turn passed them to Ronnie, who stacked them in the dinghies. The long green leaves with their strong, scoop-shaped backbones grew and grew around Enid until only the black umbrella and a little of her face could be seen. Isobel was stacked so high I had to lie on top to hold the leaves in place. All the way back to Camp Bay I lay on my back upon the rustling greenery and revelled in the love of blue sky, green leaves and hot sun. Then we finished the roof of the shelter.

G, who best knew which beams to stand on under the rickety layer of irons, first rolled out the Chairman's polythene, then steadily built up the palm thatch as Ronnie handed the leaves to him from below and Enid and I conveyed them from the boats to Ronnie. On top went the ten great bamboo poles criss-crossed into a lattice and held down with the wire that Ronnie had not forgotten to bring. By the end of the day G was tottering from heat and weariness but he was happy and proud of a job well done. Now all that remained to be done in the shelter was the preparation of the area where the tent was to go. But Ronnie was determined that we should have a cooking section built on the style of the Islander's houses, a little apart from the main building. This seemed sensible in view of the fact that a chimney arrangement through the iron, polythene and leaves above the place G had intended for cooking would not be easy to manage. Besides, I had become so accustomed to the freedom of outdoor cooking that I welcomed the idea.

The family came back several days running, always with more and more food, and while G made adjustments and improvements to the 28 Ronnie put up my cooking shelter. It was utterly simple, just a windbreak on three sides with a half covered roof to keep rain off the fires. Enid would prowl around with a spear stabbing mullet or squid to go with the rice and damper I cooked, and I alternated between concocting the novelty of sweet rice puddings for Sarls, steadying the 28 while G tested her for compression, and handing Ronnie nails while he banged on the tin roof. When the sun began to set they would go, calling out many times as they left our shores, "Yahvoh!"—the Island word used as both greeting and valediction. Then the time came for Ronnie to go off crayfishing again and we did not see them for a while.

We noticed that when the No Mores were around—we later discovered that their name was in fact Nomoa, but No More stuck—Ronald did not visit. Having been the first to "discover" us, he was fairly possessive and liked to have our attention to himself when he dropped in. Even though he had been the one to bring the other Islanders into contact with us, with the exception of Titom, he remained aloof in their presence or bided his time until he knew we were on our own again. In his own way Ronald was rather exclusive and made no bones about disparaging those of his fellow Islanders who had never been to Thursday Island or heard of a carbie. He was immensely proud of having a grown-up daughter at school Down South who could read and write "same like white girl." During her holidays he brought her to see us, a pretty, talkative girl slimmed down to conform to the beauty standards of a culture other than her own. She was an avid soccer fan and told me that more than anything she missed watching the matches on television Down South. In the sand she wrote with rapture "Dalglish" and "Liverpool," and said that she had carved those sacred words on all the palm trees near her father's house in Badu. She described life on Badu as "slack" and it was clear that she was longing to make her life among the bright lights Down South.

It was difficult, from the contrasting snippets of information gleaned from our visitors, for us to gauge just how far under Western influence the Islanders were. On the one hand they seemed positively modern with possessions such as outboard motors and perambulators, but there was another side, of which we were occasionally given a glimpse; the side that despite the work of the missionaries still believed in the older lores of the Beforetime, and that saw the world of the white man as existing on another plane, mysterious and unattainable.

One of the beauties of Tuinlife was that up until the hour when a "Third World" people came to share with us the benefits of progress, we were governed purely by the laws of survival. Organisation and administration lay in the hands of the sun and the tide. Because of the lack of perhaps the most vital resource, water, without aid from another nation, life on Tuin would have come to an end, but as time went on and our Third World benefactors drew us further and further into their own sphere of influence, it became clear that life as it had been, the Fourth World dimension of Tuin, would die under the pressures of advancement unless something were done to keep it alive. And at least fifty per cent of the population of Tuin was in favour of maintaining a grip on independence.

Diary

I don't know what is happening to me. Over the last few weeks I have changed inside and out with such rapidity that I feel nothing to hold on to any longer that I recognise as being me. It is as though the nucleus that held together all my inner resolve during the lean days of isolation is dissolving under the pressure of plenty. I cannot stop eating and yet there is no joy anymore in the gluey mouthfuls of rice, the battalions of white pappy buns I turn out to go with the endless cups of tea I make for the Islanders who come with their engines. We have masses and masses of suet pudding. And the quantities of food seem suddenly to have ceased to build up my body healthily. Arms and legs have become heavy with a layer of unmuscular flesh, and my chest and back, clear and smooth before, are now covered with a rough mass of pimples. My energy level has dropped lower than ever it fell during the lean times. I feel ungainly, unfit and strangely afraid.

Thank goodness G sees nothing of this. He is thriving on the heavy intake of carbohydrate and he still gets great pleasure from his cigarettes. My admiration for all his skill with the engines grows daily. The camp is now littered with rusty heaps; broken-toothed flywheels, pieces of dented cowling, discarded propellers with large bites out of the blades, engines without shafts, shafts without engines. And out of this muddle and wreckage G manages to piece together things that actually work. With cardboard from the boxes the Islanders bring their oddments of often unrelated machinery in, he fashions gaskets. He uses an emery board as a feeler gauge to set points and he makes new washers out of dried milk tins. He never gives up if there is the faintest chance of getting life out of what seems to be a hopelessly dead engine.

He is always saying how he likes me to be around camp, he likes my company. Particularly when the Islanders come he likes me to be there with him. If I am not there they invariably ask where I am. He made a lovely catapult just before the engines started coming in but he has never gone out and used it because he stays near the beach all the time "in case people come." Alfie has the catapult now. It is so good to see G's confidence and self-respect returning to him. I never really knew him when he was not "down." He still had the go in him to make him want to do the island project when we met, but he was nevertheless very down. It was all he had left to cling on to after

Ronnie helps G balance our water drum as work on the final
shelter begins.

The tent, half iron-clad at this stage, stands in the scrub left after the melon patch fire.

The 'Governor and First Lady of Tuin', under One-Plum-a-Day Tree outside the completed home.

The life-saving water of Yaza. Ronnie fills a container to take back to drought-struck Tuin.

Baduleegas on their own territory take a break between dances.

losing a great deal. But now I can see the reality of the kind of man he has up to now only talked of being. He has rediscovered something that fascinates him, that is challenging and demanding and has as its reward not only a guaranteed supply of tobacco and rice but also the satisfying "poum!" every engine makes when it finally responds to his days of attention. He is so absorbed that he has almost forgotten to remind me of the uselessness of being "a cunt that doesn't fuck," but not quite. Not quite. And as the gifts of the Islanders make me increasingly redundant as hunter/gatherer, I begin to feel that uselessness too.

The confusion of it all boiled over in me after an incident that occurred a few days ago.

Ronald was here. He had come over early in the morning and instead of immediately sitting down in camp and immediately launching into a talk about the latest engine he had brought over, he announced that he was off to cut down some scrub and prepare the ground for planting water melons as soon as the first Big Rains come. Eager to learn and to discover where Ronald considered the most fertile soil on Tuin to be, I went with him and, under his instructions, helped to fire the scrub.

After this I made a damper lunch for G and Ronald, who would spend the rest of the day on engines, and then decided to take myself off fishing. There was a brisk chop on the water and the wind was changeable, but the sun was high and warm and the tide was just low enough to enable me to wade and scramble out to Prize Parrot Rock. Ronald said that was certainly the best place for fishing now and he would come round and fetch me in his dinghy when the tide was full.

Out on the rock, able to take off the ugly half shirt and now too tight pants that were all I had to cover a figure no longer boyish, I felt a sense of release and the re-blossoming of simple sun contentment. I did well, catching first a fair-sized coral cod and then a beautiful spotted coral trout, G's favourite fish. The small parrot fish that came on the line in between I cut up for bait. After a short while the fish stopped biting. There could be only one explanation for this with the tide in a good position, the moon in the first quarter, and plenty of fish about: shark. Some big old monster had cruised in and was scaring off the rest of our dinner. (It was my intention to give Ronald some of the best fish to take back to his family, so I wanted a large and varied catch.)

The sun was twinkling so brightly on the water that I could see nothing below the surface out where my line was cast. A great jerk on the line caught me completely off guard, and before I knew what was happening or could think to let go, I was dragged in off the rock scattering the fish I had caught as I fell. A second jerk snatched the line from my burnt fingers and when my head came to the surface I saw the zooming triangle of a fin turn and head in fast towards me, making a long clean arrow through the water. The rock was slippery and I was bruised and coughing but I scrabbled up onto the ledge faster than I would have thought possible. As I turned round it was in time to see the shark finish his long run in with a flashy swerve and gobble up both my lovely fish. I was livid and shaken, sans line, bait, fish and composure. The tide was rising fast and there was no possibility of my being able to get back to land without the current sweeping me away. There was nothing to be done but wait for Ronald.

It was a long time before he came and meantime the sun had clouded over. I sat quietly, rather vacantly, and when I finally saw him round the corner of Camp Bay I had to rouse myself to wave. When I explained how my line had been taken by a shark he quickly rectified the situation by giving me another one and indicated that there were some winkles for bait under the water at the back of the rock. He said he would come back later, when I might have some fish, and motored back to rejoin G. I had been treated as any Island woman would have been.

For a while after he was out of sight I stood motionless on the ledge, the brand-new line on its plastic spool in my hands. Then I saw a familiar shape move languidly in the water a little way out from the rock. Something helpless and full of rage rose up in me in a great harsh sob and I hurled every available loose missile at the brute until there was not a stone left on the rock. Then I hurled the bucket and reel as well. My mouth was clamped against a breaking-up movement that threatened to crumple my face. Control went suddenly and I stood there and howled. As the tears came, broken words choked out, and glaring furiously over the darkening water, I gave way to a childish fit of self-pity, swearing and moaning and berating myself, G and the world in general. There was finally something satisfying in the voluptuous relief of "giving way" for once.

Inevitably the tears subsided and I did practical things like retrieving bucket, knife and reel from where they bobbed up against the rock, the knife fortunately caught by a piece of shirt on the handle of the bucket, lucky I had not flung it separately. Before the water rose too high I went around to the back of the rock to look for the winkles Ronald had mentioned.

When a warm strand of orange wavered up through the grey sky over Tukupai and the fish had long gone and the water risen so high that I was perched right on the very top of the rock, Ronald and G came round to collect me. I had just two parrot fish and G commiserated, "Poor old Lu, that all you got? Hey, we got the engine going!"

I was burnt out and calm, smiling at his enthusiasm. It did not matter about the unappetising parrot fish because, remembering at the last minute, as was his habit, Ronald had brought us . . . a tin of baked beans.

Last thing, when we were testing the engine once more for sparks, G said, "You all right, Lu? Your face is a bit red."

"Must be the sun."

That night as we lay in the tent I kept thinking I was hearing strange clicking and whispering sounds. I imagined I saw a shadow moving along the outside of the tent between the irons and the Terylene. I closed my eyes. When the shadow bumped into the side of my head I sat up and yelled. G stirred and we both clearly saw the outline of the ruffled intruder. It was only dear old Poo Poo, our rain bird, on a nocturnal blunder. But when towards dawn I got out and saw the red crackling line to the south of camp I was led to wonder if Poo Poo's visit had been entirely unintentional. The fire from Ronald's melon patch was sweeping right across the waist of Tuin.

There was no immediate danger. The glowing, smoking line was advancing very slowly. From time to time a ball of flame would seem to hover in the air like a beacon when a spark caught the head of a screwpine. The tide was far, far away and we had one bucket, a washing-up bowl and a billycan. Sand was the obvious answer, sand and irons. We had not a hope of beating out the fire all along its length, all we could do was try to save the wooden structures of the camp area and prevent a spark from setting alight the newly dried palm thatch. All through the morning the fire crept nearer and nearer at a steady pace.

G was calm. He knew what he would have to do if the wind blew the bigger flames in our direction. He took the precaution of burning off a patch of high dry reeds closer to the shelter under "controlled conditions," standing by with the spade and a bucketful of sand. Then he carried on, meticulously cleaning a set of reed valves he had started on the day before. I removed some of the irons from the north side of the tent and made a wall of them, banked up with sand, along the grassy side of the creek where the danger of flying sparks would be at its worst. I could not resist wandering in to take a closer look at the approaching ribbon of flame, reflecting as I walked that this would be the last time for a while that I would have to search for places for my feet in the thick straw of the underbrush. Soon it would all be cleared to a stubble, as it was already behind the line. From time to time there would be a noise like a shot as a tee tree cracked as it went up in flames towards the eastern side where the fire was most lively. I wondered about the lizards and goannas, and the spiders that wove their nests in a funnel shape on the ground. Thank goodness the fire had not been started farther back; the hanging nests in the paperbark grove would be safe.

Retreating from the crackling advance, I rejoined G, who now stood ready with the axe to chop down the small trees on the other side of the creek in case a spark from one of them flew over onto our roof. He felled them briskly while I banked more sand around the area of the tent, which fortunately was almost free of scrub. When the fire came up level with camp, everything happened very quickly. With spade, irons and sand we beat down and smothered the part of the line which threatened our territory. The rest of the fire swept on, finally dying out two days later somewhere around the top of northern hill.

It was a while before Ronald came back, but news of the fire reached him via other Islanders. The general verdict was that it would be good for the ground. This was doubtless true, but I mourned the new bald face of Tuin.

Tuin was not, of course, entirely bald; the expression is relative, shock giving drama to a first impression. It was rather like seeing a lover, the mysterious shape of whose eloquent skull, formerly waved over with a tactile tangle of locks, now suddenly appeared clipped and shorn as though ready for a feathering. Poor Tuin was already well tarred with black. It was possible now, if one walked just a little way into the interior, to see all the way through to the eastern side without difficulty. Sometimes disfigurement or sickness in a beloved face condemns because it peels away the secrets that give rise to passion. Then the depth of attachment is exposed to both. With the mask of Tuin's wonder stripped off and my own centres of sensuality dormant, I felt at a loss, and powerless to overcome a weakened state of mind.

G saw the process of the dissolution of my character as being a mellowing. With the security of food and water coupled with the simple passage of time, he saw me as at last beginning to soften, to be a more approachable, a more womanly being. Naturally, this went along with my new figure, the rounded generosity of which he found alluring. The "scrawny Scotch harridan" I had been in his eyes in the past had been much easier to ignore sexually. Were the progress of our emotional well-being to be drawn out on a graph at this point, our individual lines would be seen to cross; mine on the way down, his on the way up. Whereas in the days of insecurity and adversity I had seemed to thrive and G become a victim of depression and pain, now it was G who was full of enthusiasm and I who became the drag. With the mending of the engines more or less established as an ongoing occupation for G, there was only one thing marring his happiness—me, because for all my softening, I was still, where it most mattered to him, essentially unyielding.

With the news spreading of G's ability to effect apparently miraculous repairs for no more than the tacitly agreed price of a bag of rice, events followed a not unpredictable course. One day a message came about an engine on Badu too large to transport over to Tuin. The fact that it happened to be the Chairman's tractor added to the significance of this development. Tuin, even though it was an uninhabited island before we arrived, came under the auspices of the Badu Island Council, the white Australians' given name for the Chief and his entourage of elders and deputies. Even though the Islanders had no real over-riding power in the matter of their own administration, as a courtesy the Chiefs were always informed of anything taking place on their territory. That is why, after having been granted full, documented permission to live on an island in the Strait for the year of our project, we still had to go through the formality of consulting the relevant Island Council through its representative on Thursday Island. This man had informed us in no uncertain terms that if we were to attempt to live on Hawkesbury, the original Strait island mooted for the project, we would "pass away pretty quick." This island had, he told us, three resident twenty-foot salt-water crocodiles, a doubtful source of fresh water, and no known fertile ground. It boasted a single palm tree with one coconut. G and I ate the coconut for lunch when we were dropped there by helicopter to check whether it was really as out of the question as it sounded. It was. We had no such preview of Tuin, going on the strength of Islander recommendation. No one knew that it was going to be an exceptionally dry year.

However, although there was undoubtedly an element of respect for the Islanders' wishes in G's mind as he climbed into the boat that was to take him to Badu, it was really the idea of getting to grips with the innards of a tractor that made the trip irresistible. I did not go with him because having set out with the intention of spending one year on an uninhabited island, I did not want to puncture the rim of its isolation by stepping onto the shore of inhabited territory until that year was up. I was to discover shortly that this was in fact the only principle I had left, and because of this, it was to assume perhaps unwarranted importance in my mind.

Alone on Tuin, I moved about its face all day, reacquainting myself with areas long missed during the hostess weeks in camp and searching out new parts to love beyond the charred acreage through the centre and to the north. Ronald had mentioned two mango trees that were supposed to exist right up on the highest point of Northern Hill, the haunt of the big pythons. Bearing the snakes in mind I equipped myself with the machete and made the location of the mango trees my personal mission for the day.

Walking up Northern Hill was now a considerably easier business than before the fire, so much of the scrub had been burned away. But near the top the great tall gums and other trees, for which I knew no name, had remained undamaged. As I plodded upwards—how different now from the dancing days—the intertwining branches above formed a darkness, an envelope into which I tucked myself as I passed the last lumps of smoke-shrivelled shrub and entered a wood that, although full of things dead, was rich in shapes and mystery. Some of the tree trunks were powdered rust-red and ridged with even furrows of bark. Petrified lianas gripped them in dry, choking spirals. Bubbly green clusters of a mistletoe-like parasite plant hung on thin grey twigs high up, and two- and three-foot-long scallop-edged pods, the round flattened form of the beans clearly visible, dangled lower down. I remembered Ronald's description of these; they were not edible, but were used, dried out in the proper season, to make rattles, or "kulaps," for the traditional dancing. That was something I looked forward to seeing sometime.

I found the mango trees eventually by keeping my face turned upwards on the look-out for snakes. I would not have been able to identify the trees by the trunk, but recalled the shape of the leaves, having had them pointed out to me in Australia. There was no fruit on the trees yet. I took some leaves to show Ronald, just to be sure, as it was rather a long time ago in Australia. I only saw one snake, which was pretty and not of formidable dimensions.

The day passed quickly. I was still lost in a vague reverie some way along the north shore when I heard the phut-phut of a cautiously driven engine. It was G, alone, in Ronald's dinghy. He was coming in carefully

over the reefs, following the path Ronald always took. Running down
to the beach to greet him, I realised that although it meant shutting off
my "other" life on the island, I was genuinely happy to see his funny,
eager and yet curiously closed face. Nobody has ever made me smile
as spontaneously as G.

" 'Ello, Lulu! Know what? I haven't half missed you, you old
bastard. I've got loads to tell you. And look what I've brought you!"

"Good Lord!"

A peculiar feeling of semi-panic took hold of me as I turned over
the two objects he had placed in my hands. There was a whole box of
stuff in the boat as well, and G was talking fast. I was holding a frozen
chicken—"That's specially for you from the Chairman of Badu, Crossfield Ahmat"—and a large bunch of letters: "They're all for you, lucky
little shithouse, wasn't any for me." Not sure which to deal with first,
I postponed the decision by hanging both chicken and letters in a rope-
suspended coconut husk in One-Plum-a-Day and making a cup of tea
for G. I hoped he was not too hungry because I had not been fishing.
He said he could not eat a thing and proceeded to describe in ecstatic
detail all the wonderful food he had had on Badu.

"It started as soon as I got there, Lu. I went up to Ronald's place
first, he was there on the beach, and sat down with him on this kind
of porch outside, and his daughter, you know the one with the little
baby, she brought out this fucking great plate of sandwiches with tinned
Spam and tomato sauce *and butter* in them and a mug of coffee with
so much sugar in it, it was like syrup. I had another one straight after."

"Coffee!" I echoed, faintly.

"Well, you know, that stuff in a jar—but it was fantastic . . ."

He went on to describe all that had happened in the course of his
day. He had spent some time in a shed that Ronald had on the beach,
which seemed to be a sort of dump for every piece of broken engine
on Badu. Then they had been called up to lunch.

"God! You should have been there, Lu. We had dugong and rice
and then tinned pears . . ."

"What was the dugong like?"

"Just like meat, kind of a stew, but I had to have two shits in the
afternoon, over in the Chairman's toilet. Oooh, the maggots, Lu . . .
great heavin' mass . . . but you should have seen the tractor! They call
her Red Rose."

He told me that he was to go back tomorrow early on the tide in the dinghy that Ronald had lent him. He knew how to get there, they had come part of the way back with him and left him when Tuin was in sight. Wasn't I going to read my mail?

Oh yes, the mail. There were about eight letters from my mother, all very out of date. She had moved into a new little house, was longing for me to go there, had had some trouble getting the freezer level . . . do tell her about my house . . . My grandmother had written, very correct, very Scottish: "You've not told us very much about your G, dear, I understand that he has been twice married. I hope you have made a wise decision . . ." Two letters from a lover with photographs of his new house: "It's going to be very cosy . . . I'm growing vegetables . . . are you well? Are you ever coming back?" Letters from my French grandmother, from a disabled lady I visited in Kew, from children I used to babysit for, from an artist friend who had run out of money for canvases and used a wardrobe door in a hotel for his masterpiece. He had been caught walking out of the hotel with the door under his arm—the letter came from H.M.P. Brixton . . . Other letters from friends and finally two warmly affectionate scrawls from my father enclosing half a dozen shark hooks and two rabbit snares.

I read the letters to G, but even reading them aloud did not make them seem any more substantial than an irrelevant and incongruous daydream. Somehow only the tangibility of the snares and hooks felt like solid evidence of thoughts from another world. Days later I began to re-read the letters but had not got far before I abruptly stopped and left them with the kindling in the paperbark drum.

I remember the feel of the chicken. It was still semi-frozen, and held against my cheek, it gave a delicious cold ache to my jaw. Tomorrow G would be working all day on the tractor, why didn't I go? Everyone had asked about me. But because in his way G had not entirely forsaken his loyalty to the island project, he accepted my reasons for wanting to stay on Tuin.

Several days running he went to Badu. The long journey there and back and having to keep a constant eye on the tide took away some of the enjoyment he experienced in solving the problems of Red Rose, but by no means all. The work was hard but he assured me that he had plenty of willing help constantly on hand, and refreshments brought to him at frequent intervals by the ladies. Islanders were queueing up to tell him their engine troubles. At the end of each day I would have a fire lit and the billy boiling as soon as the distant speck of G's borrowed dinghy appeared to the west of Wia Island. He told me never to bother to have a cooked meal ready, as he had always eaten amply, but each time there would be more rice, more flour or packets of sweet biscuits in the bottom of the boat.

With each day that G was away my return to the inner Tuin world became more complete, and wrenching myself back into another reality to be with G again felt more and more like switching into a role. But underneath my languorous daytime contentment lay the confusion and restlessness of my redundancy. And in the early mornings, when G, awakening rampant from an erotic dream, met with his frustrated eyes my friendly but unyielding expression, there would be a painful tension in the air.

Inevitably it came to:

"I don't know why I bother to come back. It's not as if you're a proper wife. I meantersay, look at all the stuff I'm bringing you. It's not that I'm asking you to be grateful, Lu . . ." When someone says that, you know that that is precisely what they are asking you to be. And therein lay the basis of my confusion. I was not grateful. I did not want to live off the things he was given in exchange for the work he did on the engines. I was grateful indeed, more than I can ever adequately express, for the initial help which had saved us from perishing of thirst and malnutrition, but things had got out of hand, and, with the exception of the times when I was deep and lost in the heart of the island, all feelings of independence had gone out of Tuinlife. With G commuting off to Badu like this, "survival" on Tuin was rapidly becoming a farce.

However, something else very important was happening. G was rediscovering himself as a man; a lively, resourceful, confident man, well respected by others. This was something of more lasting value than a mere project. In my muddle-headed way I was beginning to reach a conclusion. I wanted G to be happy and to go forward, but I did not want the price of his successful re-entry to the world of other men to be the death of Tuin. So somehow, somewhere, a compromise had to be found.

Diary
There is a time that is no time and plenty of it on an island, to reflect upon all the things you could, should and would have said or done. The people you might never see again. Chances missed where warmth could so easily have been given, hurt so simply alleviated, and you did not do it, or say it, though you probably thought it but something

proud or clever stood in the way. The issue in civilisation tends to be more complex than here on Tuin, each additional consciousness being a potentially reactive vessel, every word uttered, every move made open to misinterpretation. Wires crossed in all directions.

Yet here is G and here am I and it is apparently beyond me to do the one thing that would make him happy. Tuin has done much to dissolve the concept of rights and reasons. Want, plain uncomplicated want, is underlined; call it desire, call it need, it stands out clear. G knows what he wants. He wants to enter my body. My reluctance towards, no, my complete rejection of, his body is a slap in the eye and a kick in the bollocks. *Don't* want begins to seem petty, baseless. I yearn for something I cannot name. He longs for just that one so simple-to-make-possible thing. I only know that I do not want to be parted now from whatever it is that, through the sounds and the touches, almost it feels through the very soil, Tuin is teaching me. I can call that *not* wanting my want.

Never have I used my body for sex without wanting the man. In a world of choice, that mattered. Now, here, not even its not mattering matters.

"It wouldn't hurt you."

"What's so sacred about that thing between your legs anyway?"

Yes yes. But looking apart from, beyond all that, which after all is only talk, gross words spoken through pain, there is the issue of genuine care, for I do believe that as I care for him and about him, G cares for me. The trouble is that it is not in the same way at all. His love is man to woman in all respects. Mine, and I will not quibble about calling it love, is a warmth born of a shared struggle, a thing that, growing slowly, catching me unawares, at odd moments, despite and because of all that has happened between us, has sat down firmly in my being and I do not believe it will ever go away. How brutally unfortunate that it is not the love of a woman for her man.

And what of those days in London when I slept with him and there was sex? And I was the one to talk of sex on the beaches. It is Tuin that has entered my body. It was Tuin, any Tuin, that was in my mind when I looked at G's red hair on the pillow and knew that we were going to go to an island together. If only he had wanted the island as badly as he wanted a woman. If only I had wanted him as badly as I wanted the island. Oh, to hell with ifs. It is no wonder he has called me a little whore.

Woman is a vessel. Good luck to all who sail in her.

These thoughts rolled and fumbled in my mind as I patrolled the Long

Beach shore. There had been anger that morning. G had made no bones about telling me that yet again he had woken up with "a fucking great hard-on" and the sight of me calmly bending over and casually moving about naked, drove him bananas. He knew that my periods had started again. "There's nothing wrong with you, no excuse now." We were both still unhappy when he left for Badu after breakfast.

At some point during the walk back to camp I became resolved. But one last final fling of confusion manifested itself before the transformation preparations began on the new woman G was going to meet on his return from Badu. The last proud spoil G had won for his engine efforts was a store-rejected carton of fifty-four packets of Scotch Finger biscuits. In typical female fashion I had not been able to leave them alone despite the fact that their very presence on the island annoyed me as they seemed to symbolise all that was most unnecessary and irrelevant for simple survival. Back in camp from my decisive wander, I automatically gravitated towards the despised carton. But without consciously thinking what I was doing, instead of taking out a packet, I picked up the whole thing and carried it down to the shore where I set it up on a rock. I then went back and picked up the faulty air rifle and the tobacco tin of pellets. Walking slowly round, I shot the carton twenty-six times. It must be somewhere around my birthday.

POO POO BIRD

11

BIG RAIN

When a man has slept for the first eight or nine months of your relationship with his back towards you and his face and mind folded away, and then he is suddenly turned towards you at all times during his sleep, and wakes with a smile in his eyes, then you know you have either done something very good or very wrong. What I did may have been very wrong, but G did say it was also very good. I have never seen a person undergo such a radical change. Once given the freedom to express his warmth in the way he most desired, G became warm all the time. He whistled, his eyes twinkled and he agreed with me that the engine bartering system was a good modern way of coping with survival but need not be taken so far as to wreck Tuinlife. He was quite happy to stay on Tuin with me and have the engines brought over to him. Those that were too large would just have to wait until the end of the Tuin year.

The rains were now imminent. We used two large sheets of hardboard, another contribution from the Chairman of Badu, to make a dais inside the shelter for the tent. This would keep us out of the range of sandflies and a possibly wet floor. I was pleased to have our bed finally installed inside the house, and it proved not a moment too soon. The first Big Rain swooshed down onto our thatch the very night we moved in. It was exciting lying there listening to the extravagant streaming and hissing of the water while we remained perfectly dry. The hardboard was not ideal for the new tent games, but we managed with a strategic arrangement of pads.

I was strongly affected by the change in G on two levels. One, I was ashamed that all this time I had had the power to make his life on

Tuin so much more enjoyable than it had been and had denied it to him. Two, the reminder that I had any power at all came as quite a shock to me and opened up a whole new inner vista. The Golden Gazelle days were long gone; I was just Mrs. Fatty Tuin, but now Mrs. desirable Fatty Tuin, and G made it clear that he desired me all the time. I wished I could break myself away from the knowledge that my acquiescence had been calculated as opposed to spontaneous. But I could not forget it and neither would my body. G was so lovable now that it was not difficult to open legs as an extension of loving arms. I only wished I had never experienced the aching joy of my own body answering another's. Not to have that shocked me far more than the original act of prostitution. Because of the warm other love I felt for him, unconnected with the foreign actions of my body, the sight of his pleasure filled me with unease.

How can you tell a person you love that you love them but not as a lover? You cannot, if you have made yourself their lover, so you lie. You lie there lying in the full knowledge that with each breath taken in misunderstanding, the dawning of the realisation of the truth will be the more cruel. If only I had never known what it was to soar, to arch and ache and wing, G would truly have had his woman from that time on and I need never have had to answer the demand to fly again. Whereas the mind will compromise, the body will go so far and no further, and my twentieth-century body spoke louder than my mind and belied the "little woman" inside who, when horny urges struck, saw no reason not to throw in her all with this man who loved and wanted her.

But those were night thoughts. Momentary furrows in the naked plain of aftermath that should have been so full. As far as the geckos and the goannas, the red-back spiders and the moon knew, two on Tuin had never been so happy.

There was one last little job that G had promised Ronald he would do on Badu. He would go across and do that quickly one day soon, and explain to the Chairman at the same time that he had his own work to attend to on Tuin, and would be happy to look at engines that people brought over from time to time after the bulk of his writing was finished.

Meanwhile, in the shining mornings that followed the night rains, G and I, with our new touch relationship adding a quality of poignance to the most banal routines, gradually rekindled an interest in the "project" which was supposed to be behind our life on the island.

"Now Lulu," G would say, rubbing himself affectionately against my bottom as I kneaded damper, "we ought to make a map, you know. Hey! why don't we take Isobel and we can go fishing at the same time and have a picnic?"

The intention would be there, but what with G's now open absorption with things physical and my vague, dozy placidity, organisation was distinctly lacking. Paper, pencil, picnic and persons would be loaded into the boat. We would argue politely for a good ten minutes while G, overnight imbued with gentlemanly urges which manifested themselves in a Coral Sea version of the Cambridge punting spirit, ineffectually wound us round the rocks with the aid of the spear while I kept trying to jump out and tow Isobel by unladylike main force. Eventually, by a combination of efforts, we would get her far enough beyond the sandhill shallows to begin rowing, only to discover that something vital had been forgotten. Paddles, for instance. Hearing of our escapades in the improperly powered dinghy, Philamon had sent over two paddles, if not precisely matching, at least in very reasonable condition. With practice, G and I had become quite proficient at negotiating the whimsicalities of our home waters. So long as we never attempted to go against the current we managed very well, sitting side by side with a paddle each and pulling in unison. In this way we took ourselves out to some excellent fishing spots recommended by Ronald.

Nothing further came of the map idea until we acquired the use of Jemima and Dolores, respectively a Johnson 6 h.p. and a highly idiosyncratic Mariner 20, rejected by the mechanic on Thursday Island but coaxed into sporadic life by G's patient care. Her trial run was very nearly a disaster. G had been given the 20 by Crossfield, the Chairman, who said that if he could do anything with it, he would be free to use it. This was an irresistible challenge to G, who, impatient after three days' work to try her out, neglected to strap her adequately to Isobel's diminutive stern. Halfway between Tuin and Wia Island she simply jumped off and, prop still whizzing, sank gracefully through the blue water to land with a twitch and a stream of bubbles on the sea bed. G and I were aghast. We were also adrift, again. Exhausting efforts with the paddles brought us at last within reach of Prize Parrot Rock, and the day was saved when Ronnie No More appeared and dived for the 20. He brought it up balanced on one hand and popped it over the side of the dinghy as though it weighed no more than a crayfish. G set upon it at once with diesel, oil and lubricant spray, and within twenty-four hours Dolores was once more in working order.

It was with Dolores that G and I were to chug round Tuin with a map in mind, but that was some time ahead. A series of events was now to begin which made a mockery of all my determination to stay on Tuin.

When G went over to rig up a lighting system off Ronald's generator as promised, both Ronald and he pressed me to go, if only for the boat ride. I was finally persuaded by the lure of some freshly caught turtles to photograph. Also, in view of the way G and I were so warm together now, and he was so genuinely proud of me, it would have seemed absurdly petty to have insisted that I stay behind on what was to be the occasion of the last visit to Badu before the end of the Tuin year. The news that Tuin man had Tuinlady with him flew up quickly from the Badu village beach, first to the ladies of Ronald's house and then to the large complex of the Chairman's settlement.

Having nothing more presentable to wear, I was in my usual in-front-of-others uniform of half shirt and frayed knickers. The first woman to find me on the beach, Ronald's daughter, immediately gave me a huge Mother Hubbard–style dress to wear. She took me to where G and Ronald were having a cigarette at the table outside Ronald's house and within a few minutes a message came from Crossfield inviting us to eat with him. A large following of curious children accompanied us as we made our way to "Centre Village," where the Chairman lived. The main reason for this invitation was that it provided Crossfield with an opportunity to issue another, much more important and formal invitation. He asked us to attend an official Tombstone Opening Ceremony in about two weeks' time. He would send word to Tuin of the exact date, and a boat to fetch us. G said the latter arrangement would not be necessary, as we had Philamon Nona's little dinghy and the 6 h.p., which was waiting in Ronald's shed to be taken back to Tuin today.

"Huh," said the Chairman expansively. "Might by and by I give yous one dinghy more better. Yous guest belong me now."

I remembered Crossfield's face from the first time we had met so many months ago on our way out to Tuin. He was a handsome man, lighter-skinned than the average Torres Strait Islander, having Malayan blood in him on one side of the family. He had a delightfully forthright way of expressing himself.

"Well, hello, Meesus Governor of Tuin, I been meet you 'usban', Governor of Tuin, befo'. I think I don't know you prom befo', nother time you been proper white lady. Now you come like Island woman. You been try Island tucker? I think you go try onetime."

One of the things that most endeared the Islanders to us was the way we sat down and shared their food without the slightest hesitation. We did not fully appreciate this at the time, as it seemed the obvious thing to do. Crossfield did not join us at table, but sat to one side, a gigantic mug of tea before him. There was enough food on the table for a dozen people, but until G and I had consumed one plateful of turtle each, nobody else sat down. Then eight or nine young men joined us. Women handed them mugs of tea and stood by fanning the flies off the table. A serious-faced child seemed to have been given the exclusive detail of swiping any flies that hovered near my face or neck. Several times during the meal I felt her small hand timidly stroking my hair, but when I turned round and smiled, she fled.

"Hah hah, she fright prom Tuin Markai, get away you mongrol!" Crossfield made mock fierce lunges at the child and stirred the air wearily with his hands. "Them kids! I got plenty kids, these all sons belong me"—he gestured at the silent eaters—"when you come Tombstone Opening you see all Ahmat pamily. They go come prom everyway; T.I. [Thursday Island], Mabuaig, Down South, and yous come prom Tuin."

I was so unaccustomed to talking and mixing among numbers of people that I did not take in a great deal on this brief visit to Badu. After lunch G showed me Red Rose, the tractor, which was waiting for spare parts, and then he went to finish the wiring in Ronald's house before we made our way back to Tuin. I was settled at the porch table under a tree with a soccer magazine and a large group of children. Ronald gave me some melon seeds to plant now that the ground had been refreshed by the first Big Rain. Before we said goodbye to him I tentatively enquired if he knew of anyone on Badu who would be willing to tell me stories of the Beforetime. If, as it seemed, our lives were now entwined with the Baduleegas, I wanted to do more than read soccer magazines while on their home ground.

Back on Tuin it seemed only a few days before news of the day on which the Tombstone Opening was to begin reached us. The thought of being away from Tuin for the night made me feel strange, but as the time drew nearer we both found ourselves looking forward very much to being included in the traditional festivities. G washed himself from head to foot in shampoo in honour of the occasion and I carefully rinsed out the dress I had been given and washed my hair in the sea, with a final fresh-water rinse. G watched me combing it out, sitting on a rock in the hot sun.

"Cor," he said, "imagine if you had a pair of real silk knickers. What colour would you have?"

"Blue."

"That's done it. Look, Lulu, the Member for Tuin West is standing to address his constituency."

Indeed he was. G was making up for lost time.

We left soon after breakfast on the day of the Tombstone Opening Ceremony as we had been told that festivities were to begin in the early afternoon. Isobel, driven by Jemima, the 6 h.p., was reliable if not fast. She rode the chop and unexpected eddies of current remarkably well for a small dinghy. Philamon put this down to the fact that he had blessed her before sending her over to us.

I had noticed, when washing the billy in the sea that morning, that the air was unusually cool and that although there were no off-putting seas visible out to the west of Wia Island where the journey over the most unsheltered patch of sea began, the surface of the water was fretted by a strangely tight, small pattern of waves. Now, kneeling up in the bow to help G steer safely through the reef-blotched waters by Prize Parrot Rock, I saw around the northern tip of Tuin an apparently endless expanse of very dark sea. Moa Island, generally clearly visible, was totally obliterated by an enormous black cloud.

"Golly," I said. "Sort of thing the heavy drops called prophets fall out of."

"What you on about?"

"That cloud, do you think it could be heading this way?"

"I bloody hope not, I've just done my hair," and he gave a wonderfully affected little wriggle.

As we passed the end of Wia Island we saw that Badu, too, was slowly being enveloped. The tiny chop on the water seemed almost to tremble, as though there were some great pressure beneath it. Then all at once the water stretching ahead of us was dead flat. Never, in river, lake or pond, have I seen such perfect immobility on the surface of deep water. And it was opaque. As the dark clouds released pale rollers of mist which swathed us in on all sides, the solid colour of the water broke, seeming to yield upwards to the lowering atmosphere the finest vapour of milk green particles.

G cut the engine. We could see no land ahead, behind or to either side. The ripples spread by the boat's slight movement seemed huge and loud in the stillness. Then, from the direction of Moa, swelled a crescendo hiss that covered the distance from pianissimo to forte in the space of a second. A myriad arrows of rain hit the water simultaneously and bounced a clear two feet off the surface. Between the sea surface and the dancing hem of the rain shimmered a phosphorescent green mist. We sat stunned for a moment, drenched, awed. Then we began to bail.

It was impossible to make any word understood under the high-pressure hiss of the monsoon downpour, but the obvious thing was to get to land as quickly as possible. Isobel was filling up with alarming speed. I continued to bail while G started the engine again and we nosed our way slowly forward. Although the mist gradually began to clear with the release of rain, land could only be glimpsed in the wink of an eye as the rain poured masks of water over our faces like blind-folds. Somehow, by watching the wake more than anything else, G managed to maintain a steady course until we were running parallel with the coast of Badu. We caught a split-second vision of the rough stick fence in the sea which used to be part of a corral in the days when a turtle farm had been started on Badu. Using this as a guide, we moved in closer until we reached the place called by the Islanders "Dogai," after a female spirit creature with great long ears down to her feet who lay in wait to suck the virility from desirable young men. We dared not attempt to follow the coastline any further, so here it was that we left the ghostly green world of deluge on sea and took like a pair of drowned spectres to the land.

It was not a long walk to the part of the village where the houses began, but before we reached it the weather had undergone a trans-formation. As the cloud trundled off the western hills of Badu and presumably on to create further green wonders on the way to Papua New Guinea, a bright wet yellow sun winked at us from all the troughs and puddles on the Badu sand track. On either side sun-bleached veg-etation dripped and glistening runnels of rainwater spilled from leaves still furled from drought. As we approached the shuttered houses a cry went up and passed from one to the other until we came to Ronald's house, where we found the doors already open to welcome us.

The majority of the Islanders' houses were built on stilts, either of wood or, in the case of the more modern ones, of concrete. Although some had been shored up with traditional arrangements of mangrove poles, they were all basically made of sheets of corrugated iron, with hardboard in the interior to divide the rooms. We learned early on that it was not the custom to invite visitors indoors straight away. We had been exceptionally honoured at the Chairman's lunch. However, Ronald, as already mentioned, was something of an exception himself to traditional Islander ways. He greeted us now from the top of the rickety plank steps leading into his house. At home the Islanders very seldom wore trousers, feeling more comfortable in the traditional lava-lava, or calico. This was only worn by the men and consisted of a broad length of heavy cotton, in a single colour, folded over and wrapped around the waist like a skirt. It was tucked over in a special way at the front, forming a neat flounce to show off the hem of crochet stitched onto the edge. Ronald favoured shocking pink as the background colour. A bright blue one was produced for G to change into out of his sodden corduroys. It was some time before he mastered the art of the frontal tuck and I had to keep warning him about the obtrusive evidence of the Member for Tuin West. I was given the temporary garb of another bust-around-the-waist Mother Hubbard and told that a ''sulo'' had been set aside for me to wear at the feasting.

As we were officially the Chairman's guests, we were encouraged to show ourselves at his house before G could be distracted by any Baduleegas with engines on their minds. It was clear as we approached Centre Village that preparations for the feasting were in full swing. A long shelter, open the length of the side facing an expanse of cleared ground, had been erected out of sheets of iron contributed from all over the island. Trestles of mangrove logs and hardboard were ranged in a double row all the way up the middle. At one end a bank of earth had been built and sided in with irons. Over the top of this were laid two twenty-foot-long iron pipes under which a continuous line of fire smouldered. Blackened petrol drums serving as large pots were steaming and bubbling on the pipes, and what appeared to be a gigantic fish tail was smoking in solitary state at one end. Large women in Mother Hubbards or shapeless floral frocks prodded and stirred over the fire.

''Woa-o!'' Crossfield's voice rang out to greet us. He was seated, surrounded by a number of his progeny, at a solid drum-and-plank table. His wife, Teliai Ahmat, occupied another. She was proportioned as befits the First Lady of an island people whose criterion for beauty is size. On her broad face was a slightly shy, warm smile of welcome. A group of her senior daughters stood nearby. Crossfield made the formal introductions in English.

''This Teliai, my Meesus, First Lady of Badu. This Lucy, Meesus Deral, First Lady of Tuin. Nows yous sit down an' have cup of tea. And how are you, Mister Deral, Governor of Tuin? By an' by you an' me go fix up them lights for feast. I been buy plenty wiah. I think I go make you work like bruddy nigger, befo' them other buggers catch you por them engine!''

Since G had earned Crossfield's eternal respect by exposing the innards of his beloved Red Rose and explaining by demonstration and in plain terms all that was needed to make her work again, the two men had been on familiar terms.

Soon Crossfield and G went off in the direction of the lean-to which housed the Centre Village generator and I was left to the attentions of the ladies. I took to Teliai straight away, although at first she was very hesitant about trying out her English on me. When she did speak her voice was low and clear and her pronunciation careful. Back on Tuin I used to practise the way she said ''coconut'' simply because it was so attractive. She told me the names of all her children who were present and then began a list of those due to arrive in time for the ceremony which was being held in honour of her father. I lost track of the number of children after fifteen. As we talked a group of young girls who had been watching my every move, edged closer and closer. Among them was the child who had kept the flies off me before. Now she stepped forward proprietorially, touched my still damp hair and announced something to the others.

''She say,'' explained Teliai, ''might yous got long 'air. Dey like make 'im same like Island woman. Them girl been made bath por yous.''

Suddenly she gave a startlingly loud command in her own language and a woman with a limp and even fewer than the average quota of teeth hobbled off to fetch something. Teliai lit another cigarette from the one just finished and seemed to settle deeper into another layer of majestic adipose. A tiny naked boy came squalling into the shelter and refused to be comforted by any of the women who lifted him up. Teliai signalled and he was placed in her arms.

''Sut-up, sut-up nee migi bastard.''

She pinched the run from his nose with her fingers and set him down in the wilderness of her lap, where he lay happily in the shadow of her great bosom.

A shout came across from near the house and I was escorted to my bath by the limping woman and a crowd of children. Halfway across the ground between house and shelter all the little boys in the group were chased back by the older girls. The woman, hiding her face under her arm and giggling nervously, was evidently trying to frame a question. A confident girl of school age spoke for her. They wanted to know if I would take my bath in the bath shed or in the creek. I asked where the ladies usually bathed and was told in the creek during this season. It was clear that Badu had already had considerably more rain than Tuin, for among the brown and bleached grasses a few fresh shoots could be seen, and the short "lawn" under an orchard of mango trees was evenly green. The creek lay beyond the mango trees in an area thick with reeds. A woman was already down there scrubbing clothes on a stone. I suddenly smiled to myself at the irony of having gone for months and months without a fresh-water wash, and now I was going to be bathed twice in one day. My smile provoked nudges and grins among the girls. "Look 'em. 'Em happy."

They talked rapidly among themselves. Then one, a girl of about eight, took me by the hand and led me into the water, still wearing my dress. I was handed a bar of Sunlight soap. Several of the girls came into the water with me. They took off their clothes when submerged up to their chins. I followed suit and there were appreciative squeals. Two little girls dived under water to get a better look at my curious white body and when they came up gave an animated report to the others. The children splashed and played for a while, lustrous droplets beading their wild mops of hair, their taut little bodies lithe as fish. A large black lizard sat calmly in the mud at one end of the pool and looked on like a bored attendant.

Wrapped in a length of cloth—this was my "sulo"—I was taken back through the orchard to a table beneath a single spreading Hammond tree right in the middle of the yard area. Here a dozen eager hands removed the pins and string from my coiled plait and waved the hair, dried in long fluffy crinkles, all round my head. Small fingers combed through the mess, deftly dividing it into uneven sections over top, back and sides. Nineteen plaits were made and each one spat on to make it stick together at the end. My stylists were not happy about the way the plaits hung down, so they looped them over each other and secured them with pins, one or two of which seemed to stick straight into my skull. Then I was shown how to wrap the pale blue silky "sulo" in the traditional manner so that it hung gracefully from armpit to calf, knotted over the bust with folds falling away at the front in petal-like scrolls.

Amadan, the giggling woman who had come with me to the bath, hovered in the background uncertainly waving an old soy sauce bottle filled with a mysterious thick liquid every time she caught my eye.

When the children had finished with my hair she approached and held the bottle under my nose making sexy swooning motions to indicate how delightful it was. It did indeed have a strong, rich, sensual smell: pure coconut oil, reduced and reduced to a sweet heavy lotion. When I willingly consented to having it stroked over my face, neck, back and arms, Amadan went into a rude ecstasy of anticipatory pleasure. "Mmm, mmm," she moaned, lips compressed, hands clasped and body rotating from the hips. "Deral go love you up, love you up," and encouraged by my smiling response, broke into a scream of laughter and kneaded my shoulder with her fist.

Back under the shelter with the Ahmat ladies, having been critically approved, I watched three women struggling to help Teliai cram her feet into a pair of shoes. They were brand-new cream plastic, bought specially from Down South for this big occasion. Sadly, it was an impossible task. Even when the backs of the shoes were beaten down and the sides split, her massive legs, when she tried to balance on them, obliterated each shoe like a tree trunk in an egg-cup. Eventually the effort was abandoned and Teliai attended the ceremony comfortably in her bare feet. Her dress, an elegant tent in pink and purple with elbow-length sleeves each the size of a normal skirt, was not unlike something the Queen Mother would wear to a garden party, although on a considerably grander scale. When Crossfield appeared in a fresh green lava-lava topped by an exuberantly decorative shirt, I made suitable complimentary noises about how well they looked.

"You look your 'usban'," said Crossfield, pointing over to where G was emerging from the bath shed. "He proper Island boy now." G's already slender legs were encased in a slim tube of bright pink, so tightly and modestly closed all down the front that he had difficulty in moving one leg in front of the other. In fact the sugary colour complimented his tan very well, as did the ice-blue striped shirt he wore on top. His hair was carefully parted and combed. He drew nearer very slowly, forced almost to take pigeon steps, hobbled as he was by the skirt. When he saw me with bare shoulders and special hair-do his face broke into a lovely warm grin.

"You look beautiful, Lu," he said as he sat down carefully beside me, and then hissed loudly, "The trouble is they took away my trunks with the trousers and I haven't got any knickers on!"

A wicked little devil got into me. "I have," I boasted, "and they're pink silk."

"Don't say that, Lulu, don't say that. You know what it does to me!"

I giggled and smiled straight into his eyes.

"Look at them two Tuin lovebird," came Crossfield's booming voice, and obediently all eyes were turned on us. Amadan's high mating cry of a laugh rang out from somewhere at the back.

All during the middle part of the day, boatloads of Islanders arrived and strolled up from the beach to greet their relations. Because of the rainstorm earlier, those coming from Thursday Island had been held up and the official beginning of the Ceremony had been delayed. New arrivals settled themselves under the mango trees and along the outer edge of the long shelter. Rows of coconut mats were spread out on the sand at the back and these were gradually covered with layers of small children and babies. Those of their mothers or aunts tired out from a long dinghy ride stretched themselves out and went to sleep calmly amid the increasing din of preparations. I was intrigued by something that was going on in a crowded corner of the mango orchard and politely asked if there was time for me to go and have a look.

"My 'ouse, your 'ouse," said Crossfield grandly. "Go!"

G had sat quietly for a while in his finery, then muttered about some final little jobs he needed to do in connection with the lighting for the evening. As he walked off, surreptitiously loosening his lava-lava, I trotted after him to admonish him in true wifely fashion not to get his clothes covered in oil. He retorted by telling me not to collect any black fingerprints on my pink silks.

Under the mango trees it was pig-slaughtering time. A helpful old man shouted for the swarm of fascinated children to step back so that Tuinlady could have a good view of the killings. He explained that the four large pigs tied up on the ground were not like the little black wild ones they ate on ordinary days, but had been specially kept and fattened for this particular feast. The turtles, he said regretfully, had already been killed and were now cooking under mounds of what I had taken to be randomly heaped earth. These were the traditional "Kapmaurie" ovens of the Islanders, an ancient method of cooking which, unlike some of the customs we were to see later on, survived from well before the arrival of the first missionaries who had "civilised" the Strait Islands. One of the ovens had not yet been covered over and I went to take a closer look. Lying on the hot embers of a well-burnt-down fire lay a great turtle shell filled with roughly chopped meat and clean white coils of intestine.

"That the guz," said Walter Nona, my guide. "Very good."

On top of this natural cooking vessel were heaped banana leaves and more hot embers. A few stones held the leaves in place. Then the whole thing was mounded over with earth and sand and left to cook slowly.

"How long?" I asked naïvely.

"Oh, 'til we's ready for eat 'em, when we's been peenish eat nother ones."

We walked past several ovens which had obviously been cooking their contents for some time. The last oven, larger than the rest, about five feet square, was not covered with earth but had over it instead a thick layer of smoking leaves. Underneath the leaves were long loaves of freshly made damper individually wrapped in carefully woven parcels of palm leaves. A group of ladies sat on a tarpaulin weaving still more casings; a huge man in a slipping lava-lava kneaded the dough, and a child passed on the ready loaves to the wrapping team. Gappy grins cracked out at me from all sides and one excited little boy rolled himself before my feet like a carpet and then squirmed to one side chanting shrilly, "Tuinlady! Tuinlady!"

"That Phoebe," said Walter indulgently, "she don't know if she boy or girl."

A badly crippled young man hovered jerkily on the edge of a lively knot of boys who were busily grating coconuts on long sharpened spikes held in their laps in blocks of wood.

"That Dan, he been look Deral fix up Red Rose."

Dan moved towards us in wobbling, puppet-like spasms. His legs were thin and short, pressed together and bent as though he were in a permanent side-saddle position, his spine was curved so that his buttocks pointed upwards like the bottom loop of a "J." An abnormally long arm shot up and waved about in the air, shining eyes gazed into mine and a large, wet square of mouth struggled to form words. I took the floating hand and shook it in both of mine. He let out a husky sigh of pleasure and managed an "l"-less hello. As shouts from the group he had left called him back, his eyes rolled up in the unmistakable mock exhaustion of a prima donna who is always in demand but really loves it. His part in the proceedings was to hand them the coconuts, which they could perfectly well have picked up for themselves, but Dan was never left out of anything.

An appalling shriek rose above the hubbub, climbing a demented scale like steam escaping from a pressure cooker. It went on and on, increasing in intensity as though the animal being killed gained rather than lost strength with each pint of blood that gushed from its open throat. Walter hurriedly steered me back to my prime viewing position. Pawnee Ahmat, Crossfield's eldest son, a Colossus of a man exuding steamy sexuality from every pore, performed the role of chief slaughterer. From the avid and yet curiously distant expression in his eyes it would have been impossible to tell whether he was making love or committing murder had one not seen his strong hands directing the shrieking creature's blood into a saucepan held by a kneeling woman. Three other men lent their weight to keep the pig still while it died. The words of a white man on Thursday Island jumped into my mind: "Long pig, they used to call human meat, long pig."

Even the children were hushed in the excitement of the killing.

The procession down to the graveyard where the tombstone was to be unveiled was ragged, but its slow pace and silence gave it dignity. G and I, not being allocated any specific position, tagged along behind Crossfield's party. As we passed through the village, more and more people joined until the entire population of the Island, plus all the guests from further afield, were gathered together in a long line six persons wide. In all there were in excess of 300 people.

Teliai had explained to me beforehand what the ceremony was about, for it was to be conducted in Island language. It was a native extension to the Christian tradition of burial. After a person had been buried, his relatives saved up for the whole of the next year to buy him a tombstone. The size and grandeur of the stone would depend on the position held by the individual in the community and the size of his family. Sometimes it took two years to save up for a stone big enough to honour the dead person. Parties would be given on the dates of Christian festivals such as Christmas and Easter, with the theme that the names of the dead should be remembered on every occasion that marked his absence during the first year in the grave. The unveiling of the tombstone was a confirmation that he had finally been laid to rest and all honours had been observed. It coincided with the time in the old beliefs when the person's spirit should have taken its final form and not still be floating around in the shape of a totem beast such as a shark or crocodile.

It was clear that no unnecessary time was wasted on the official part of the ceremony. A few prayers were intoned, solemn faces pulled and a couple of "hymns" were chanted with much whistling and stamping from a semi-blind man with vast wet lips who appeared to be a sort of town crier figure. It was he who brought the graveside meeting to a close and with happy, expansive gestures released the Islanders to get on with what the whole business was really about: celebrating.

On the way back to Centre Village the procession, now moving quickly and chattering gaily, was met by a troupe of costumed figures spread across the dirt road and occupying a large clearing. An old man sat to one side nursing a long drum shaped like a double ended vase and covered with a stretched skin at one end. Women sat on the ground to either side of him with petrol drums and bamboo drumsticks at the ready. The procession fanned out into a standing crowd and the first notes of the ''warup,'' beaten with the palm of the old man's hand, hushed the noisy jostling of the people. After a few moments of the slow, hollow beat, the metal drummers joined in doubling the baseline rhythm of the warup. A tiny woman, with white hair and hands twisted tortuously with some disease, produced an astoundingly loud and vigorous note which seemed to burn straight out from the very depths of all the life that was in her. She was supported physically on either side by two younger women who took up the note and were gradually joined by every Baduleega present, with the exception of those who now began to dance.

They moved towards the crowd in five long lines. At the front were the largest men and those who were most sure of their footwork. Behind came the next most proficient who were followed by a strong line of the younger men. Second from the back were the adolescent boys, mimicking with their lighter bodies the weighty movements of those in front. The back line of dancers consisted of all male children, from efficient, well-practised boys of Alfie's age right down to toddlers so small their lava-lavas were no bigger than handkerchiefs. All the dancers wore swinging skirts over their red lava-lavas made from the pale insides of a particular kind of palm leaf. On their heads were tall, painted masks with the elected symbols of their clans marked like heraldry on a shield. Around their dark ankles were tied white bandages—''maka-mak''—which gave the impression, as their feet lifted in rhythm, that the dancers were all one creature moving like a spirit just above the ground. Some of the leading men held rattles made from the type of bean I had seen on Tuin; these they shook in rhythm with the warup.

I learned that the dances, although all based on a known series of traditional movements, were individually choreographed by the old man with the warup to fit the words of a song. Any Islander could come up to him in the months before an occasion at which there would be dancing and say that he would like a song composed on the theme of a subject close to his heart. For instance, as Ronald explained to me, supposing he missed his daughter Reuben while she was away at school Down South, a song and dance could be made on that theme which would demonstrate the mixed sadness and happiness of missing someone and anticipating their return to the island of their birth. In older times similar songs had been created about families missing their young men who went away for periods of time to take heads on other islands and make trade with the Papuans for canoe wood.

After the men's dance came a performance by the women and girls who all wore royal-blue Mother Hubbards with white piping on the sleeves and hems. But these afternoon dances were only a prelude to the "big dancing" which would follow later. They were merely an underscoring of the fact that the festivities had begun. Once started, the drumming of the warup did not stop for three days and three nights. The instant the old dance leader let up his beat it was taken up by someone else. Gradually it became impossible to imagine life on Badu without the continual presence of the drumming, swollen sometimes by the click of split bamboo "palgas," stamping, singing or dancing, but always there in its most basic form, the steady, commanding heartbeat of the warup. Although it was there illegally, hidden away behind bushes and iron screens, alcohol was unnecessary; the Islanders had the age-old intoxicant of mass race rhythm on tap and flowing stronger than any wine.

There was one more formality to go through before the people took the reins of their celebration entirely into their own hands. This was the speech-giving prior to the disinterring of the first food. Back at Crossfield's place the entire company assembled around the area of the long shelter. First spoke Joey Nona, a Badu Island Council representative. His speech was entirely in Island language. Then the floor was yielded to Crossfield, who spoke to his people with the confidence of a popular elected chief and then, right at the end, broke hesitantly into English, though still in a ringing tone that reached to the furthest ears in the assembly.

"Here we are, all Island people prom par place, our pamily an' priends. Prom T.I., prom Down South, my pamily prom Mabuaig an' them two prom Tuin. We all Island people por celebrate here togedder. O.K."

G and I were tremendously touched that we should be included in this speech, coming as we did from another world and engaged upon a project incomprehensible to the Islanders. It also served as a mass introduction to those of the crowd able to see us, who from then on greeted us as Deral and Tuinlady without any bashfulness. As our acquaintance with them lengthened I was called Lucy to my face but always referred to in Island language as Tuinlady. As I gradually began to pick up a few words I was flattered to hear myself spoken of as "capu caz," a complimentary term for a good person. When, much later, I tried to explain that although I loved the islands I missed my homeland, too, and would be leaving when the year was over, they smiled and assured me that I would be back, for I had been seen to eat the wongai, and those who eat of the wongai will always return to the Strait.

Official speeches over, the town crier, whose name was Yopele, spread his great arms wide as though to embrace every person present, and raising rheumy old eyes above the heads of the crowd, called down a blessing from the Christian God and then exhorted the people to begin eating. This seemed to be a well-known joke; when the people did not immediately rush at the food Yopele stamped and yelled, half in "Yarca," which was the only name he would give me for the Western Island language, and half in English, "Come on, don' be shy, pill you belly here, pill plate two tree time! Ayey wal!"

All at once everyone was doing just what he said.

Wheelbarrows full of steaming turtle meat were brought over from the Kapmaurie ovens; great dishes of boiled and roasted dugong were spread the length of the trestles between mountains of rice, sweet potatoes and yams cooked with coconut; two- and three-inch-thick slices of roast pig were piled on to the plates alongside heaps of orange pumpkin and coiled lengths of gut. Small dishes of raw chillies were placed by each mound of rice to encourage people to eat more. When I went forward in the press, helpful hands reached out on all sides and filled our plates with what is considered to be the finest part of the dugong, the fat. We watched the Badu dogs having a field day as the children, drunk on the plenty, tossed away the steaks of despised meat and concentrated on chewing the blubber. There were knives and forks on the tables but few people took any notice of them. When people went back for second and third platefuls they heaped up beside their meat squares of spongecake rolled in cocoa powder and coconut. Other sweet dishes were custard and sago made with reconstituted dried milk. There was tinned fruit too, but I made a beeline for fresh watermelon, commenting en passant to a gigantic woman who was also helping herself that on our island there was not yet enough water for growing things, my melon seeds were only just in.

"Wa," she said, echoing Titom's words, "small island funnykind place."

Heavy evidence of impending rain did nothing to spoil the feasting. Thunder ("duyoum") and lightning ("panipan") were greeted with expressions of approval. The Wet was late this year; let it rain, it would not stop the dancing. As darkness came on, the devastated tables were pushed back and people relaxed on benches or sprawled contentedly in the sand. Bodies of tiny children were everywhere underfoot, some so full-bellied they were snoring already. Remarkably, nobody seemed to get crushed. Somehow the dancers had got themselves into their regalia. There was a roar of pleasure as G's lighting system snapped on with the judder of the generator, which was now drowned out by the drums and singing. Teliai stood up and led the women in a magnificent dance clearly about the sea. Lines of blue-clad swaying women undulated back and forth holding semi-circular blue "seeks" in front of them, decorated with downy white heron feathers which when waved in harmony looked like white spume on waves. A "pussycat" dance followed with amusing black and white cat masks thrusting forwards in the shadowy dance area and turning to face one another in fierce mock combat. But of them all, perhaps the bow and arrow dance was the most exciting. A large number of men took part in this, and each one had a great bow taller than himself and a single, brightly painted arrow. The smallest boys had their "bunera" and "tiak" scaled down to size. In this dance the sound of the arrows being shot was used to great effect against the basic rhythm of the drums. The arrows were not actually released or the majority of the audience would have been slain.

If the Islanders had seemed vague about time before, we were now to learn that during a period of celebration it ceases to exist as a notion altogether. Singing and dancing carried on all day and all night. When one lot of performers dropped with exhaustion they were cleared away and others took their place. At some point, after the rain had started, G and I, accustomed to bedding down as soon as the sun left the sky, began vaguely to wonder where we were supposed to sleep, or if we were supposed to sleep at all. Eventually one of Crossfield's daughters took us to the mango orchard where a tent had been pitched for our use. Its erection had evidently baffled whoever had tried to set it up and it took some adjustment in the pouring wet before it was ready to enter. By that time both of us would have been happy to lay our heads down anywhere, which was lucky, as the tent proved 100 per cent non-waterproof and one has to be fairly tired to sleep in the middle of a monsoon on a strange island with non-stop native singing competing with the rain.

Amazingly, perhaps because so full of food and impressions, we did manage to get some sleep. When we awoke in the morning the rain had stopped but we might as well have slept outside. The tent had caved in totally on one side and the bottom of it was a pool of water, the deepest parts of which were the two troughs in which we were lying. Stiff and groaning, like, as G aptly put it, ''a couple of geriatrics,'' we crawled out to gaze upon the aqueous vision of Badu in the Wet.

Over by the long shelter a seemingly indefatigable woman was performing a solo dance to the beat of the warup. Her sodden dress clung to her great shuddering body, and her eyes were closed as she softly mouthed the words of a song. Across the yard area ran fast-moving streams of water, forded in places by heaps of palm leaves. The kitchen end of the shelter, towards which G and I made our dripping and inelegant way, was ankle-deep in mud-blackened water. Amadan was paddling about, heating up breakfast for the hundred or so souls who had spent the night in the environs of Centre Village. A great bubble of strong-smelling fat popped with the sound of a fart off a massive piece of dugong roasting over the fire.

''Control yourself, Lu,'' said G, and I aimed a smack at his wet backside.

''Ah,'' he said, stopping before a mountainous black form which blocked the way to the only dry seat not occupied by a snoring body, ''I've been meaning to introduce you, Lu; this is Yaya, he helped me with Crossfield's tractor.''

Yaya's huge round head, spiked on top like a mine with corkscrews of stiff hair, lolled sensuously in a puddle. His fat dark lips, pushed outwards in sleep, kissed the mud in innocent obscenity. Amadan, a filthy dishcloth stuffed against her giggling mouth, made rude prodding movements at his belly with her foot. When he stirred she leapt back behind a table, but she need not have worried; it was some time before young Yaya was fully compos mentis. He had celebrated last night with a bottle of methylated spirits flavoured with green cake-colouring essence, the same mixture used by Island women when they wanted a break from childbearing.

Gradually, as G and I sat sipping a welcome mug of tea, the bodies about us began to stir. Pawnee's pretty wife, Lily, extricated herself from her sleeping brood and loudly hawked up a gob of phlegm before emptying her nose on the hem of her dress. As she waded past us through the mud and children she gave a lovely sleepy grin. Pawnee himself appeared from another direction looking temporarily satiated. He patted Lily's bottom absently as he passed by yawning and she jabbed him crossly in the nostril. Amadan did a wicked pantomime of double adultery behind their backs for my benefit. Tousled children, their wide-open eyes still dreamy from sleep, picked themselves up dragging their smaller brothers and sisters towards the trestles for morning food and bottom wiping. My small companions from yesterday's bath smiled blearily at me.

The all-night dancer was by now on her knees, but her body still moved to the sound of the drum. As the man beside the warup beater woke up, his hands found the two sticks he used on the petrol drum and he began immediately to play. A small boy dragging a full rag that had been used as a diaper bent his knees in the dance position and waved his fist as though shaking a kulap: At once a woman sat up and began to sing, and the words and rhythm were picked up throughout the length of the shelter. The feasting began all over again as though never broken by a comma before dawn.

There is a tale in every encounter, the story of a man's life behind every phrase he utters, the history of a race in the actions of a child. On Badu island, marooned by the nor'westerlies which suddenly blew up and in cacophonous concert with the rain made any attempt to cross back to Tuin temporarily unthinkable, G and I met many people and heard many tales. We learned of the strong belief in "pourri-pourri," the mysterious dark force which, commanded by certain men, had the power to kill. A young man viciously strangled by the rope attached to a harpoon sunk deep in a struggling dugong's shoulder was not the victim of an accident; he had refused to touch palms with the pourri-pourri man the day before. The birds that flew low over the houses screaming at night were not birds at all, but angry devils with wings. A man had been banished from the island as a sorcerer because he was found bending over with his face to the earth and flames shooting out of his anus. My irreverent suggestion that this was because he had eaten too much wongai fruit caused shrieks of ill-stifled laughter, but the belief was nonetheless real and founded in a culture that, although superficially obliterated by the "Coming of The Light" in 1871, had never been entirely crushed.

At first I was treated rather carefully by the Baduleegas who had not been to Tuin, and until the penny dropped that I was "Tuinlady belong Deral" a number of them automatically called me Sister, assuming that I was either a nurse or something to do with the Church. Yopele, the town-crier character, who was old and had very interesting stories to tell, was hard to convince that because I came from England, home of the original London Missionary Society, I was not necessarily a special emissary from the Lord. Attempts to get him to open out on the subject of the Beforetime were often interrupted by one of his wailing speeches about the love of God and the goodness of the white man. In the same breath he told me that as a young boy he had been jailed for being seen on the same path as a white woman. One day I struck a bargain with him: if he told me a true story of the Beforetime, I would tell him a true story about the British Beforetime, before the present Missus Quin. Unfortunately he was so enthralled by my detailed account of the marital history of Henry VIII that he rushed over his part of the bargain and proceeded to translate my story into "Yarca." However, he did tell me that Ol' Doroky, a relation of his, had been the first man to witness a baptism on Mabuaig and had brought the custom himself to Badu, with the refinement that the baptised individual had to fight as hard as he could while under the water, and the "Priest" had to be sure to hold him down until there was no more resistance. He also informed me, with embarrassment, that the last person known to be eaten was "Tamate," who had suffered the ignominious end of being cooked with sago on the shores of Goaribari Island at the beginning of the twentieth century. I was later to find out that "Tamate" had been one Reverend Chalmers. Immediately after telling me this he asked what had become of "that nother ones" on Tuin. I assumed he meant the girl photographer who had come across with us in the dinghy all those months ago. It struck me then that a number of Islanders had called the mysterious words after me as I walked past their houses: "Wish way that nother womans?"

I had always assumed they were making a mischievous allusion to feminine glances cast in G's direction, but now I had the real explanation. Because no boat had been sent to fetch our young photographer it had been assumed that she had either perished or been disposed of in some way . . . Old Yopele shouted with relieved laughter when I told him that the chopper had picked her up safely on the very first day.

I was to discover that the Islanders' long-abandoned habit of cannibalism, far from being the gruesome screaming-figure-in-a-cauldron business one tends to imagine, was a highly ritualised and in many cases respectful custom. Usually only the meat from the brow area of brave young men was consumed, in the belief that their strength and admirable qualities would pass into the eater. The dried hands and feet of deceased loved ones would be carried around the neck of the bereaved, and in certain cases the skull would be carefully cleaned and then built up with moulded cheeks of wax and used as a divining object. It was not the sort of thing one hears of happening in back kitchens during civilised wars. I had learned by now that need creates a situation of potential savagery in an individual, but it takes the savagery of refined civilisation to create need among thousands.

The sodden night in the tent had not been fun. Because it was known that on Tuin we slept in a tent at all times, and had even moved the tent into our house, it had been assumed that we would not be happy with any other form of accommodation. Once this misunderstanding had been cleared up, we found ourselves in a position of considerably greater comfort. We were given a room in Crossfield's house with a double mattress and all children who laid claim to the floor space during the day were regularly removed before we went to bed, although they had a clear view of all interesting activities through a window in the hardboard dividing wall. There were nits in the pillows and small biting things around after dark, but the luxury of a thin mattress more than made up for the discomfort caused by these. G, with his still bony spine, was in seventh heaven on the mattress. I, who had not suffered so badly from the hardness of the bed on Tuin, found it difficult to get used to the sounds of other human beings around again. Sometimes, when he was asleep, I used to wave to the rows of little faces peering in at the window. Yaya was banned from the house on account of the unbearable racket of his snores, which could be heard shaking the table in the mango orchard at least a hundred yards away. Crossfield slept on the floor outside our room with a score of children and grandchildren, and Teliai alternated between a bed in the house and her daytime table over in the long shelter.

With each day that passed G was becoming more and more of an asset to the Islanders. A tiny woman, reluctantly respected despite the smallness of her body, sent word that her son had bought her a modern fan Down South to ease the last days of her dying husband and she had no electricity to operate it. We went up to her house every day for nearly a week and by the end of that time G had made her a generator from all sorts of odds and ends lying around the island. Her gratitude was pathetic, and over a month later, when her husband died, she sent a special message immediately to ask ''them two on Tuin'' to pass the statutory hours beside the body with her. The old man, who had been Chairman of Badu for twenty-three years before a stonefish sting confined him to his bed, used to sit and listen with a gentle smile of pure pleasure when I told him how much the Badu people had helped us. He had a large number of children, amongst whom were two teenaged daughters, both very sexy in totally different ways. When he spoke of them he raised both his twisted hands in a gesture that expressed all the older generation's bewilderment at the ways of the young. Peena, the older one, resembled her mother in that she was unusually slim and would have been pretty had her front teeth not been missing. Her proudest possession was a large cassette player on which she played only one song: ''If I Said You Had a Beautiful Body, Would You Hold It Against Me?'' Once when G and I were there she played it thirty-two times, lovingly stroking the machine from which the sound came. The younger girl, Olita, generous-bodied to a fault, would wander around wearing nothing but a lacy-edged nylon half-slip resting just above her nipples and just below her knickers. She had huge, warm, indolent eyes and a smile that was ten shades bluer than shy. It was probably just as well that dear old father Nona was virtually blind.

I was tremendously proud of G's success with the engines, and during the weeks we were stuck on Badu I saw how easily he could make a future for himself there. All over the island stood proofs of his dedication and ability. Red Rose was working beautifully now and at night strings of lights from Centre Village down to Dogai were the marks of his success with generators. After all the urgent jobs were done, he would spend the days in Crossfield's garage poking around in all the corners until he came upon a part he could match up with something else and create one working engine. Crossfield was most impressed and spent many hours watching and helping. Yaya was G's constant companion and soon confided in him all his personal problems. He was desperate for a girl, but as none of the Badu women would go near him because of his terrible snores and gross body, he had to make do with little boys occasionally and the trouble was they sometimes wanted more than a can of Coca-Cola and Uncle Crossfield would not give him any more money. He had a secret mirror and a three-toothed comb hung up in a corner and he would spend hours gazing sadly at his vast, bloated image, prodding vainly at his hair.

Most of my time was either spent sitting on a petrol drum with G in the garage and handing him wrenchs, or under the Hammond tree with the ladies. Although nobody prevented me from going off alone to visit Ronald, Yopele and the No Mores, I was aware that this independence was considered eccentric. Inevitably, after the novelty of observing and sharing in the Islanders' way of life wore off, the restrictions for me of life on Badu began to make themselves felt. Coupled with this was a growing awareness that as the mild spells between the winds and rain grew longer and longer, had G really wanted to get back to Tuin as much as I did, we could have gone.

There was much vague talk about the future at this time. Crossfield was very enthusiastic about the idea of G starting a mechanics school for young Islanders and used to say, "When yous peenish on Tuin, write that book an' all that thing, yous come over live here Badu. That time we make them buggers pay por yous fix engine. No more tucker, only dollar!"

It was a possibility that G considered very seriously and when, lying together at night on our urine-scented mattress, he used to speak, full of warmth and optimism, about the life we could make here together, it would have been so easy to fall in with the waves of his enthusiasm and see myself not as the Lucy I used to know, the determined woman who would see a thing through from start to finish whatever, but as everyone saw me here, "ipeca belong Deral," Deral's woman, and as G wanted me to be.

In my miserable confusion and guilt—for was I not once again in a position to be the only thing marring G's happiness?—I almost caught myself giving in, accepting the slow, well-fed life as a mechanic's wife on Badu as my lot. I had lost sight of the notion that I had any personal abilities, any character, or strength of mind. Intellect was useless to me; it saw my yearning towards Tuin as illogical, lacking in sensible reason, even mad. It saw what it was told. But my heart and body had a louder voice, and because in them was a power I could still relate to, still recognise as being essentially me, I followed what they commanded me to do.

Every day my feet took me down to the sea shore, where I stood gazing out over the grey waves, straining to catch a glimpse of Tuin. I always checked to see that Isobel was ready should the wind suddenly die down. But there were days when there was no wind at all and I was well aware that if I proposed our departure to G he would offer some viable reason for procrastination. I did not want to hear it so I did not ask. I merely continued weakly to pine. It was understandable why G was reluctant to face going back to the island; there lay ahead for him the task of settling down in our rough shelter and starting on the book that was to tell the story of the island year, and there were only a few months of that year left. What was going to happen to us then?

In a secret corner of his heart where he did not often care to look, I believe G always knew that for all our loving, to me our marriage, as it had been in the beginning, was only for the sake of the project. He knew that when the year was over I would leave him and that is why he had to look to his future. But it was something he did not want to believe, and in all justice I must confess I found it hard to keep telling him to his face. In the same way as he clung on to the hope that there was a future for us as a couple beyond Tuin, I still believed, equally blindly, that G was going to go back and write his book. But beliefs aside, for there was no analysis of reasons for doing or wanting things at the time, as I stood beside Isobel, every pulse in my body singing a hymn of homesickness to Tuin, I knew that somehow I must get him back, and soon.

Lacking in confidence and full of nervous uncertainties as I was, my initial efforts at steering G back to the island were feeble in the extreme. He was right when he said that the main part of the "survival" was over, but I was not so certain when he assured me that the book would write itself. Appeals to the principle of sticking-to-what-one-sets-out-to-do having little effect—and it is true that Tuin had given the finger to most principles—I resorted to the age-old feminine device of restricting my favours. The "cure," so to speak, was always just over the hill, or rather, just over the sea, on Tuin. It was hardly a subtle ploy and it made neither of us feel good, but gradually it did begin to start having the desired effect, at least in promises that we would go soon. But still the days of sitting in the garage continued, so I made every effort to break the routine and do something more in my line.

I took my solitary resolution into the Badu bush. So long as I was stuck there, I wanted to keep as closely as possible in touch with the things that made me feel and gave me strength. At first these sorties were conducted on a semi-official basis, Crossfield providing me with one of his sons-in-law, Albert, as a guide. With him I would go off before dawn, ostensibly to take photographs, glorying in the sharp scents of the lush interior thrown up by the heavy night rain. Albert was a good guide and a pleasant companion, but still I longed to be quite alone, to throw off my clothes and bathe freely in the tonic of lawless air. Little did I know that I was stirring up a situation which was to make our departure from Badu even more pressing.

One afternoon, when there was barely any wind and the sun had been drying the spongy ground all day, I went into the bush alone. I followed the deep stream which supplied the village with water, far into the Badu interior and away from the pig hunters' tracks. Teliai had given me a bright length of cloth after the feasting which I had made into a simple wrap-around dress. I was wearing this now and it felt hot and unnecessary. Slowly as I moved forward I unwound it, and it was as though the fertile heat of the damp ground rose up through my unhampered limbs like sap. My heart quickened with the joy of that naked freedom in solitude which is at once so rich and so empty. I found a flat rock beside the stream that had widened out here to a calm brown glistening river. Lying down, I closed my eyes and let the sun work its cleansing wonders. Faithful and ardent, it closed on me and took my mind. I heard the sound of a snake rustling the grasses nearby, but feeling so serene and still, I did not bother to look. However, when the snake took a quiet step forward, I opened my eyes.

The boy's pupils were dilated so that his shining eyes, reflections of the dark river, seemed almost black. His lips were folded inwards to control his fast breathing, for he had been running. There was sweat at the edges of his hair. His eyes, swimming with intensity, were fixed on my face. Neither of us blinked. It was very quiet.

At last my arm moved slowly to find the bright wrap. I pulled it across my body and sat up. At the same time he hunkered down with his weight resting on his calves, face towards the ground so that I could only see the top of his woolly head.

"Albert, you have been running," I said lightly.

"Wa, yes. I like it, running." He ran a hand down his bent face from brow to chin, as though to wash it. Then he sprang up and adopted a relaxed pose. "I feel hot now. I like to swim."

"Where do you swim?"

"I show you. Come." He turned away and began walking at once. I followed, tying the wrap as I went.

The part of the river he took me to was broad and deep. A shallow waterfall ran across it, tumbling fast white water down smoothly worn rocks. Above the fall was a long stretch of slow-flowing river overhung with pale tee trees whose graceful, leaning branches were perfectly echoed in the mirror clear water. Below, there was a wide round pool, upon which floated a sprinkling of shining bubbles, escaped from the turmoil of the fall.

"Not that one," he said, pointing to the lower pool. "Might be croc there."

Kicking off his black undershorts, he dived in above the waterfall. Brown ripples lapped the bank and splashed up against the root of a tree. His head appeared on the other side, the invisible oil in his hair chasing off glittering droplets in chains.

"Swim!" he called. "Swim!"

I stepped across the few dry rocks at the top of the waterfall, and as though drawn irresistibly down, allowed my body to fall into the water. Pushing away from where the stream pulled towards the edge of the fall, I lay on my back, the folds of my wrap drifting before me. It was like floating in liquid satin, feeling the caressive resistance of the water whispering at my bare back.

With a splash Albert's head appeared at my side. "Take your dress off."

"No." Unrelaxed, my legs sank down and I trod water, facing him.

"Take it off. I won't do it to you."

The dress was already half dragged off by my paddling legs. I turned away, and keeping my body under the water, unwound it and hooked it over a branch. Albert disappeared and a few moments later I felt his arms clasping me around the waist from behind. Slowly I turned round, my hands gently pressing his shoulders away. His hands were grasping my hips, pushing my upper body out of the water so that his upturned face was below me.

"Are you frighten'?"

"No."

One of my thumbs was in the dip of his collarbone. I shook my head, aware, as from a distance, that I was speaking the truth.

"No," I said again, and it was telling him no to everything.

"Please."

"No, let me go. Let us swim."

His eyes were rich with his plea but he let me go, first quickly imprinting a child's kiss to one side of my mouth. He dived and stayed under the water for a long time and then swam upstream once strongly and back again. I got out and retrieved my wet dress.

On the way back he was mostly silent, contemplative. Once he said, "What if I rape you?"

"Everybody would know, because you would have scars."

He smiled slightly at this. "I don't mean that thing, only I feel little bit wild. What time yous going to Englan'?"

"After May."

"Deral go with you?"

"No."

"I like go Englan'."

As we drew near the settlement he became agitated and begged me not to tell G or any of his family what had happened. I told him I would not, but he must not follow me again.

It would have been idiotic to have gone alone into the bush again after that, for I knew the boy was watching me, and despite what had been said it would almost have seemed like an invitation. However, on a few mornings, when I was sure that he was safely occupied elsewhere, I could not resist going back to the pool again, but when he found this out, listening to chat at mealtimes and glancing at my damp hair, he looked at me with great reproach. He was incapable of hiding his feelings and it was not long before the situation became intolerable. He sought to catch me alone at every opportunity, telling me in urgent whispers that he loved me. He knew that I was interested in books for he had overheard me asking Crossfield if he had any, so he brought me cartoon comic books from the school, using them as a pretext to come into the bedroom when he knew I was alone. When he began to hang around at night waiting for me to go out to pee, I told him this would have to stop or I would be forced to tell G, who would no doubt complain to Crossfield. It did not stop, and I did have to tell G, who told me to tell the boy to fuck off, and not be so stupid as to go wandering off on my own.

So from that time on I was more than ever riveted to G's side, and the longing to get back to Tuin grew in me like a pain.

PHASE IV

Getting Away Again

AUSTRALIAN BLACK-AND-WHITE PELICANS

12

CIRCLES

As far as G was concerned, my insistence on going back to the island was a pain. A pain in the arse.

"You and that fucking island," he grumbled. "I don't know why I put up with it, really I don't."

But as we ploughed through the sparkling waves, rolling and bouncing madly in our over-loaded little craft past Wia Island and Snapper Rock, all the dear familiar places, some of my joy at homecoming transferred itself to him. Ronnie No More had presented him with an illegal six-pack of beer for fixing a kerosene freezer; this he now broke open and knocked the caps off a couple of bottles on the side of the boat. We took swigs in the downward heaves of the waves so as not to get our teeth knocked out. Having been so long without it, both of us were highly susceptible to the smallest amount of alcohol. It made us very hilarious, and what with the sun, the sleazy roll of the boat and G looking so utterly himself, reprobate and dear, any lurking inhibitions I might have had were released, and I gave a performance in the bow of the boat which ensured that our first day and night back on Tuin were spent in a horizontal—or mostly horizontal—position. And in my pleasure and gratitude at being safely brought back to where I wanted to be, I relished our touches, and my eyes, as G sought them, were not veiled with the foreknowledge of pain and guilt which had so often left me feeling beached and lonely when it was over before. If I was aware that the finer the feeling, the higher the price to be paid in the end, I refused to consider it then. My guile on Badu had oppressed me, the feeling was "to hell with caution now" and when he was in buoyant mood G had the same attitude. Whatever lay ahead, we would make the best of the time we had left on the island together.

It was several days before I ventured to re-enter what was for me the real Tuinworld, for the various accoutrements of civilisation we had acquired on Badu had to be organised, and places made for them in our home. Afraid that back on our small island we might revert once more to the skeletal and primitive state in which we had been discovered before the Wet, the Baduleegas had made sure that we were well stocked up before leaving their shores. Gone now were any feelings that we "should not" have anything like a tin of beans on the island; such judgements were anachronisms. The most basic survival commodity for a castaway is adaptability; he must be prepared to accept positive changes in his circumstances as well as negative, and generally keep up with the times.

The mod. con. which was to alter domestic life in the shelter most profoundly was a kerosene ring. This had been a gift from the wife of crippled father Nona. It was extremely rusty and possibly more of antique value than useful in the kitchen. However, with a great deal of pricking and shaking it could be persuaded to function, although I never found it as reliable as a fire. Another gift was a brand-new kettle, which thoughtlessly I thrust straight onto the fire, treating it as a fancy billycan. Shuddering inwardly at the suburban symbolism, I unearthed the old packet of Brillo pads we had been given before and dutifully scrubbed off all the black. I had forgotten how life with possessions could be so complicated. Arranging all our bits and pieces on the shelves G had made was an exciting new game for me; having a permanent corner for tea, dried milk and sugar felt like the last word in civilised living, and when I found among the Baduleegas' gifts of provisions some small jars of preserved cheese, we ate the contents quickly so that I could line up the jars on the shelf as glasses. Drinking water out of a glass felt wonderfully posh.

Domestic articles were not the only things to be unpacked from Isobel. There was the shell of a 40 h.p. Johnson outboard and a box full of rusty parts which might or might not belong to it. There were also various parts to go with Dolores, the 20 h.p. fated to go on a journey to the bottom of the sea, and several rice bags full of jumbled nuts, bolts and sockets which eventually would find themselves neatly sorted into milk tins. The idea was that between writing paragraphs of his book, G might occasionally divert himself by tinkering with these engines. There were also some musty-smelling tattered manuals which could serve as sedentary diversion when the weather prohibited practical mechanics.

We had returned to Tuin towards the end of what we were later told was one of the latest and shortest Wet seasons in years. We were fortunate not to have landed one year later than we did, for there would have been no water to greet us at all. However, the monsoon rains which had fallen, and continued to drench the ground at night, had wrought a number of changes on the face of Tuin.

Diary

Home again! and to a whole new world of smells, touches and sounds. And visions! The first thing I ran to see when we got back was how my watermelons were coming along. There is so much new green grass and undergrowth that it took some time to find them. The vines have wandered higgledy-piggledy in all directions and some have been swamped and drowned, but those which have climbed away from the creek in the direction of the woodpile are flourishing and there are three healthy-looking melons already and some others just starting. Barren little Tuin is not so barren, after all.

The second thing I saw, as I went to fill up my new kettle at the drum, was a dead gecko floating belly up on the surface. This would have been very bad news before the rains came, as his poor little bloated body has probably polluted the whole drum, but now there is so much water around we can sling this out or use it for washing. G found a pile of old rags in Crossfield's garage and he has brought some back for wiping engines, but one or two will do to soften the floor of the tent and improve our pillows. G hates the hard floor after the mattress on Badu. I put on so much weight with dugong fat and damper I don't need any external padding.

Poo Poo came back the second evening after we were back. He has a mate now, a shocked, mousy-looking little thing who never says a word. Poo Poo makes his Poo Poo noises every evening before the rain begins.

It baffles me where the frogs in the creek come from. Where did they hide during all that time of drought? G called my attention to a new arrival the other day, a small black bird which hovers vertical in the air, wings beating too fast to see, and catches insects as they swarm. There is a new kind of snake, too; a bright green whipsnake that perfectly matches the new grass. They are not reputed to be poisonous. But the red-backed spiders are, and they are all over our house. There are so many that a wholesale extermination policy would be impracticable, so we have decided simply to leave them alone. They seem to respect us as much as we respect them.

I had a nasty shock a couple of nights back when I rolled over onto something hard and prickly in the tent and thought I had discovered some horrible new insect. It seemed to have a large slimy body and two sharp horns at the front. G was outside having a pee when he heard my yell. He came rushing in to find me crouched in a ball at the back of the tent and gibbering at the thing on the floor. To my astonishment he picked it up and put it in his mouth. It was his two front teeth. I found it very touching that he had bothered to hide them from me all this time, as if that sort of thing were of any importance. But I was not insensitive to the fact that it was obviously something rather private and personal to him, so for once I did not burst out laughing, at least, not until he did. Now that he knows I know about his teeth he doesn't bother to put them in any more. I am rather afraid they have got lost in the sand.

Excited as I was with the business of playing housewife and, ironically, a little distanced from Tuin because I felt closer to G, it was not until I went on a long lone trek in search of a rumoured mango tree in the south that I took in the changes properly.

Diary
This morning Wet Tuin touched me properly for the first time. The smell of the mould in the shelter struck me as soon as I went in; the cheesy reek of mildew, musty cloth and damp. But that was somehow an imported smell, to be wiped off with the fluffy green lines of mould that had grown on my damper board, cleared out with the droop of rotting cloth which was once my best shirt, washed away like the termite trails with sluicings of sea water.

Tuin's own wet scent gradually came in on me as does the special tang of a loved body. It made me kneel down in the damp grass and stay still, just to smell. Then the touching. There are flutes of curled grasses filled with water in the early morning. When I find one at just the right height I can tip it onto my tongue as I stand or kneel and it is like a final return to my sensual ache; and when it spills upon my throat and breast I love it. I love it.

The paperbark grove, so stiff and grey and dry before, is now a black swamp. I barely recognise it as the same place where I used to dance, brushing the flaky trunks of these trees that are now up to their waists in water. So much water, and so dark and still. Can the trees soak up enough water now to feed life to their arid convolutions for all the rest of the year?

How quickly the grass had shot up in the deep interior. It is strong and fine, the power of youth still flowing in Tuin's dry seed. Year in, year out this goes on happening, careless of watchers, of whether it is loved or loathed or noticed at all. And the mango tree I found, standing all alone on flat damp ground in the south, has borne its fruit and let it fall, to enrich the dark mulch under the round shadow of the branches.

"Here, shitface, come and test for sparkypoos."

"Hang on a mo, my hands are covered with dough."

"It's not your hands I want, cunt, it's your eyes."

"All right, I'm coming."

"That'll be the day."

This is a very common performance nowadays. G has got one or other of the outboard motors ready for testing. It is now just a question of making sure that there are two, preferably matching, operational sparkplugs. G pulls the starter rope while I watch for sparks. He looks at me invitingly over the top of the engine: "How do you fancy a pleasure trip then, Lu?"

"Oh no!" I strike Lady Macbeth attitudes of distress. The term "pleasure trip" is a special joke between us because of the breakdowns that almost invariably occur the first time one of the old engines is tested. However, after I have reconciled myself to the worst that can happen—drifting off to Papua—I simply go prepared, packing along with G's shorts (present from Crossfield) and my wrap, two bottles of water, fishing gear and some damper.

One of the most memorable testing occasions was when G tried Crossfield's 40 h.p. on a twelve-foot dinghy. When the crayfishing started again, Isobel went back to Philamon, and, true to his word, Crossfield provided us with a better dinghy. The trouble was that it was not better at all. It was the most wayward little boat G or I had ever come across, bent at the bow so that it never went in a straight line, stuck all over the hull with inadequate caulking and so badly dented in the stern that it made three squint lines of wake.

Somehow, G and I lugged the hefty Johnson down the beach. It was a foul job and made both of us swear. If the engine bowl was not cramping G's fingers, the shaft was bashing my ankles. Once by the boat, which was not worthy of a name, my job was to hold down the bow so that the weight of the engine did not tip the whole thing over backwards. When it was securely lashed on, G pulled the starter rope from where he stood in the water, as he could never have kept his balance in the unstable boat. Luckily, this engine was not stuck in gear, so he was able to climb in before we sped away. To our mingled horror and delight, the engine went very well and the boat began to plane at once in a hectic fashion. We shot off in the direction of Tukupai and G, using all his strength to keep the thing in a straight line, squawked at me over the engine roar, "Mum-look!"

The aluminium bottom of the dinghy was shaking and flapping as though it were made of paper.

"Oh my God!" I wailed. "Slow down, stop!"

"I can't. I never put the stop wires on."

"You maniac!"

"She goes all right, though, don't she? It's all right, there's not much petrol in her. You enjoying it?"

"Yes! Yes! You know I am, you daft doddering old fart!"

It was true. I loved all the crazy little trips we took and I did not care when propellers fell off and pins fell out and we were stuck for hours drifting more often than not towards rocks or vaguely out to sea. G always got us home in the end, even if it meant using me as a sail. When many, many months later I was stranded in a smart broken-down motor launch off Monte Carlo, with frivolous companions who knew nothing about leaking gaskets and big ends, I would have given a hell of a lot to see G appearing with a grin and a wrench.

In those days I learned how much I did love G. This happened once I had stopped thinking of the past or the future and fretting guiltily over the fact that my love was not an equal return for his; once I had blocked off the knowledge that there were vast tracts of inner space in our lives where there was nothing to share; in a way, once I had stopped thinking at all. In the clear blue days after the Wet, when life on Tuin was all boats and sun and G bending over an engine and me lolling luxuriously in the bow, there were things we could share, and we did. Together we went trolling with a "lucky" line blessed by Crossfield. G steered the boat and I held the line, both of us delighting in the tense anticipation as the lure chased through the sun-dazzled water. Flocks of white birds flew up from a rock and circled in the air ahead of us, working the water for small silver fish. When the great tug of a queen- or kingfish came on the line I would cry out and G would slow the dinghy. Hand over hand we hauled the fish in together, and our smiles and exclamations were all joined and yet free, because out there on a big sea under a bigger sky I was not dreaming of a lover who could share my music and tap the wells of my senses, and G was not dreaming of the messy realities of a future in which I might or might not feature.

After a while, because it reminded us of the impasse in our relationship, we abandoned talking about the future except in a most casual way which had very little bearing on the realities we would have to face sooner or later. There had been one or two painful occasions in the tent when we grappled uselessly with words, flinging irrelevancies at each other which always skirted around the main issue. Those times were agonising for us both. As G's salient jabs struck home I retorted with phrases meant to sting, and the vicious ball bounced backwards and forwards, hurting us both, helping neither. Very rarely did we argue during the day, and if we did, it was triggered by some visitation from the outside world, demonstrating how fragile was the veneer of our harmony. Once Ronald brought over another batch of mail for me, and amongst the letters were a couple from men I had known in the other life. One I risked opening and reading straight to G, as I did with the rest, because I knew that if it did contain anything risqué it would certainly have a humorous slant. But the other I did not dare even open. It seems a bizarrely exaggerated thing to do now, but at the time I was so desperately anxious to avoid another wrangle with G that I burned the letter without reading it. Not surprisingly, this very action struck G as being highly suspicious and was itself the cause of a bitter exchange.

It was around this time that G admitted to me how earlier on in the year he had honestly believed that I had a secret lover on the other side of the island, possibly even a man smuggled out from England in some way. When he told me this I was open with him about how my mind had been affected at that time; the vicious thoughts about the shark channel and my hatred of him over the "swift kick in the belly" comments. He said that he too had entertained some violent ideas during the most extreme period of antipathy and stress. It made us feel close to be able to smile at such things now. However, there were still enormous differences in the ways in which we regarded our relationship which could not be reconciled. When G said outright that he wanted me to get pregnant, or as he put it, "Come on, Lu, it's chico-making time," it stirred up all my confusion and I pretended to make a joke of it. It was not, of course, a joke to me at all. I am as subject to broody urges as the next woman and during those times when I fell heavily under the nest-making spell I made the fatal mistake of voicing my feelings. The warmth between us bred a laxity of control which made us both reveal our tenderest spots, leaving them wide open for later wounding.

G's way of coping with pain was to sheathe himself in indifference. To see somebody one cares for doing this, shuttering himself away behind a chink-filled shield, is a painful thing. How much more painful for the person doing it. A man who is rough around the edges and not ashamed of it, who has no pretensions towards refinement and yet is a very sensitive being, does not find it easy to give way to tender feelings. It was a long, long time before G's way of showing his love became comprehensible to me. I remember him describing, with so much warmth that his voice went gravelly, how his youngest son used to say to him when they were playing darts and G kept getting the bullseye, "Dad, you're a cunt," or just, with quiet emphasis, "cunt." Yet one month away from the time when we were due to leave Tuin, I could still feel angry when he used that word on me. When I was being rather inept once at holding up a boat we had just finished sluicing out he said, "Listen, cunt, can't you hold the fucking thing properly?" He was totally mystified when, suddenly fed up with the treatment, however well meant, I simply dropped the boat flat in the sand and marched away without a word. By that time I was using the commonest vulgarities in the language almost as frequently as he, so my behaviour must have seemed unreasonable. Later I was to discover how profound an effect being called a cunt for a year had on my feelings of worth as a woman. Because it was all I could really be to G, in the end, I felt that it was all I really was.

There are two sides to every coin. If, careful analysis aside, all I felt I could be to G was a cunt, what did he feel, after all this time, he was to me? "An island, that's all I fucking am to you, a fucking island," and the truth in that made me feel like a cunt.

But between the man who placed an ad for a "wife" for a year on a tropical island, and the woman who got the job, by the end of that year there was a great deal more than just thoughts about cunts and islands. The most revealing thing G ever said to me, when I demurred one night before a second onslaught of sex without preliminary touching of any kind, was: "Well, how can I, how can I, Lu, really make love to you when I know you're probably just going to go?"

He threw himself back angrily onto his side of the tent. Then I understood why he behaved as he did and it touched me to the core.

*   *   *

It was not long after this revelation that a third character came to live on Tuin. She lived in a manor house not far away with a long drive running up to it and a gamekeeper's lodge in the woods. She seemed to have plenty of time on her hands because she spent hours chatting to G on her golden telephone and shamelessly leading him on. Her name was Millicent Farquharson and she was to become the "other woman," G's fantasy ideal.

Millie had a voracious appetite for men and she made no bones about letting them know it. She wore black silk stockings with seams up the back, and a broad-brimmed picture hat with a black velvet ribbon under her chin. Sometimes she wore pink silk knickers as well, but her lacy suspenders, sketched on with a stick of burnt wood, were apt to rub off on them, especially when she wriggled with excitement when the vicar came to tea. It was clear that, stuck in the rut of dutiful domesticity as I was, hands always covered with fish or rinsing out oily engine rags, I had not a chance of keeping G's eyes off that sweet-talking vamp of a woman. I would spend all morning "slaving away," filling a forty-five-gallon drum with sea water for G to test his engines in, or holding down some block for him to tighten up the nuts, and then his voice would suddenly come fluting into my ears in a studiedly casual tone: "Hey, Lu, is Millie coming to tea this afternoon?"

"Well, I don't know, she's been feeling rather strange lately."

"Oh dear, not well? I think Dr. Frobisher had better pay her a call and cure her with his special tool."

Dr. Frobisher was a lascivious old country doctor who went around introducing distressed young women whose husbands were away to his famous relaxation method. Like the vicar he wore a stiff khaki jacket, but with the omission of a bandage at the throat. However, Millie had most of her fun with the chauffeur and the gamekeeper because she liked the warm sound of their Buckinghamshire burr, and it excited her to watch their eyes go round and swimming as she gently encouraged them to help her arrange her stocking tops. Millie received all her visitors indoors and would call out in her distorted-vowelled snooty voice when she was ready. When honoured with a call from the Member for Tuin West in person she sometimes used to describe exactly what she had been wearing before reaching her present state of what G called "dizabil." As she verbally strip-teased away each layer of silken finery, the M.F.T.W. would sit up tall and straight and look her boldly in the eye.

After a while, Millie and I became quite close friends. I learned how to handle her and even let her use the one cosmetic I found I had in my suitcase, a shiny roll-on lipstick with a scented, sexy taste which made her feel randy. She accentuated her eyes with the same charcoal she used to draw her suspenders, and stroked Vaseline from the medical box onto her eyelashes. Because she never went out in the boat or took her games outside, I did not feel that she impinged too heavily on my own Tuinlife, and she brought out a side of G that I found endearing in its honesty, if not in any other way. She was perhaps the most entertaining twist in the castaway's religion of adaptability; one makes the best of absolutely everything one's got. As a cunt I was beginning to feel almost professional.

The question of G's writing did not completely fade out, but it became, like the future, a subject one just did not talk about. In a way it was an impossible task for him at that time because it was so closely linked up with the future. The island to him was so much the woman that if the woman was going to leave, the bottom fell out of the story. Just occasionally, when he was happy and had convinced himself that if I was not going to go and live with him straight away on Badu at the end of the year, at least I was going to come back after a short visit to England, he would tell me that he had thought of a good first line. But good first lines, like good last lines, have little relevance to real life stories. If life were a neat thing to be packed into pages like fiction, I would not now have to recount the messy series of events which interrupted what should have been our last month on Tuin.

At some point G began to run out of tobacco and there was no more tinned butter to spread on our damper. Also we were running low on mosquito coils. On Badu we had been spoilt; the Islanders burned shavings of a special kind of wood that helped keep mosquitoes away from their eating areas, and coconut husks burning in small piles all around the area of the dancing square had left the dancers free to concentrate on their pre-planning movements rather than having to break off to scratch every few seconds. But on Tuin the special wood did not exist, and although I burned husks, it was almost as bad to have the smoke blowing into the tent as to suffer the attentions of the insects. A coil slowly burning at the foot of the tent was the perfect answer, although it never lasted all through the night and at some dark hour I could be sure to be woken by G going through one of his extraordinary extermination routines. It took me right back to the first nights on Tuin when we were plagued by sandflies on the beach. The sound of a mosquito in the tent made G's whole body go rigid with a tense fury that built and built as he lay trying to work out where it was from the high-frequency persistence of its lunatic whine. In the grey darkness I could see little but the rolling movements of his wide-open listening eyes. There was a rag we kept in the tent for various mopping-up purposes and it was ideally stiffened in parts. This G employed as his weapon of destruction. Into the midst of slumber his taut whisper would crack across at me from a distance of eight inches: "Where's that spunk rag, Lu? The little bastard's over here."

Weapon in hand, he would fling himself at the enemy with the energy of the demented, thrashing ceiling, back, floor and sides of the tent until no life of any sort could possibly still survive. In blissful relief he would sink down and say wearily, "'Night, Lulu."

Thirty seconds later his head would shoot up, again questing madly to trace the source of the renewed torment. Smoking a cigarette in the tent helped, but then, he was running out of tobacco. He would just have to make a trip to Badu. Besides, there were some engines to return—and no doubt a few to be collected.

During the time we had been back on Tuin we had had fewer visitors than before, as it was generally known that we had come back to concentrate on purposes of our own, but one or two people had not been able to resist coming, among them a worried little man called Timao who became panicky as the tide ran out, thinking he might have to spend the night with the Tuin Markai. He had made himself hysterical with fear by telling us the story of how, when fishing on the reefs beyond Mabuaig Island, he had once been stranded on Sarbi, a place with an evil reputation. He had been so convinced of the existence of a harmful spirit on the island that he abandoned his boat with its broken-down engine and paddled out to sea on a log. He had been picked up the following morning, in a state approaching catatonia, by fishermen from Badu and had not uttered a word for days. He was so terrified a similar experience would befall him on Tuin that I was obliged to carry his boat with him miles across the sandhills while he muttered a pidgin version of the Lord's Prayer continuously, at the same time casting fearful glances in the direction of our Northern Hill, expecting at any moment to be set upon by devils from his old religion, or indeed, to judge by his looks, waiting for me to transform myself into the beast of my totem clan and devour him.

The most significant visitor we had was a stranger from Moa Island.

He was a great bull of a man with almost plum-black skin and a face set in stern ridges like roughly heaped mud. His name was Osa and he was the Chairman of the settlement of Kubin on Moa. Osa did not compare to Crossfield as regards finesse and command of language, but his concern for his people shone out as, in broken phrases, he told us of their difficulties. The government had provided the people of Kubin with a communal freezer run off a diesel generator. This enabled them to store their cray until they had a big enough load to take to Thursday Island without a large percentage of the profit going on petrol for transporting single catches. The freezer had not been working for some time now and since the start of the new cray season Osa had had to make the long journey to Thursday Island frequently. He had heard about G's genius with engines; could he come and have a look? The people of Kubin would be happy to give us as much petrol, food and tobacco from the store as we wanted. No need for that trip to Badu, after all.

G packed a few tools into a rice bag and off he went. Predicting that there would be plenty of opportunities to visit Kubin in the future, I elected to stay on Tuin. Somehow, the Baduleegas found out that G had gone to Moa that day.

It had not occurred to us in these good-will-to-all-men days of advancement that there could still be the seeds of an age-old enmity lurking beneath the surface. Later reading was to inform me that until the "Coming of the Light" the relationship between Badu and Moa, less than half a dozen miles apart at the narrowest point, had always been one of raiding, head-taking and full-scale war. The great peak of Moa, standing out high above the rest of the island and overlooking Badu, was the site of the original blowing of the "Bu" shell, the trumpet call which rallied all the men of the two islands to prepare for war. For a Baduleega to have set up house with a Moan at that time would have been as scandalous and unlikely as a white marrying a black in Victorian England. Even since the missionaries had burned all the artifacts pertaining to the old culture and the habit of murderous inter-island raids had been curbed, relations between the two peoples had hardly been cordial. Fatal injuries in Thursday Island bar fights were not infrequently the result of an island-versus-island squabble, and in fact the social areas on Thursday Island were quite rigidly divided: non-mixing whites in one bar, half castes and mixers in another, Baduleegas and men from Mabuaig clanning together in one corner, Moans and non-Western group Islanders in another, and running through both white and black factions a combustible thread of animosity between those in favour of pearl trawling and those not. Altogether an outpost in which the high concentration of incompatible feelings and lifestyles made for a pressure-weary atmosphere. However, we were not then on Thursday Island, but on Tuin, which just happened to be bang in the middle of the sea between Badu and Moa. With G's innocent defection, we had landed ourselves in something of a diplomatic pickle, but we knew nothing of this until our next visit to Badu. Perhaps G had something when he spoke of "Kingsland luck," for it was by a fortunate coincidence that the next time we walked into Crossfield's settlement we were armed with a gift.

When he came back from Kubin, G was full of enthusiasm and loaded down with petrol and stores, including mosquito coils and tobacco. All he needed to fix the host of engines he had been greeted with on his arrival—the freezer was only one job out of many—were one or two things from Crossfield's garage. Even we realised that it would be the courteous thing to make sure all Badu jobs were finished before G seriously embarked on the Moan engines, so we made our plans accordingly. G began by sprucing up Crossfield's 20. I had accepted by now that although he was not unhappy on Tuin with me, and Millie, keeping him well distracted in between sunny hours of fishing and engine mending, sooner or later he would want to get back to where there was a soft mattress and even the possibility of a beer. As the thought of going back to the days of endless sitting in the garage on Badu was intolerable to me, we reached the compromise of going on day trips only, so that I did not have to accompany G if I did not want. On that first occasion after the long break it was perhaps of diplomatic benefit that we went together.

Early on the day we made the crossing we went trolling with Crossfield's line and caught a fine haul of both king- and queenfish. When we reached Badu we took our catch straight up to Centre Village, not at first consciously aware of the absence of friendly greetings as we made our way there. Crossfield sat at his table at the end of the long shelter surrounded by his council and family. When we stood in front of him, not immediately invited to sit, his eyes wandered from the gift of fish to G's face and back again, his face inscrutable behind the traditional Islander mask of non-expression. Finally he spoke: "Yous been have tucker? 'E gud tucker here, but might be yous been feed over there that nother place." He was not even going to utter the name of Moa if he could help it.

"Oh, what you mean over there on Moa?" said G, barging in with both feet. "Well, no, we've just come from Tuin, caught these fish for you on the way."

Still no expression lightened Crossfield's features. "Wish way Tuin, Lucy?"

"Tuin is good, but"—and here I became deliberately diplomatic—"we missed Badu and you and all your family."

"*Yarga* . . ." Teliai's gentle voice, speaking the Island word which could be made to mean anything from "give" and "share" to "sorry" or "love," floated through from behind her husband. A signal was given and Lily came forward to relieve us of the burden of fish. We were invited to drink tea.

"Guess which engine we came across with?" I teased, smiling at Crossfield.

"Wish what engine?" he asked suspiciously.

"Your 20, she went beautifully, didn't she, Gerald?"

"What? Oh yes, there's one or two things not quite right. I was wondering, Crossfield, you know in your garage you've got some really big sockets? Well, I could do with them and a couple of other bits and pieces, over on Moa."

"You want take them thing for them buggers? Get away! I don't give nothing for them!"

"Oh well, I only meant to borrow . . ."

"They go over that flace they never come back." Like many of the Islanders, when he became excited, Crossfield completely lost the ability to pronounce "p" and "f" where they belonged.

G tried to reassure him, "I'd make sure they came back. I could send Lucy over with them as soon as I'd finished, couldn't I? Osa would lend us a boat."

"What you need Osa boat por? I got nother boats here por yous, sixteen-poot proper good one!"

The conversation went on in a similar vein for some time, Crossfield clearly concerned that G was being lured away from him. The deciding factor was the mention of money.

"Well, you see," said G, scratching his ear carefully, "they did talk about quite good money over there, and I've got to start thinking about my future now."

Crossfield leapt in with counteroffers: "Nother time yous stay here Badu I give yous money. All them buggers give yous money por fix engine."

The "no more tucker, only dollar" time had come sooner than anticipated, although in fact we stuck to the voluntary barter system for the time being, with the difference that if it was a major job, I was encouraged by the "client" to tell him what we needed from the store rather than risk getting all the same items from everybody. Crossfield was persuaded to lend G the tools. Although Teliai had made very approving clucks when I told her that I had stayed on Tuin on the previous occasion G had been to Moa, I was now "allowed" to go with him, although not before I had virtually promised not to enjoy it. Half way through the day on Moa I crossed the channel between the two islands in a boat driven by Osa's eldest son and manned by a stern group of his cronies. They waited firmly in the boat while I went up to Crossfield's place. With slyly exaggerated deliberation I placed the borrowed tools in his hands and was rewarded with a smile and a guffaw.

"Oh!" he shouted, clutching his stomach. "Oh! Meesus good por them thing, good por 'member thing, Oh ho ho! and make tea!" Loaded with a second lot of borrowed items, I returned to the shore and was whizzed back to Moa by my escort.

Was this, I wondered, a small step unwittingly perpetrated by us along the hazardous path of progress? Before very long we were to see Osa and Crossfield standing next to each other at a church meeting on Badu, discussing the only thing they had in common besides a polite lip service to Christianity: G.

Once again our horizons had broadened considerably. Not only did G now have the promise of all Moa's mechanical business at his fingertips, but also the security of knowing that after our year on Tuin was over, a definite means of making a living awaited him if he cared to take up the challenge. The possibilities for expanding a mechanics business need not stop at Moa; there was the whole of the Torres Strait to be visited, the Eastern Islands and the Central group, which went right up to the coast of Papua New Guinea. If he could fit out a boat as a travelling workshop, maybe have one of his sons over from England to help him, he would be "made," if that was what he wanted, and it might have been with the right woman at his side. Instead he was saddled with a dreamy creature with a thing about an island and a powerful sexual device up her sleeve which shattered his resolve to treat her as the bitch he suspected she was. With the new power of a potentially profitable future he was in a strong position to feel justified in vacillating between the idea of chucking Tuin altogether and plunging straight into his new life, or conceding generously to my wish to remain based on Tuin right up until the end of the year.

In the event, compromise stood in where pride and fear prohibited irrevocable decisions. G knew that if he abandoned Tuin altogether and moved over to Badu permanently, I would leave the minute I had the means to do so. It had already been established that there was no chance of my being permitted by Crossfield to remain on Tuin alone; G only had to hint that this went against his wishes and the very notion would be swept aside. If I were seen openly to defy my husband, his status would be severely undermined. It would have been in no way advantageous to me to have tried, quite apart from the fact that my real feelings for G would never have allowed it to happen. I would do anything, fall in with any plan, so long as I was not parted from Tuin until the end of the year.

Almost on the very day I concluded that submission was the most powerful aid to my wishes, its force was taken out of my hands. We were over on Badu and Crossfield mentioned that he was planning to go to Thursday Island the next day. Would G like to go? G went, ostensibly to look at the prices charged by Thursday Island mechanics and help Crossfield pick out some spare parts, but really because there was no reason not to go. Looking at it now, my reaction seems absurd and even melodramatic, but at the time, the word which leapt to my mind when I heard him casually agree to go was "traitor." All that time we had struggled on Tuin with not enough food and barely any water, and nothing in the world would have persuaded either of us to give up on what we had set out to do. Now that everything was so much easier, so cushy and laissez-faire, it seemed as though the margins defining determination and single-mindedness had blurred, and what did it matter anyway?

On that day, while he was away in "town," I bribed an Islander with the promise that I would take his photograph if he would take me over to Tuin and leave me there for the day. He would pick me up from the end of the sandspit before the sunset. During the day, unable to lose myself completely in the inner world of Tuin, I mused on how things had changed recently.

Diary
When I move over the body of Tuin now, it is as though its impressions come into me through two separate sets of senses. Looking at it consciously at all, feeling thus distanced, I have lost something.

Naked feelings don't sit comfortably within the safe cup of compromise; they are not to be fitted in at routine's convenience. To tell
myself: "This morning I will cook and be around to help G if he
needs me, then after lunch go for a walk alone and be back in time
to make tea"—it does not work. I go for a walk and that is all it is.
I am not absorbed. It is too obvious an effort to grab a quota of
spontaneous feeling for the day. G does not demand that I am there
to present him with all his meals, but if I were not, the tacit contract
which holds our base here would stand for nothing. It is my part of
the bargain to be around. G has not agreed to stay based on Tuin in
order to be left alone all day while I go off on my aimless wanders
as if he were not even on the island. No, I cannot half-play my role,
but neither can the world of Tuin enter a divided, half-given person.
I have never felt closer to non-existence, mumbling my way as I do
between two insubstantial lives.

Definition and spontaneity—spontaneity being my approximation
to the notion of freedom—do not easily marry and yet without a
balance of the two, one is faced with havoc or a rut, at least with
reference to relationships. In a way I am surprised at how seriously
I play my role of wife. I think G would be surprised too. It even
extends to fidelity. I suppose that is why I become so incensed when
he accuses me of fucking other men. He does not understand that for
this year I am his. As Tuin is my definition of place, bounded on all
sides by sea, its horizons my horizons, he is my definition, my limit,
of man. Even when I was despising him, ashamed of him and not
sleeping with him, I would not have stepped right outside the sphere
of our tie by having another man enter me. I am glad that he has been
married before, glad that he has had homes and children and lovers,
for I could not set these seals upon a younger man. His love makes
me feel enough of a criminal as it is.

But as for the feeling that freedom can only exist within clearly
defined boundaries, it is still there. Among all the beliefs I never
knew I had and then discovered and abandoned, this one has been
reaffirmed. The extent of a person's mobility is too enormous to be
contained, so he reduces it either consciously by decisions, or by
simply following the path that appears most directly under his nose.
For those who make their own decisions it is comforting to think that
chance or a God takes a hand; the responsibility is too great to face
all alone.

All I came to do today was walk on the drying earth and trace the
vines of the passion fruit that have flowered and fruited again. I have
eaten some, but they do not taste so sweet this year. Maybe it is
because we have jam. I flattened a square in the long grass with my

drowsing body but I did not lie long and drift. Three times I have crossed the sandhills and patrolled the sandspit. At first the tide was going down, a gap appearing on the smooth seal's back of the spit when the two lapping seas rolled up but failed to meet in their snaking white line. Then the water was gone, and I took two patrols on the long tongue of dry sand striped by my lines of footprints. The water is coming in again now. I hope there is time for it to come together over my toes before I am collected.

G's face was warm and dry from the sun and salt wind when he returned to Badu from Thursday Island. He had been given some dollars for mending an engine and had bought me a present. I was amazed. It was even wrapped up in coloured paper. I held it in my hand all the time while I was pouring tea and setting food on a plate for him. The Badu ladies always gestured for me to fill plates for G and myself before the others. They were all watching me now. I opened the parcel when I sat down. Inside were two pieces of soap and a pretty comb. One of the soaps was apple-scented.

"I thought you'd like that, and there were pink and blue combs but I thought you'd like that tortoiseshell-colour one. Look, you've missed something."

Folded into the paper was a wooden spike as worn by some of the Island ladies in their hair. I stuck it through my plait immediately. Although I kept smiling and saying thank you, I could not express how surprised and touched I was, and he was even right about the choice of comb. He knew that much about me.

The next day we went back to Tuin but—and with what irony in the face of G's "treacherous" daytrip—within ten days I was air-evacuated from Badu to the hospital on Thursday Island where I stayed a week. I had been aware of clutching pains in my abdomen from time to time but had brushed away the thought that it could be anything that needed attention. I guessed it might be connected with starting periods again and the weight change. It was an infection caused by the IUD contraceptive I had had fitted before leaving England. To think that I had been naked all that time, the faithful body bouncing back so quickly to overcome the weakening and scars of the survival days, and now this thing, the one token of responsible civilisation I had carried around with me, had to be removed, and removed me from Tuin.

I was in too much discomfort to take in the journey or even the strangeness of white faces at the little hospital. I was asked if I wanted a single room, but I did not care, I did not know. After the infected thing had been removed and I had slept a while and the pain was gone, I woke to the sound of a woman's voice softly singing my name and breaking off now and then to giggle. I'd know that voice anywhere; it was Amadan. I pulled myself up and exclaimed her name aloud. The yellow curtain by my bed wrinkled back and her beaming, toothless face appeared. She was in bed too; we were roommates. We were delighted with each other's presence. She had been missing all her people on Badu and I was able to bring her up to date with news.

For her part, although she did not know it, she saved me from having to face the appalling blankness I felt within, not knowing who the plump tanned body lying on the white white sheet of my hospital bed was and inarticulate as an imbecile when the doctor came to see me. He made some sort of wry comments on how well I seemed, apart from the IUD problem, on living the life of a castaway. He had heard about G and the engines and probably thought we had spent the whole year on Badu. I said nothing because I knew if I opened my mouth I would sob. I cried once quietly in the night and not for long. Earlier on in the evening I had taken a shower and afterwards looked at my face in the mirror; the only expression I could find in it was one of a sort of crumbled apology. What had happened to the proud golden girl of the island? Who was this fat anxious-looking housewife? After the pause and the absolution of weeping I lay calmly and made up my mind.

G was well looked after on Badu while I was away. Crossfield sent messages, via relatives on Thursday Island who came to visit Amadan and me, to say that I was to let him know as soon as I was well and he would send a dinghy to fetch me. He had insisted that I should not go penniless to Thursday Island and had given me twenty dollars which I had in a tobacco tin. I was being treated as one of his own, for he sent Amadan money too. I bought some candy from the tiny hospital kiosk to share with my island visitors and spent nearly all the rest on stamps and writing paper. I hoped there would be enough left to buy some contraceptives, not that they would be such a pretty present to G as his had been to me. In fact there was not enough, but it did not matter because G came in to Thursday Island on the dinghy sent to collect me and he had earned some money with repairs. He gave most of it to me for "housekeeping" and I went into a shop and spent it on groceries, just like real husbands and wives. The rest he blew on half a bottle of champagne, which we drank warm out of paper cups in a park littered with passed-out Islanders in the middle of Thursday Island.

We had talked in the early days of how we would celebrate and revel in the luxuries of civilisation when we left Tuin at the end of the year. It had not been quite like this in our fantasies, but I loved G for the gesture, and as I sat across from him at the wooden table and looked at his dear, slightly inebriated face, I knew that the process of leaving him was going to be no fun at all. He had been right in an earlier speculation; as soon as the year was up, I was going to "fuck off," and now I had to tell him, once and for all, and make him accept it as a reality.

When I was a small child my sister and I shared a tricycle. It was large, or so it seemed to us at the time, and had a useful bin at the back. Because she was the elder and therefore the boss, it was my place to travel in the bin. As we rode along the pavement past our neighbours' houses my job was to scatter hedgeleaves over the ornamental walls of their front gardens. Whether this was intended as a form of benediction or simply as a dare, I do not recall, but what happened when I threw too far and landed a heap of poisonous leaves in the middle of Mr. Browne's goldfish pond is crystal clear in my mind. Unbeknown to us he had been observing our progress all along the road, and by the time we were level with his garden had worked himself up into a proper Sunday-morning fury. The leaves in his pond were the last straw. My sister, agile and swift to act, was off the trike and behind our own garden fence in a flash. I made an effort to follow but found to my horror that I was unable to move; my bottom was wedged in the bin, and I had to face the full brunt of Mr. Browne's righteous rage from that low and ignominious position. Eventually I tipped the situation my way by turning the whole machine over in an effort to free my seat. Inadvertently poisoning goldfish may be a crime, but upsetting little girls on tricycles is infinitely worse; Mr. Browne calmed down and pretended to be nice, but from that time on I vowed always to pedal my own tricycle and never get into a situation from which I could not escape.

Having made the decision before going back to Tuin to pull myself together and recover my identity at any cost, I was now, so to speak, pedalling my own tricycle, but what I had yet to realise was that none of the wheels under me was going the way I was aiming. I had learned from G a long time ago that a decision taken is not a move made, and later that inconsistency had shown itself in my own behaviour. I had about-faced on so many issues, broken so many personal rules in the course of the year; what solid basis of personal credibility had I on which to build the conviction that what I wanted to do was neither impossible nor necessarily criminal, when all the influences around me implied that it was? I had to find something to latch on to as proof of my own integrity. The one thing that had never wavered was my determination to see the year out on Tuin, and now I needed that knowledge of constancy to remind me that I had the strength, if only I could believe it, to pull myself out of the mire of self-doubt into which I had fallen. In the first months I had learned of the adaptability of the body; later on the need for adjustment had been extended to the regions of mind and emotion, and it was somewhere here that I had lost track of what was real and what was compromise.

"I will never have sex with you again!" I had screeched at G across the creek. I had gone back on that. "I will not stoop to bitchery and pointless rows," I had told myself. What vanity; I had certainly not kept my own word there. Nothing formed in the mind is immutable. It is those things beyond words, unconnected with intellect, that are the real force behind the major steps one takes. The driving lust for living and the energy that had made me love Tuin even in the worst days, and had been used later in another guise to keep me there, would now be redeployed again to secure my release and get the reins of my life back in my own hands.

Relieved to be on Tuin again, I found that although we fell back easily into the routines which had developed before the interruption of the hospital, there were subtle differences in my own attitude to the island and in my behaviour. I resumed patrolling the sandspit, walking to Long Beach, crouching in the hot salty soil of the south east, but, instead of waiting for the sun and scents to take me as they had before, I would find conscious reflections creeping in. Aware of being a creature with a will once more, I was thinking. It was both a loss and a gain.

G was going over to Badu and Moa fairly frequently these days on engine business and occasionally I would accompany him. If he had a major job on, we would stay a night or two. But more often than not, I stayed on Tuin. The days were very short, as they had been a year before when it had been an effort to fit all the jobs that made mere survival possible into the hours of daylight. To help guide G back home after the sun had gone down, I would light a beacon fire at the top of the beach in Camp Bay. Now that I was no longer physically weak, I was able to drag along big branches to make a splendid blaze. I would stand by a grey pyramid of rocks just outside the fluttering limits of the light cast by the fire. Long shadows of flame danced hectically over the sand, and bright red chips of spark shot high into the night air. Flaring a brilliant challenge to break the grey haze of sea and islands, the fire seemed like a wild shout of life.

Sometimes, knowing the journey well, I let my thoughts travel with G, seeing him in my mind's eye pushing off from the gritty mud of Badu beach, poling over the beds of sea grass which undulate like streaming green hair, then opening out the throttle past the old turtle farm. He would align the dinghy to run parallel with the two islands before Wia, craning his neck to watch for the wicked trio of rocks which lay just below the waves at high tide and then, relaxed once the danger point was past, aim straight at the three palms which were our guide as soon as he caught sight of the shape of Tuin. And if it was too dark to see, he would be guided by the joyous beacon of my fire. Sometimes there was a long time to wait, and the flames would die down and have to be fed again. As I worked, my thoughts would wander over the three main areas of my dilemma.

Most difficult to contend with were my own feelings for G. I was aware that in marrying in order to make the island year possible I had done him a great wrong. That he had known I viewed it only as an arrangement at the time made no difference now. It was no excuse, and backing G up in persuading me that wanting to return to Britain after the completion of the year amounted to desertion, was the whole weight of public thought on the meaning of marriage. It may be that over the last couple of decades opinion on that subject has undergone a few changes, and I would like to say I did not give a hoot anyway, but that would not be true; nobody likes to be thought of as a shit. But all that aside, for on Tuin it only came into evidence as a barb occasionally slung my way, there was the simple fact that I cared for G and hated to see him hurt. Caring, though, was not enough. What kind of a love was mine, as G put it, that I was prepared to up and go when I knew that he would rather I stayed or at least said definitely that I would be back? Certainly it was a love very hard to explain. It still is.

Complicated and all-too-human these musings seemed beside the careless abandon of the flames, but they went on.

There was the pull of the island itself, and now, coupled with the private sway held over me by Tuin, there was my fondness for the whole Torres Strait Island way of life, and the warmth and respect I felt for individual Islanders. They expressed sorrow that I should want to go when a permanent place was open to me on Badu as G's Missus, and they were somewhat mystified as to my reasons. Some of the women, attempting gently to probe, had said with the hint of a question in their voices,

"*Nee migi ipeca, pakai* [You are a little woman, a girl], 'em little bit old bloke''—this they saw as a possible clue. Also, much to the disappointment of Yopele, who claimed to pray daily that I should be delivered of forty-three children, there was the mysterious fact that I had no babies. Teliai, who I felt to be imbued with a special wisdom and serenity of spirit if only because she was mother, grandmother, great-grandmother, aunt and sister to so many, was someone to whom I would have liked to try to explain.

One morning when we were over there I presented her with my prize melon from Tuin. Teliai and Crossfield had melon patches all over Badu, but Teliai kept the melon I gave her in her lap all morning, and after she had divided it ceremoniously when Crossfield came for his lunch, she told all the children to keep the seeds because "this proper good melon belong Tuin." While I drank tea with her in the afternoon we had a strange little conversation.

"Hit true you go Englan' Deral stay 'ere?"

"Yes."

"We go proper miss you. What time you go come by again?"

"I don't know. I would love to come back and see you all again."

"You come by again make 'ouse along Deral 'ere Badu. You me go for peesh." She wrinkled her lovely squashy nose at me in a persuasive smile. I tried to get out of giving a negative answer to this by talking about fishing, but she knew I was being evasive.

Looking very steadily into my eyes, she said, "You an' Deral peenish?"

"I love Deral but I do not want to live with him forever."

It sounded as feeble as it felt.

"More better you no got married," she answered evenly.

More better I no got married. I still wanted to find a few simple words which would somehow explain that I was not all bad in my desire to go, but I was perhaps not fully convinced of that myself.

The third problem threatening to pull me off the track of my resolve was purely practical. I did not have the means with which to go. I was relying on payment for an article I had written earlier on in the year to get me back to England, but I did not know when the money would come through. The anniversary of our arrival on Tuin came and went, and no move was made.

One night by the beach fire, perhaps because of my preoccupations,

I experienced a taste of fear for the first time when alone on the island. It was not long after dark but I had had the fire going for some time because feeding it gave me pleasure and I liked to watch it become the focal point of light in a grey world after the sun had set. Soon, by straining my eyes towards the dark water by Wia Island, I made out the movement of a dinghy. At first I assumed it was G, and I set the billy on to boil. Usually when he came near enough I called a greeting and he answered, but as the dinghy came level with Snapper Rock and turned in towards Home Beach, the first whisper of doubt entered my mind. The figure in the boat was too tall and broad to be G. It must be someone sent over to fetch me because G had decided to stay the night on Badu. I went to the edge of the water and hallooed. There was no answer. It was not full tide and the water in Camp Bay was shallow enough for the stranger to have to pull up the engine and punt the rest of the way. In the silence after the stopping of the engine I called again. Still no reply and the boat was coming nearer and nearer. I tried standing in the firelight and waving. The tall silhouette in the boat did not respond.

I became uneasy and ran up to the shelter for the rifle. There was only one bullet left for the .22, and as the proper magazine was missing, it had to be loaded awkwardly from the top. I fumbled and it went in squint, so that I had to drag the stiff bolt back again and tip it out. Muttering a selection of words from G's repertoire, I scrabbled it out of the sand and eventually managed to get the damn thing in. Back down on the beach the figure had left the boat and was walking slowly and heavily up the sand. It looked monstrous and yet not the right shape for an Islander. I gave one more friendly yell and then as there was still no answer, crouched behind a rock and took aim. I suddenly realised that I was frightened; frightened of an unknown man who was not an Islander and therefore not one of a known group of people. I had been lost in the hospital with the doctor and white nurses, unable to communicate even though I knew they were "goodies," but how on earth would I cope with someone who was not even friendly enough to return a greeting? I followed his progress with the aimed rifle, and then lowered it in surprise as the figure broke in two, dropping its top half in the sand, and saying "Fuck" loudly.

G's voice wafted plaintively up the beach: "Lu, where are you? Come and give us a hand."

How come his voice reached me and mine did not reach him? Walking past the fire to help him with the cloth-wrapped engine he had been carrying, I saw the answer. The sparks leaping off the top of the fire were performing a wild fandango; the wind, as whimsical as the tides in the area, had flicked round to the north west and was sweeping in high gusts inland over the sea. G laughed over the business of the gun and rightly pointed out that I would not be able to face every stranger back in "civvie" from behind the safety of a rock and a gun.

As the days of boat trips, firelight suppers and long nights in the tent went by, and the wind settled to its proper direction for this time of year and the sandflies returned in force, we were reminded that this was the second time we had seen the island in its present season. I looked at G and saw how much he had changed. For all his hurt, which came across largely as disgust alternated with genuine wonder that I could be so stupid as to fly in the face of the happiness we did share, G proved his love for me by not insisting, as he could have done, that now that the set time for our stay on Tuin was over, we should leave the island and move over to Badu. He would do that after I had gone. An incident, again caused by the caprices of the wind, brought home to me the depths of his feelings about me and about Tuin.

One night when an unexpectedly strong wind swept over the island and buffeted our shelter violently, the greater part of our lovely palm-leaf roof blew off and the canvas section of wall was torn away at the top. G showed no interest in making a repair and, sadly, I understood why. There was no point, now that the year was over. After I had gone the shelter would cease to be occupied, would cease to be home for anything but red-backed spiders and geckos, and G would have no reason to come to Tuin. I pulled a few of the leaves back and found some heavy rocks to hold them down. Then I left it, and the sad realisation it had caused, and went to continue helping G pack up all the odd engine parts lying about camp. He told me that after I had gone he did not want to come back for anything, as there was nowhere on the island that would not hold a memory of me for him. It is hell sometimes when people are honest. He was so very different now from the resentful, directionless man who used to lie on the green towel all day. I only hoped that I was just as far away from the "scrawny Scotch harridan" who had spattered him with the spittle of my invective in days gone by.

To some extent, as the weeks wore into months, the anxiety of wrenching my being physically from Tuin itself began to recede. Because my mind was made up, my heart was partially steeled against too close contact with those aspects of Tuin which had meant most to me. Although I explored its surface, marvelled at a strange new nubbleskinned fruit I found, touched the trees and shells that had so touched me, in the deepest seat of my reactive being, I was already gone; and this left me free to give more of my perfidious self to G. In those days, any one of which might have been the last, it was by no means all tugging away and pain, for there were moments of joy and still many a laugh shared.

It was unkind of fate that since the removal of the IUD I was unable to follow the desire to be giving with the full, uninhibited use of my body. Expressions of care and tenderness meant little when it was brutally obvious that I was desperately anxious not to get pregnant. Although we made a joke of it, having to use ''jolly bags'' was grim for both of us, and it put Millie off to such an extent that we almost abandoned having her around. However, we found ways of overcoming the mechanical side of the problem, and when our supply of ''JBs'' ran out, in response to an urgent message via Badu, the helicopter from Thursday Island kindly dropped in an economy pack.

GREEN TURTLE

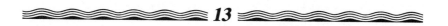

13

FLYING

Dawn over Tuin is never sudden, and the crow of the scrubfowl cannot be guaranteed. But when you have lain for over the sum of nights in a year and received through sleeping ears and skin the subtle signs of its imminence, you know, before you open your eyes, when it will be there. That night I left the tent twice, once to pee, once just to bathe in the air. It was so silent that when I brushed the sand and tiny particles of shell from between my toes, the small sound rasped in the atmosphere.

I was down by the sea before the first white rising of light, in time to see the last stars blink and vanish. Strange how with no direct source of light the rocks seem so insubstantial; in the graininess of dark they look as though they might drift away if pushed.

The dinghy rode at anchor far out where we had purposely left it the evening before. We would have to go very early to catch the tide. I immersed myself in the shallows for a moment to beat the sandflies, and when I rolled over to face inland, a pale breath flaring over Northern Hill announced that it was time to move. In the shelter I made tea and spread jam on damper, then wandered out again briefly to look at the tide. From the tent came a stern question: "Where's my tea?"

I pushed the red mug in past the torn mosquito netting. G's head was raised up and I could hear, rather than see, the grin in his voice as he said hello. He lay under the shroud of a once white sheet which was now unequivocally peaked in the middle. He pointed to it: "What am I going to do with this, Lulu?"

"Not a lot at the moment I'm afraid, tide's on the way out fast."

"What? Already? Is the boat all right?"

"Yes, I was just going to take it out a bit further. I'll do it now.

We'll have to move." A groan from G, rushing being his particular horror.

"Come back in the tent for a minute, Lu."

"I really have to go and do the boat, besides, I'm all wet and sandy. Here, feel"—I touched his leg with a damp forearm.

"Ugh! Get off! Bloody old cow!"

The tide was moving at an alarming rate. It would have been sensible to have left yesterday and spent the night on Badu, but I had wanted to stay on Tuin. I pulled the boat a good way further out but we would have to carry it over the sandspit. There was not a moment to lose. I raced back to the shelter, wishing to God I had a bra as I bounced painfully in all directions. G was standing near the entrance having a long sleepy morning pee. He yawned and smiled.

"God, that damn tide," I panted, "we'll be lucky if we make it."

"Ah well, said the soul, arsehole said the well," said G.

"I'll take the cases down."

"Right-o, shithouse."

By the time our things were ready to load, two very dilapidated suitcases containing more termite trails and beetles than anything else and several boxes of engine parts and tools, the boat was standing on dry land. We worked furiously, in silence except for the occasional gasped obscenity. By removing the outboard, we managed to get the dinghy over the hump of the sandspit in a series of heaves. We would move forward in short bursts and then stop for a few seconds to pant. In one of these breaks G said crossly, "Serve you bloody right if you do miss your plane, insisting on spending your last night on this arsehole of an island. I just don't know why I listen to you."

"Oh, I know, I know, this is bloody awful, but we can do it. Come on, let's go again."

In the end we were half way to Snapper Rock by the time the boat was floating properly. I rushed back for camera and typewriter while G fixed the engine on again. My eyes swept hastily over the shelter and caught on the little black bowl I had filled with wongai and passion fruit in their time. I left that but picked up the small red-handled knife I had had since I was sixteen. There was no mutual property to divide; I had already slipped the rest of the Jolly Bags into G's case.

The engine fired on the fourth pull. I sat right on the apex of the bow to keep the propeller out of the sand as much as possible. I was keeping my eyes skinned for rocks but there was one clear patch where

I could have looked away for a moment. I prayed inwardly that G would not say: "Aren't you going to turn round for a last look, Lu?"

I was so glad he did not. Before he opened out the throttle I plunged once quickly in the sea, then knelt in my usual position on the bow seat. Past Wia Island the currents were bad and it was all G could do to keep us at a safe distance from the rocks. We put on our clothes when we came level with the turtle farm and I tidied my hair, which I had not had time to do earlier.

We left the boat and our luggage at Dogai and rode back for it together on Red Rose the tractor. Because the Islanders were bad about leaving the key switched on, which left the battery flat, G had rigged up a special light that winked until everything was correctly switched off. Unfortunately this device proved so fascinating that the battery was almost dead through the light being left on to be admired. However, she went with a push from Yaya, and soon my case was sitting in a little cart ready to be taken to the airstrip and G's was in the room he was to use in Crossfield's house. We sat down with Teliai and Crossfield to have a second breakfast and after a while G excused himself to attend to an urgent call of nature.

There were people I wanted to say goodbye to, so I excused myself from the long shelter gathering while G was still absent, saying I would be back shortly.

"Better not be late," called Albert's wife, Leah, "I think Deral go pourri-pourri that plane." Lily and Teliai joined in the fun:

"Deral go miss you!"

"Badu go miss you!"

"Small island go miss you!"

"Deral go cry!"

Their bright bird voices fluted after me as far as the mango orchard. I cut through the creek way to get to Ronald's place, avoiding passing the garage, as I suspected Albert might be lurking there.

Ronald, who counted among his accomplishments the art of barbering, was in full session. Seated at his porch table, the lap of his pink lava-lava already overflowing with shorn curls ranging in colour from black to brassy auburn, he was peering with great concentration at the head in front of him through the single broken lens of his spectacles. This head was already quite bald; it was the animal life left behind after the shaving which intrigued him. Folding in his upper lip firmly, he made deft crushing movements with his fingers and thrust the child away from him. Those waiting in the queue squeaked and bunched tighter together. Alice was next. I took a step forward in the hope that the interruption of my arrival might delay for a few minutes the end of the glorious Afro fuzz that became her so well. The greasy knife he used to begin the operation was poised when Ronald noticed me. In the split second of his hesitation Alice, her small features screwed into a furious silent raspberry, dived beneath the table and squirmed out the other side, covered from head to foot in the rubbish which had accumulated under there. She spent the rest of my farewell visit shying unripe Hammond fruit at me from behind one of her sister's graffiti'd palm trees.

"Oh!" cried Ronald, who always exaggerated his reaction once he had decided upon it. "Lucy!"

He gave rapid-fire orders to various female members of his family and in a moment I was comfortably seated flanked by a cup of cordial and a mug of tea, made, as far as I could tell, with an entire tin of condensed milk. Unable to sip it, as it stuck to my lip in a glob, I used it as a dip for the crackers I was offered.

"Well," he said, drawing out the word as long as possible and using the exhausted tone in which he made all announcements. "Today you go. What time you coming back?"

That question was asked by every one of the Islanders who said goodbye to me. As I walked past Olandi and Kales Aragu's house they shouted it at me from the verandah, as I passed beneath the mango trees on the way back to Crossfield's settlement a gang of children dropped out of the branches and danced around me:

"What time yous going?"

"I go with you!"

"What time yous coming back?"

Giving them all vague and breezy answers tore me inside. Patti-Pat of the scarred legs and huge eyes still had no pidgin, but when I finally detached her small hands from my hair and left her, she cried after me, "*Nee melaca?*" (Where are you going?)

"*Ngai moode ka,*" I answered, fatally. (I'm going home.)

"Tuin?" she cried. "Tuin?"

The plane was due to land at ten o'clock in the morning. G and I were back in the long shelter again. Crossfield had a watch. At nine-fifty G said, "Lu, will you come outside a minute?"

We stepped into the sunlight and moved a few paces away from the shelter. Although I had washed since the exertions with the boat, and had known many hotter days than this, there was dampness under my arms and, belying the relaxed way in which I had been chatting to Teliai and the others, there was a wad of compressed emotion something like a stone behind my breastbone. Although he hid it very well, I knew that G was suffering too. His hair was flat on his forehead with sweat and the skin under his eyes looked frail. His head was up and he stood in front of me with his hands by his sides. When he began to speak, one hand came up and he rubbed the side of his head slowly, a covering gesture I knew so well.

"Listen, love, I can't stand long goodbyes. I shan't come to the airstrip with you, you won't mind, will you?" His hand left his face and came across to me. He held both shoulders awkwardly.

"Look, I know you've got to go, love. Christ, you're only twenty-six, you've got your whole life ahead of you. But I just want you to remember this: unless you've been play-acting all these months you've found some happiness here, and happiness isn't that easy to find. If you decide, as I reckon you will, after a few months back in civvie that you want to come back, there'll always be a place for you with me, you old bastard." And with that he pulled me closer and our faces bumped together in a brief kiss. We had so rarely touched in pure affection that it was almost as if we did not know how to do it.

"G'bye, Lu," he said as he drew back, "there's another old Mariner 20 in Crossfield's garage. I'm going to get it out on the stand and have a look at it. As far as I'm concerned you're gone now, your plane will be here in a minute. I've got to get on with my own life."

"I know," I said, and he nodded once briskly as though to clear his head and then walked away.

Teliai patted the table beside her for me to sit down again. More tea. At eleven a.m. Titom, whose job it was to mow the airstrip, came to tell Crossfield that someone was burning off a melon patch down there and that the plane would not be able to see to land until the smoke had cleared.

"Ho ho!" said Crossfield. "That pourri-pourri por make you stay, Lucy." This was the second time this joke had been levelled at me; I was beginning to wonder if fate was against my going as well as everything else. Amadan had made yet another pot of tea and was pouring out a cup for G. She hesitated before taking it over to the garage, and Teliai gave her a signal on which she placed the tea in my hands. It was a conspiracy. Amadan, who since her return from hospital had been busy "catch one kids" from her boyfriend Tierri, covered her mouth and giggling as ever, pushed me firmly in the direction of the garage. God, this is unfortunate, I thought.

"What, you still here?" said G, not looking up from the engine. "Oh well, might as well make yourself useful, pass us a twelve-millimetre spanner, would you? And roll us a fag." It was the best thing he could have said. I went on passing wrenches and rolling fags until at last came the faint drone of the plane as it approached from the direction of Moa. I touched his arm briefly and left to take my place in the cart.

I was not the only passenger. There was a very old man with a wooden leg called Aporia and one hugely pregnant woman. Crossfield and Teliai, puzzled that G was not coming to the airstrip, but accepting my explanation that we had already said goodbye, did me the honour of accompanying me all the way. The cart, pulled by Red Rose, trundled out of Centre Village to a loud chorus of "Yahvohs" from the women in the long shelter, several children ran alongside until Crossfield barked at them. As we passed the garage I caught a last glimpse of G's back bending over the engine, then he was hidden by the trees.

The noise of the tractor and the rumbling of the cart made speech impossible, but just beyond the point where we had to slow down to cross a broad stream, a loud and unmistakable voice rang out. It was Yopele. Blind as he was, he had posted Ronnie No More to tell him when the cart carrying Tuinlady should pass.

"Hah! Tuinlady, where you are?"

His long arms paddled in the air until he found one of my hands, which he trapped in his gnarled paws. Ronnie No More stood lined up with Sarls Torres and Enid. Big smiles everywhere.

"Now I touching small hand belong Tuinlady for say yahvoh," boomed Yopele. "She go plenty mile, long way prom Badu people, but she no porget all Island thing. I been teesh her Island word, she no porget. That time she go Englan' she go tell every peoples story of Badu and that day she coming back we all happy. Now I give you Yahvoh."

"Yarga, Yopele, ka-i esso. Yahvoh!"

"She talk Island word, she say thank you! Yarga! Yarga! Yahvoh!"

He danced up and down on the sandtrack as the tractor went on its way, his yellow lava-lava flapping round long bow legs. The No Mores waved and waved; so did I.

The small plane had already landed. I was to sit up by the pilot, as this was the best position for taking an aerial photograph of Tuin. He said it would be no trouble for him to fly right over the island so long as I pointed out to him which one it was. I said I was sure I could do that. Just before I climbed in, Teliai handed me a parcel. In it was a lava-lava she had specially made for my brother, and a full bottle of precious coconut oil for myself.

"This make prom good coconut prom Gaobuut [a place the other side of Badu]. Me an' them ladie, we been make this three day por you."

"Teliai," I said, bending forward to speak to her alone, "thank you very, very much." I hesitated, then realising that I had to try, said, "Please understand, I am not a *bad* woman to leave Gerald."

She smiled as if she had been waiting for me to say something like this. Very softly she said, "Might I know. Yahvoh, Lucy."

I shook hands with Crossfield, who had gone very formal. "See you" were his last words, something like a command.

Away, away over the pinky reefs. Goodbye Badu. A lugger ploughed north towards Mabuaig. Not much of a sea but it would be bad between Kubin and Wia, it always was. How soon before I saw the outline? If we kept this course we would be heading in for a side view. Already I had made out the round tussock that was Death Adder Island. Gesturing that Tuin was ahead on the left, I focused the camera for a shot of Tukupai, then suddenly realised we were losing height and veering to the east; the pilot was going to take me right in close. There was Wia Island, flat on top where the crocodiles had their swamp, a splash of white where waves hit the rocks on the eastern side. And there was Tuin. Oh my God, hold, hold, don't go so fast.

The green darkness of Northern Hill, where I had scrambled and craned to find the mango trees; Green Ant Woods where we had found the uprights for the first shelter and G had cursed blue murder and worse; Prize Parrot Rock, Snapper in the distance, and there within that curve Home Beach and our camp behind the trees; First Fishing Rock almost covered, Palm Beach narrow, tide coming up. But here right below us, the Other Side. My low flat dais of the days of the golden gazelle just a tiny tablet of grey rock; the secret pandanus clump within which lay the dead remains of one woman's idol; less than a second to cover the length of Long Beach, every footprint there my own; the shells like Grecian urns; the wongai grove; my diary rock, the southern tip . . . missed the paperbark grove but there is the headless palm above crocless Croc Bay. Too fast, too fast, too much—let me touch every rock and blade of grass just one more time . . .

The plane pulled away for a full shot of the island. It was a perfect view, but the camera was shaking and the scene began to blur. All I wanted to do was reach out and throw my arms around Tuin's lovely waist and bury my streaming face in its thick chest hair of green. I knew that I could never, never recapture those first wild days of wonder, there where I had once belonged so utterly.

The pilot, encased in his radio earphones, was oblivious to my breaking down, but the pregnant woman in the seat behind leaned over and gently patted my shoulder.

"Yarga," she said, " 'em cry for leave."

Then she summed it all up better than I ever could: "Small island funnykind place."

And Tuin was gone.

January 1983
Summer Isles Hotel
Achiltibuie

FRIGATES WHEELING

About the Author

LUCY IRVINE was born in 1956 in Whitton, Middlesex, England. She ran away from school very early and had no full-time education after the age of thirteen. She has been employed as a charlady, clerk, monkey keeper, waitress, stonemason's mate, life model, pastry cook and concierge, as well as having worked with disabled people. Her father, Robert Irvine, is proprietor of the Summer Isle Hotel in the Western Highlands of Scotland, where she lives when not traveling.

REEFS

REEFS

ROCKS

CORAL WASTES

VERY TIGHT UNDERGROWTH

NORTHERN HILLS

CLAMS OYSTERS

TWO MANGO TREES

MY SUN ROCK

LONE P

PURPLE GRASSES

1st SHELTER

IRONCLAD TENT

FINAL SHELTER

PRIZE PARROT ROCK

CREEK

COCONUT ALLEY

HOME BEACH

ARMCHAIR ROCK

CAMP BAY

MANGROVES

CORAL REEFS

WINKLE ROCKS

CROC BAY

SCRUB HEN

FLYING FOXES

PA

SANDSPIT

SHARK CHANN

SNAPPER ROCK

FIRST FISHING ROCK

SNAPPER CHANNEL

REEFS

R